Hidden in Plain Sight

Hidden in Plain Sight

A Deep Traveler Explores
Connecticut

David K. Leff

WESLEYAN UNIVERSITY PRESS
MIDDLETOWN CT

For Nick Bellantoni, archeologist,
and in memory of
Les Mehrhoff, naturalist,
and Walt Landgraf, historian and educator.
Friends and mentors,
masters all of finding
what is hidden in plain sight.

Wesleyan University Press
Middletown CT 06459
www.wesleyan.edu/wespress
© 2012 and 2014 David K. Leff
All rights reserved
First paperback edition, 2014
Manufactured in the United States of America
ISBN for the paperback edition: 978-0-8195-7466-4

Wesleyan University Press is a member of the Green Press Initiative. The
paper used in this book meets their minimum requirement for recycled paper.

5   4   3   2   1

The Library of Congress has cataloged the hardcover edition as follows:

Leff, David K.
Hidden in plain sight : a deep traveler explores Connecticut / David
K. Leff. — 1st [edition].
pages cm — (Garnet books)
Includes bibliographical references and index.
ISBN 978-0-8195-7281-3 (cloth : alk. paper) —
ISBN 978-0-8195-7282-0 (ebook)
1. Connecticut—Description and travel. 2. Cultural landscapes —
Connecticut.
I. Title.
F94.L44 2012
917.46'04 — dc23   2011049405

For most of us, knowledge of our world comes through sight, yet we look about with such unseeing eyes that we are partially blind.

—Rachel Carson, *The Sense of Wonder*

Contents

Ghost Towns and Graveyards

Through Artists' Eyes

For an online version of the map, please visit
http://www.wesleyan.edu/wespress/maps/hiddeninplainsight/

Preface to the Paperback Edition

Objects, places, people, and phenomena hidden in plain sight are always at the mercy of mercurial time and human whim. They deteriorate, disappear, are remodeled and restored, find new uses, are rediscovered, or fall deeper out of mind. In the two years since the first edition of this book, there has been no hiatus in the tug-of-war with change.

The Quonset hut that once housed well driller E. O. Phelps & Sons on U.S. Route 202 in Litchfield is among several of these curving steel structures that are now gone, replaced by a conventional building. Mike Meehan's eighteen-year revival of historic brownstone quarrying in Portland came to an end in 2012 after harvesting 20,000 tons of rock, some of which restored landmark buildings from the eighteenth and nineteenth centuries. The pit is quiet now.

Long vacant and deteriorating on a Torrington street corner, Skee's Diner now resides in a storage facility where it awaits restoration. The Torrington Historic Preservation Trust plans to move it to a new location where it will once again serve eggs and home fries. For years a victim of vandalism, Frog Rock, the state's most venerable painted roadside stone, has been sold by the Department of Transportation and given new life. An entrepreneur bought the site and added a fresh coat of paint to the dour-faced frog, a small gift and antique shop, a tiny stage for entertainment, a food truck, and picnic tables so that families can once again enjoy a meal or snack in the shadow of the big green boulder.

The bucolic Pleasant Valley Drive-In, delighting carloads of patrons since 1947, is threatened with closure because, beginning in 2014, virtually all movies will be distributed as digital prints rather than film. The cost of a digital projector may prove prohibitive for the family-owned operation, one of the last three outdoor theaters in Connecticut. In contrast, the volunteer-driven family movie program at the municipally owned Southington Drive-In is thriving, generating $17,000 in 2013 for non-profit civic organizations.

Many historic cemeteries continue to suffer from neglect. But Old North Cemetery in Hartford, where luminaries like Frederick Law Olmsted and Daniel Wadsworth rest, has received a significant monetary commitment from the city to restore the monuments and grounds. In Bristol, Boy Scouts and a volunteer commission have made improvements at the Downs Cemetery, where more than two dozen Revolutionary War soldiers are buried.

A sign of the state's changing landscape is the decline of small local agricultural fairs. The Association of Connecticut Fairs listed nineteen local fairs in their 2008 brochure. In 2013, twelve were listed. Among the casualties was the Cherry Brook Grange Fair, which had a small-town, country atmosphere that delighted me whenever I visited over the years. Dwindling membership caused the organization that ran the fair to disband in 2012. Despite these closings, larger fairs have continued to thrive with their varied entertainment and greater commercial appeal.

Icons of once dominant agriculture, barns continue to be torn down to make way for development or slowly deteriorate. In response, the Connecticut Trust for Historic Preservation has done much to improve the public's appreciation of these intriguing structures through an inventory project that has produced an online database of over 8,400 barns. They've also created a Connecticut Barns Trail iPhone app that is sure to stir interest in preservation.

A long-time deep traveler is bound to find new marvels even in familiar haunts. Among sites I recently encountered by chance are a painted roadside rock alligator at a bend and rise on Goodale Hill Road in Glastonbury, a milestone along U.S. Route 44 in Ashford near the Windham line, and an octagon house in the West Mystic section of Groton. In addition to subjects covered in these pages, new adventures await those intrepid enough to seek them out, and I'm on the trail of public fountains, canals, fire towers, caves, repurposed churches, and many other intriguing places that beckon with stories.

Regardless of the transformation or disappearance of ordinary wonders hidden in plain sight, the intrigue of our landscape and our interest in it will increase as long as we tell the stories of change and loss. Deep travelers know that well-told tales create community, are stronger and longer lasting than masonry, wood, and other materials. They take their narrative obligations seriously because, as writer Lucy R. Lippard has observed, stories "articulate relationships between teller and told, here and there, past and present." The number and variety of quirky features sprinkled throughout our landscape is limited only by our own imaginations and our willingness to see. Get out and follow your instincts to where the clues and questions lead. Wonder beckons just beyond your doorstep.

Acknowledgments

Thanks to Tom Condon, my editor at the *Hartford Courant*, where many of these pieces originally appeared in a different form. His interest and insight into Connecticut's landscape is unrivaled.

Deep gratitude to my brother firefighter Juan C. Gonzalez for his friendship and magic with computers, which has more than once saved my words from disintegrating into cyberspace and has preserved my sanity despite the most perplexing (to me, at least) technical problems. I'll try not to bang on my keyboard as if it were the mechanical Underwood typewriter I learned on.

Thanks to Bill Keegan, historical geographer and GIS specialist, for his generous contribution of time and expertise. Not only can he see spatially, but in time as well.

My appreciation goes to the librarians at my hometown Canton Public Library, especially Beth Van Ness. I value her friendship and admire her patience with my frequent requests to track down obscure facts, books, and documents.

Finally, I'm grateful to my friends Alan Weiner and Bette Abrams-Esche, boon companions on many a bizarre quest.

Prologue to Deep Travel
The Merritt Parkway

All curious things, above, below,
Hold each in turn my wandering eyes.
—Oliver Wendell Holmes, "The Flâneur"

At fifty-five miles per hour I feel the twist and roll of the landscape as the road rises and descends, winding past gray ledges and clusters of pine and graceful hardwoods that stand in the median and along the shoulder, shadowing the pavement and in places creating overhanging arcades. Bound south for a routine meeting at the Greenwich Audubon Center, my senses are on high alert after exploring an old Nike missile base hidden behind roadside vegetation atop the Merritt Parkway's highest point in Westport. One of the old radar towers is now a domed observatory, and there's a public works facility with heavy equipment as well as offices at the site. Finding the old military installation, which had been invisible to me during hundreds of drives, leaves me feeling wide awake with the adrenalin rush of discovery.

Conceived seven decades ago as a northern alternative to insufferable traffic congestion on U.S. Route 1, the parkway was the state's first limited-access thoroughfare. Unlike any other route at the time, it was intended not just as a means to get from one place to another, but as a purposeful connection between vehicles on the pavement and the surrounding countryside, a link among transportation, nature, and art. When the first half of the road opened in 1938 it was hailed as "a special kind of highway whose design emphasized the pleasure of driving without sacrificing such mundane considerations as speed, efficiency, and safety," according to historian Bruce Radde. Of course, motoring for fun has long since lost some of its allure, and the parkway at rush hour is often a clogged nightmare of pulsing brake lights.

On a sun-washed June afternoon, when blooming clusters of mountain laurel look like so many eyes peering from the undergrowth, I feel as if I am driving back in time. But the time-travel high doesn't last long. Soon I enter the relatively new interstate-style intersection with U.S. Route 7, where the road is straight and flat. Trees and rock outcrops no longer hug the pavement, and red maple swamps yield to wide, barren shoulders. Modern changes to the parkway are not always kind to its intimate scale and meticulous detail. Fortunately, the road quickly plunges back into skunk-cabbage-filled wetlands, towering spruce, and remnant stone walls from long-gone farms.

Following a decade of spirited debate, political intrigue, scandal, and planning for location and design, construction of the Merritt Parkway began in 1934 during the heart of the Great Depression. Completed in 1940 at a cost of $22.7 million and running from the New York state line to the western end of the Sikorsky Bridge across the Housatonic River, it featured a pair of vanilla concrete strips of two lanes each, with a wide median between. Only the northern half of the right-of-way was developed as a roadway, the remainder left wooded for future lane expansion.

Approaching the Ponus Ridge Road Bridge in New Canaan, I notice broken and spalling concrete from decades of harsh weather and road salt, which have been gradually dissolving its art deco geometrics, balustrade, and state coat-of-arms centered over the arch. At High Ridge Road, laurel blossoms near the stout abutments and around a dark ledge, where gnarled stems wedge themselves into rocky crevices. Uneven grassy areas appear, often dotted with dusty green cedars. A few miles later the Guinea Road Bridge, faced with rounded stones above a wide arch of granite blocks, radiates rustic grandeur as I speed beneath it.

Each of the Merritt's sixty-plus bridges is unique, almost all using concrete with surprisingly subtle artistry. Pylons and wing walls seem to embrace the countryside with whimsical art deco designs and concentric receding surfaces. Details feature historical images of Indians and colonists, mythological creatures like griffins, freestanding Nike wings, botanical motifs, and even spider's webs and butterflies (in the cast iron railings of Fairfield's Merwins Lane overpass). In some places the concrete has been scraped, tinted, or carved to reveal the texture of various rock aggregates. Conspiring with topography and vegetation, the bridges inject theater into the road, enhancing the drama of a drive when suddenly they appear around a bend or over a rise. Seeing all the detail in a single pass or tens of trips, even below the legal speed limit, is impossible.

Not surprisingly, the parkway has garnered many well-deserved accolades over the years—listing on the National Register of Historic Places, designation as a National Scenic Byway, and receipt of a Centennial Medallion from the American Society of Landscape Architects. But the Merritt is not so revered as to be above peril. Cracking concrete bridges, unkempt and invasive plants, interstate-style signs, and the bland, massively out-of-scale new overpasses at the Routes 7, 8, and 25 interchanges all provide evidence that lack of imagination and insufficient maintenance dollars will forever remain threats.

In recent years, lawsuits have successfully halted widening schemes and other despoliations by the Connecticut Department of Transportation, an agency impossibly tasked with both the road's preservation and ensuring traffic efficiency. Thankfully, the parkway's singular artistry has not been lost on the public's affection, and people have rallied to protect it. After years of petitioning by private individuals and groups, restoration work at last slowly proceeds.

Once heralded as "the Gateway to New England," the Merritt's lush mix of natural and built landscapes may well be a gateway to the kind of "deep travel" that enables us to see what is hidden in plain sight. Deep travel is purposeful "power-looking" at our surroundings. It is about seeing in time as well as space, enabling us to weave fragments of the past into coherent stories that help explain the present or anticipate the future. As writer Tony Hiss observes, deep travel "has the feeling of waking up further while already fully awake."

The Merritt is rather an ideal avenue of deep travel because, as any veteran or novice driver will confirm, the road demands constant attention. Having accidentally entered the parkway within an hour of receiving my driver's license at sixteen, the memory of that first white-knuckled ride has left me ever respectful of the road's heaves and swells, tight curves, narrow shoulders, and pinched exit ramps.

Unlike interstates with their long, monotonous straightaways, the Merritt never lulls me into the hypnosis of white-line fever. Instead, I've found myself exhilarated by those curvaceous rolls caused by glacial scour, which emphasizes longitudinal ridgelines and river valleys on a road largely traveling against the topographical grain. Though construction crews flattened many high points and used the blasted rocks to fill the dips, the parkway retains its geological imprint. These rising and descending rhythms send me into deep ruminations, fusing me more securely to the road and landscape.

Deep travelers experience an increasingly vibrant and comprehensible world as they uncover what is easily recognized but seldom explored. The countryside bubbles with intriguing stories and is dotted with veiled, sometimes gossipy clues about people, places, and phenomena that reveal themselves in everyday sights such as roadside rock cuts, swayback barns, and octagon houses. Take any parkway exit and discover commonplace, yet unusual points of interest. Waiting to be discovered just beyond the road are not only Nike missile sites, but Quonset huts, castle-like houses, vintage diners, towering elms, abandoned graveyards, ghost towns, lost worlds beneath reservoirs, and old cider mills still pressing their quintessential seasonal drink.

For many, the Merritt is merely a paved road through pristine Yankee country. But in fact it is more like a garden, a cultivated space, a collaboration between man and nature. Though the road retains a natural appearance, landscapers planted tens of thousands of trees and shrubs, including native dogwoods and mountain laurel, along it. "The main objective of the landscaping," wrote parkway engineer Earl Wood, "has been to assist nature in healing the scars of construction." With the wounds long since mended, the Merritt's mix of nearby nature and wide vistas helps us see beyond the general greenery to a world where particular plants suggest something larger about the places where they are growing.

Years ago, I took a drive with my friend the late Les Mehrhoff, then the state biologist. Where I saw a world of undifferentiated leaves, stems, and trunks, Mehrhoff knew the names of individual plants, their life cycles, origins, and ecological functions. Particular species held hidden knowledge about the soil and bedrock, the insects and reptiles living there. He saw where groundwater seeped to the surface or when a particular microclimate meant heavy winter snow. The green mass was suddenly laden with meaning, order, and wonder. Clustered pines indicated gravelly, well-drained soils, maybe the remains of an esker left by the mile-thick glacier whose meltwater sorted the sediment it carried. Raggedy blue discs of chicory along the pavement brought forth stories of colonization by settlers and the plants that inevitably shadowed them from Europe.

As I approach the exit for the Audubon center, I pass a golf course with rolling grassland and neatly grouped trees obscured by a screen of woods. I then whiz beneath the North Street Bridge's rusticated concrete and see the rippled waters of Putnam Lake lapping near the eastbound lanes. In less than a mile the Lake Avenue Bridge appears, its steel arches decorated with a profuse tangle of cast iron vines that are rusting through faded electric-blue paint.

Sculpted images on the bridge recall the grape vines I've just seen climbing rocks and trees along the roadside. Remembering Mehrhoff's instruction, however, I also recollect seeing Asiatic bittersweet, a nonnative invasive vine that is girdling full-grown oaks. Japanese barberry and winged euonymus are among several other aggressive alien plants also covering the roadside shoulders. But here at the parkway's lower end the snarl of vegetation has been trimmed back. Freshly planted trees and shrubs grow along new wooden guardrails, and the characteristics of individual plants stand out among the mass of vegetation.

Because they undergo constant change, landscapes cannot be understood or appreciated only spatially. Accepting a static postcard image of our countryside risks leaving us with a flawed notion of permanence, an incorrect sense that landscapes are relatively stable. We might see a clearcut here and there, but we would never imagine that most of Connecticut was stripped clear for farming and industrial charcoal little more than a hundred years ago, or that entire Connecticut villages, like Dudleytown or Gay City, have disappeared due to economic and demographic changes. Transportation systems have likewise faded, leaving the state with spider webs of ghost roads and railways.

Observing these disappearances, I can't help but ponder how the past is still present in what I see. For example, when I encounter an old rail station gussied up as a boutique or cozy restaurant, a string of questions comes to mind: Where did the tracks lead to? What was the logic behind the cut-and-fill that went into building a relatively flat line in uneven topography? What business opportunity or geographical barrier caused the tracks to take a particular route? What freight did they move and, if abandoned, why?

Instances of things hidden in plain sight abound throughout Connecticut and elsewhere. An old earthen dam in the woods can lead me to wonder about the kinds of products made at the site, where workers lived, and why the mill closed. A farm's location speaks volumes about the quality of the soil and climate there. Downtown building facades are indicative of the spirit and wealth of the time in which they were built—and suggestive of the potential for reviving street life today.

More than reflections on the past, these places cause me to wonder about the fate of landscape objects, roads, buildings, and natural features we take for granted today. Some will undoubtedly disappear and others will lose their importance or be reborn with new uses. The effect of finding things hidden in plain sight is not reverence for history, but recognition of the humbling power of metamorphosis. Above all else, a deep traveler perceives change.

To foster finding what is hidden right under our noses, these pages are divided into five broad sections representing the ways in which we commonly experience our landscape during the course of our everyday routines. These broad topics—Along the Roadside; Places We Build; Seeing Green: Trees, Culture, and Agriculture; Ghost Towns and Graveyards; and Through Artists' Eyes—reflect that we encounter much of our world from behind the wheel, in the spaces we construct, in our encounters with nature and it's cultural confluence with agriculture, in realms where imagination meets a sometimes ghostly past, and in the interpretations of life depicted by artists.

Within each section are chapters that explore ordinary wonders from antique milestones to quarries, agricultural fairs to abandoned landfills. The list of topics barely scratches the surface of potential discoveries, and no chapter is exhaustive of its subject. My hope is that this small sample will stir in readers a reflexive desire to explore further the everyday wonders existing just beyond our doorsteps. At its best, the adventure of finding such things will encourage us to protect and nurture what is singular and idiosyncratic in our landscape, thus providing all who come after with places that will enrich and bring joy.

I slow for the Round Hill Road exit, and by the time I've stopped at the ramp's bottom, the spell is broken. The Merritt, it seems, is not merely a means for moving motor vehicles, or a "traffic sewer," in the parlance of civic planner Andres Duany. Rather, it creates a journey befitting the most scenic destinations and enhancing even mundane trips. It's a road that can not only provide an uplifting drive, but has inspired artists like the poet Denise Levertov, whose poem "Merritt Parkway" speaks to the "Houses now & then beyond the sealed road, the trees/trees, bushes passing by," or the painter Willem de Kooning, whose canvas of the same name—with its broad, edgy bands of green, blue, yellow-brown, and white—evokes the speed, linearity, and hues of the ride. As we find ourselves spending more time behind the wheel, the Merritt, perhaps, should inspire us to demand more imagination go into future highways, railways, or other new forms for getting us from one place to another.

Our evolving transportation system is just one of many different landscape changes happening simultaneously all around us. How to see these evolutions from manifold vantage points is the goal of this book. Exit this prologue and explore an array of ordinary places and phenomena as diverse as racetracks and camp meetings, used bookstores and drive-in theaters, town greens and old-growth forests.

Connecticut is hardly unique in its plethora of quirky, wild, domesticated, and artificial things lying unseen in everyday places. It's just the place I know. Like Thoreau at Walden, I have tried to offer "a simple and sincere account" of my own place, "and not merely what [I have] heard of other men's" places. Though my investigations all lead to Connecticut, such explorations can occur anywhere, as sure as a ride on the Merritt Parkway can begin a trip around the globe.

Along the Roadside

Sometimes when I walk down a familiar street,
I look around to see if I can make new discoveries.
It's a game I can never lose.

—David Finn, *How to Look at Everything*

There's a lot to see along the roadside and, as we spend ever more time behind the wheel, plenty of opportunity to experience the mundane wonders found there. I begin with milestones because they are among the most obscure and ancient of such attractions, plainly visible though rarely seen. I end with diners because they are well known, but remain largely invisible because they are taken for granted. These and the other objects and places I describe are neither definitive nor necessarily the most interesting roadside experiences. They are merely an introduction to a few of the marvels hidden in plain sight at the pavement's edge.

Milestones are the ancestors of the ubiquitous signs we see along our roads today. They were among the first things to give definition to travel routes. Totems of the past, they are fun to find and ponder. But where once they marked distance, in their obsolescence they now provide an awareness of time. Today the signs that best give us a sense of place are those that name streets, telling stories and raising questions about both the natural world and human culture. "Scratch a name in a landscape, and history bubbles up like a spring," wrote physics professor Chet Raymo. Of course, if you want deep history and an explanation of why the road twists and rolls or is arrow straight, looking at a roadside rock cut for a peak into the geological under-pinnings of the planet is your best bet.

As rock cuts and other soil-moving construction indicates, engi-neers and builders can't leave geology alone. But neither can artists, who, like cave painters of yore, occasionally delight in conspiring with natural rock outcrops to paint frogs, turtles, dogs, and other creatures on roadside ledges and boulders. Yet, perhaps the most apt form of roadside art is the drive-in theater, in which automobiles are an essential part of the experience. The ephemeral nature of big-screen images as well as the theaters themselves, over 90 percent of which have disappeared, well illustrates the car culture.

While roadside art may offer refreshment for the spirit, springs bubbling from rock and soil along the way were oases for the body in the days of slow, animal-borne transportation. Some still offer refresh-ment to those who stop and fill plastic jugs, but streamlined diners later assumed some of their role as quick stops for a drink and spots to trade gossip with other travelers and locals. They still beckon.

Counting Miles in Four Centuries
Old Milestones

Much to the annoyance of drivers behind me, I slowly cruised along in my pickup on a busy stretch of State Route 10 in Plainville, scanning the roadside for a tablet of brownstone. In an area of small shopping plazas, offices, and modest homes near the corner of Betsy Road, I suddenly hit the brakes and pulled onto the narrow shoulder. Half hidden in tall grass on a gently sloping lawn was the small reddish-brown marker. The two-foot-high slab was inscribed with a single letter, "H," directly above the roman numerals "XII. M." An early nineteenth-century milestone, it informs passing travelers that Hartford is twelve miles from this spot.

Scores of stones inscribed with numerals and initials stand quiet sentinel along many of Connecticut's roads. Measuring distances that have served since colonial days, some of these markers are over two centuries old. Often obscured by brush, detritus, or the distractions of development, many are clearly visible to (if rarely noticed by) thousands of motorists who pass them each day. But when first established they were significant monuments, helping bind the nation together by facilitating the flow of people and goods.

Typically two to three feet tall, these mile markers resemble headstones. Though most commonly made of brownstone, some are cut from local gray gneiss or granite. Distances are generally marked, as is the one on Route 10, in roman or arabic numerals, with the county seat designated by initials, such as "H" for Hartford or "NL" for New London.

I began my Route 10 milestone prowl at the nine-mile marker, a low stub of brownstone shaded by well-sculpted shrubs at the edge of Farmington's village green. Heading south to New Haven on a crisp and windy winter day, I found the mile ten marker precisely a mile away in a historic neighborhood in which some of the homes may have witnessed the stone's planting. Though I doubled back a couple of times, I couldn't locate the eleven-

mile monument. After finding the twelve-mile marker at Betsy Road, number thirteen also eluded me. Low to the ground and splotched with lichen, the fourteen-mile stone was surrounded by neatly clipped grass in front of the Plainville Housing Authority's Crest View Manor. Creeping past Southington's big-box stores, gas stations, and chain restaurants, I didn't find another marker until I was almost to the Cheshire line, as mile twenty-one appeared.

By some estimates, Connecticut once had some six hundred milestones. Without a complete inventory, no one knows how many are left. Given that they lost their function a century and a half ago and considering that they are subject to abuse by weather, snow plows, vehicle crashes, and relentless development, the survival of so many is remarkable.

Roadside milestones go back at least to Roman times, and as early as 1767, Connecticut law required local selectmen to install "stones at least two feet high near the side of the common traveling road, marked with the distances from the county town of the county where such town lyes." No funds were appropriated for the mandate; however, failure to comply subjected selectmen to a fine of forty shillings. The markers replaced irregularly situated cairns, much to the benefit of "the saddle-sore horseback rider, the weather-beaten stagecoach driver, and the foot-weary itinerant," according to an anonymous report in state transportation department files. Turnpike companies planted many of the later stones. Today's sheet metal interstate highway mileposts and road signs indicating distances to various places are direct descendants of the old stones.

Route 10 in Cheshire proved barren of markers, as far as I could tell, but shortly over the Hamden line I spied a weather-chewed stone. Standing just outside the railing of Mount Carmel Cemetery, it looked like an escaped gravestone. Pitted and barely legible, the mile marker stared across the street at a tavern, bike dealer, and pawn shop, while signaling to travelers that "NH" (New Haven) was nine miles away.

With dark descending I arrived at the severely eroded seven-mile marker along New Haven's Dixwell Avenue. Standing beside it among parked cars at an Allstate Insurance outlet and across the street from a muffler shop, I imagined the traffic and change the stone had witnessed. But it wasn't only an instrument for channeling the past. It posed questions about the future. If the stone survived another hundred years, who would be passing by and what would surround it?

Placed over the better part of a century by various public and private entities, milestones are hardly uniform. A series of stones on State Route 49 in Voluntown and North Stonington in the eastern reaches of the state don't indicate the distance to a town, but rather to "PB," or the Pawcatuck Bridge at the Rhode Island line. Not far from the New York state border, a gray marker on a grassy slope beside U.S. Route 202 in New Milford gives two distances—forty-nine miles to Hartford and eighty-six miles to New York. Further east in Litchfield, a similar stone on the same road gives not only the distance between the cities, but the name of the person who planted it and the date, 1787.

While many ancient stones have fallen victim to road widening and vandalism or have been repurposed for house foundations and terraces, those left standing are increasingly celebrated as historical artifacts with almost talismanic appeal. On U.S. Route 1 near the center of Clinton is a low, grayish-red stub of a milestone, its left side partially broken. Situated on the narrow lawn of a large colonial home known as the Milestone House, it marks twenty-five miles to New Haven. A nearby plaque notes that it's a replica, the original having been uprooted and taken to the local historical museum.

Visit the Canton Historical Museum and you'll find a brownstone marker indicating sixteen miles to Hartford bolted to the porch wall. The two-mile monument that once stood along East Hartford's Silver Lane is now an artifact at the Old State House in Hartford, the very spot to which the inscription refers. No doubt the milestones on display were saved from destruction, but, having been calibrated for a specific spot, they seem bizarrely out of place indoors.

Plymouth created a pocket park on U.S. Route 6 beside a four-foot-high brownstone that indicates it's nineteen miles to Hartford, fifteen to Litchfield. Orange and yellow lichen cover the scarred, rounded marker like rust on an old car. Surrounded by flowers and shrubbery, there's also a large sign recounting the marker's purpose and provenance.

Though retired from their original use, these ancient stones are not entirely devoid of value as tools of modern business. Often they are curiosities attracting tourists. The gracious white clapboard Longwood Country Inn in Woodbury showcases its milestone, which is embedded in the inn's front stone wall. The inn's literature refers to the prized object as "an excellent specimen of a vanishing reference to our nation's early commerce and communication." The light-colored stone bearing roman numerals is faded almost to illegibility, leaving it invisible to all but inn guests and a handful of the thousands of cars passing daily.

Hidden for years by weeds in front of a dilapidated historic house that was dismantled to make way for a Taco Bell on U.S. Route 6, the fourteen-mile marker to Hartford was saved in 2007 by Bristol's city officials working with the State Department of Transportation and the site's developer. A tiny object at the margin of a major commercial artery near fast food restaurants and sprawling big-box stores, the foot-high chunk of brownstone could easily have been destroyed but for an outpouring of public concern that came close to affection. It now sits safely in a little well-landscaped plot in front of the restaurant. I recently saw it at dusk, basking in the eerie glow of internally lit plastic signs.

Not all milestones are on main travel routes. A wrong turn onto Walkley Hill Road in Haddam one day led me to discover two sandstone mile markers on the steep, twisty country byway, where I never expected them. Amazingly, this must have been the primary route to Hartford before a straighter, flatter alternative was built. Walkley Hill climbs from the new main road, State Route 154, and winds around in the hills before returning to the state road a few miles later. This old way is a reminder of a slower transportation era when even major roads were more beholden to topography. Route 154 also has milestones, though some are replacements dating only to the late twentieth century.

Connecticut Yankees have a reputation as a practical lot, but something in a milestone captures the imagination and stirs nostalgia. How else to explain a noble, short-lived Department of Transportation program of the early 1970s to find and replace lost milestones? In addition to Route 154, State Route 85 in Colchester and Salem and several other roads in eastern Connecticut were planted with replicas that use pink granite to represent sandstone and gray granite for other rock types. Little more than a generation old, they've begun disappearing into the underbrush and show signs of weathering.

Perhaps Connecticut's most unusual milestone sits in a suburban neighborhood of well-tended postwar houses in the Griswoldville section of Wethersfield, where it marks six miles to Hartford. Though it looks like an ancient brownstone monument, it was erected in the early 1970s by Richard Lasher, the self-styled mayor of Griswoldville, now in his nineties. Fashioned from material salvaged during renovation of a local eighteenth-century church, Lasher created the stone as a tangible token of his attachment to home and its connection to the larger world.

Expensive, difficult to replace, a safety hazard in a crash, and barely visible at even moderate speeds, the old stones are obsolete now. I'm grateful for the new road markers with bright reflective surfaces, but a deep traveler's curiosity keeps me always on the lookout for these old-time monuments. I doubt that our current clutter of metal and wooden signs will last as long or be as deeply affecting once they become outmoded in a future filled with GPS devices. Regardless, as we speed faster and faster into the twenty-first century, old milestones will continue to stand sentry along the roadside, reminding us of where we've been.

What's in a Name?
Reading Street Signs

We get places by reading street signs. They enable others to find us. But more than just practical navigation tools facilitating the flow of letters and visitors, the street signs we read at road intersections are community memoirs forming a network of meaning, what William Least Heat Moon has called a "deep map," a written outline of a place that joins together history, topography, legend, and politics.

Wherever I go I not only read street names to determine where I am, I treat them like a crossword puzzle whose intersections offer clues leading to a fuller understanding of a place, enabling me to see what is hidden in plain sight. Street names describe natural features; specify uses of property; indicate landmark buildings like taverns, churches, and factories; and offer directions, such as east and west, or the name of the neighboring place to which they lead. They memorialize Indian tribes and honor families and individuals. Streets are commonly named for flowers, trees, birds, and other animals. Some names suggest good places for seeing sunrises or sunsets, such as Sunny Slopes Road in Columbia or Suncrest Lane in Farmington. Others are biblical, with events, places, or people from scripture that indicate settlement by devout people. Some are just whimsical or demonstrate the salesmanship of developers, such as Ellington's Darby Dream View.

I especially like street names that provide clues to overlooked elements of our landscape, such as the numerous Spring Streets indicating water bubbling from the ground, or Four Mile Road in West Hartford, where an old-time sandstone mile marker proclaims a distance of four miles to Hartford. Some street signs are mysteries solved with a little curiosity, like Huyshope Avenue in Hartford, a corruption of "House of Hope," the name

of a Dutch fort built nearby in 1633. Others, like Obtuse Rocks Road in Brookfield, have origins that will forever remain just … well, a little obtuse.

Topographical monikers are common, often combining the practical and the poetic. Boggy Hole and Foggy Meadow Roads, both in Old Lyme, are among the most evocative. Simple utilitarian descriptors like River Street, Hill Street, and Ridge Road are legion, and there may be more Cedar Swamp Roads than there are cedar swamps. But some topographical names are truly intriguing, like Pulpit Rock Road in Woodstock, where religious services were held in the 1600s from a large glacial boulder. Breakneck Hill Road in Woodbury is among those names inviting curiosity and stories, but whose origins are unclear.

The remains of a cider mill, quarry, paper mill, lime kiln, brickyard, and icehouse may still be found along a namesake road. Swimming Pool Road in Canton memorializes a public swimming hole, but no one's swimming there now. I once made my way up Roxbury's Mine Hill Road and, thanks to preservation by the local land trust, came upon the remnants of a once thriving nineteenth-century iron forge and the series of abandoned tunnels from which ore was extracted. Iron Works Road in Killingworth marks the site of one of the nation's largest colonial iron makers, but my visit there revealed nothing beyond the street name.

Given Connecticut's role as a breadbasket of colonial America, it's logical that farms are frequently found in street names. In developed areas, the names serve as epitaphs of fading agriculture, as is the case on Bidwell Farm Road in Canton or Farmstead Lane in Farmington. Cream Hill Road in Cornwall used to be the site of dairy farms. Town Farm Road, found in several communities, marks the location of a nineteenth-century poor farm.

Taken collectively, street names can demonstrate the mindset of an era and place. Connecticut is dotted with many nineteenth-century mill villages whose pragmatic road designations are befitting neighborhoods developed to produce practical products. In the edge-tool-making hamlet of Collinsville, where I live, three of the four cardinal directions are street names, as well as Front, Center, Main, Spring, River, Church, Bridge, and High.

Current uses are also indicated by street names, such as Middletown's Aircraft Road, Groton's Filtration Plant Road, and Torrington's Technology Park Drive. Church Streets and Cemetery Roads have probably had their namesake uses longest. Railroad Streets can lead to the train station or an abandoned right-of-way. Whenever I pass Canal Street in Farmington or Ferry Lane in Simsbury, they ignite questions about long-gone means of getting around.

Native American culture is well represented on Connecticut street signs, which tend to memorialize a tribe, like Bloomfield's Tunxis Avenue, or a great tribal leader, such as Bozrah's Wawecus Hill Road. Kent's Schaghticoke Road leads to an actual Indian reservation. There are also descriptive Native American terms, such as Massapeag ("great-water land") Road in Montville and Wopowog ("the crossing place" of a river) Road in East Hampton. Many Indian-themed street monikers have nothing to do with Connecticut tribes. Near Middlefield's Lake Beseck, there is not only a Pequot Road, but also Cherokee, Iroquois, Kickapoo, Sioux, and Seminole Roads lending an air of Hollywood nostalgia for something that never existed.

Roads are often named for a town's earliest settlers, like Case Street and Barbourtown Road in Canton. Later industrialists also get their due. East Hampton has remembered its most famous bell maker with Bevin Road, Bevin Boulevard, and Bevin Avenue. Sometimes a road commemorates an entire community that settled and then moved on, as with Shaker Road in Enfield and Somers.

Politicians often get streets named after them. Governor Morgan Bulkeley is honored in Hartford, Ella Grasso in Torrington, and Chester Bowles in Essex. Local writers like Lydia Sigourney and Mark Twain are celebrated in Hartford. Stephen Mather Road in Norwalk acknowledges the local boy who went on to become the National Park Service's first chief.

Bridgeport's Barnum Avenue and Barnum Boulevard pay tribute to the great impresario and mayor P. T. Barnum. Naugatuck pays homage to military leaders, dedicating roads to Generals Dalton, Pulaski, and Patton (none of whom were from Connecticut).

Streets named for animals, trees, and flowers often salute existing features, like the large, ancient tree on Easton's winding Old Oak Road. But sometimes road signs are like obituaries, as is the case with the many Elm Streets, whose signature tree has succumbed to disease. Over twenty-five species of trees are represented on road signs, including maple, birch, sycamore, tamarack, aspen, apple, and hickory. About twenty different birds, from raptors to songsters, are acknowledged. Deer are a popular mammal, as are foxes; Simsbury has Fox Den Road, Fox Ridge Lane, and Fox Chase, while nearby West Hartford includes Foxcroft Road, Fox Meadow Lane, Foxridge Road, and Fox Chase Lane.

My favorite street names reference places depraved or lofty, expressing the residents' fears and hopes or sense of humor. There's Beelzebub Road in South Windsor, Hell Hollow Road in Voluntown, and Sodom Road in North Canaan. Countervailing forces prevail at Paradise Street in Windham, Eden Avenue in Southington, and Utopia Road in Manchester. A visit to New Hartford's Satan's Kingdom Road didn't reveal any obvious differences in geography or the moral character of the inhabitants, though the name and others suggesting brimstone have sometimes engendered controversy due to their devilish references. Perhaps such areas are damned with the virtue of eternally inspiring stories.

The best street names invite speculation. According to former Killingworth first selectman David LeVasseur, Roast Meat Hill Road may commemorate the time a salt hay-filled wagon driven by one Deacon Avery was struck by lightning and burned before the oxen could be unhitched. Another theory is that a barn full of livestock caught fire back in colonial days. It's most likely that early settlers discovered piles of animal bones, leftover from years of feasting, since the hill served as the main winter encampment of the Hammonasset Indians.

The Hatchett Hill Road area in East Granby was reportedly sold by an Indian for a hatchet, or it could be connected to a colonial family named Hatchett. Yelping Hill Road in Cornwall might have gotten its moniker from noisy foxes in colonial times or from a family with deaf-mute children who screamed loudly when angered or excited. The origin of Skunk Misery Road in Haddam is unknown, according to municipal historian Jan Sweet, so I've yet to learn for sure whether skunks were made miserable by intruding settlers, or vice versa.

The contestants for worst street name are many. Some subdivisions bear the first names of developers' wives, children, and secretaries. No, Tolland's Chardonnay Lane, Merlot Way, and Zinfandel Circle are not on the Connecticut Wine Trail. Middletown's yellow series that includes Yellow Birch, Yellow Hill, and Yellow Roads; Yellow Green and Yellow Wood Streets; and Yellow Orange, Yellow Pine, and Yellow Yellow Circles must drive visitors and emergency responders to distraction. A species of lexico-logical acrophobia is at work with names like Hi-Lo Road in Durham, Hy Vue Drive in Newtown, Top O' Hill Road in Darien, and Hi Top Hill Road in Voluntown. Hopefully, it isn't contagious.

Of course, there are Lovers Lanes in several towns, though it's unclear whether they result from developers being cute or actual trysts. And I've often wondered about Flirtation Avenue in Washington. The name has always attracted me.

Sometimes street names are more markers of a time than a place. So-called Astronaut Village in West Hartford includes streets named after some of the Mercury Seven, none of whom hailed from Connecticut. Nevertheless, the subdivision's house styles hark back to that era of middle-class optimism, and names like Glenn, Shepard, and Grissom are worthy of being emblazoned among them.

Street names can steep a landscape in significance or turn it into gibberish. Perhaps local planning commissions, which typically have authority over such things, should require that a bit more thought go into street naming rather than merely accepting what a developer writes down on a subdivision map. There's no reason why a road map can't also be a deep map.

Seeing through Time
Roadcuts

Preferring straightaways and moderate grades, modern highways slice through solid rock, exposing the bare bones of Connecticut's countryside. These rough rock walls reveal fabulous stories about the origins of our landscape that largely can be grasped at a glance. Even zooming by them at sixty-five miles per hour, who hasn't occasionally wondered about the colors, fractures, undulations, and odd striations of roadcuts?

To satisfy some of my curiosity, I went for a drive with former state geologist Ralph Lewis on a chilly March morning when the trees were still leafless and the landscape fully exposed. With a large map of colorful swirls and blobs depicting Connecticut's bedrock laid out on the hood of my pickup as we stood on the Rocky Neck Connector in East Lyme, Lewis described the cataclysmic continental crashes, volcanic island arcs, ancient seas, the solidified remains of molten magma, and the omnipresent and inexorably slow process of erosion that formed the state's stony foundation. We perused the map, with Lewis pointing out rocks south of Hartford over two hundred million years old, and in the northwestern part of the state, rocks in excess of a billion years.

On the Connector's north side are rock faces in subtle shades of gray laced with white and yellow highlights sparkled with sun-washed mica flecks. The closer we got, the more intricate the pattern became. Like most stone in Connecticut outside the Hartford–New Haven Central Valley, these are metamorphic rocks formed under intense heat and pressure as many as twenty miles below the earth's surface during continental collisions millions of years ago. About six hundred million years old and now visible after millennia of erosion, such rocks can usually be identified by a distinctive layering, or foliation, caused by their compression. These layers are often

elaborately twisted and folded because, before fully cooling, they bent under the immense pressure like taffy.

We headed west on I-95 and, after crossing the high arch of the Baldwin Bridge over the Connecticut River, we planned to drive northwesterly on Route 9 to its junction with the Berlin Turnpike. In about forty-five minutes, we would travel through four hundred million years of earth history.

"For its size, Connecticut has geology whose complexity rivals any in the world," Lewis boasted as if he were bragging about his daughter. He's a stocky fellow in his late fifties with a bushy gray beard, heavy glasses, and salt-and-pepper hair who talks about the state's bedrock as if describing familiar objects at home. "You'll see more geology in an hour than you would traveling from Ohio to Colorado," he added with a smile.

Despite decades of vehicle exhaust, the exposed ledges along the Connecticut Turnpike are fairly bright and clean, a soft light gray, sometimes bearing a pinkish cast. We pulled over at a cut just east of exit 70. Traffic whizzed by at a fearful speed and was so thick there wasn't a moment of quiet. Foliation was even more pronounced here, a stone layer cake in the thinnest laminations. But what garnered Lewis's attention was a crisscross of irregular bands of lighter-colored rock, some with fairly large crystals indicating they cooled slowly. These so-called intrusions formed when hot mineral-laden liquids percolated into fractures and solidified. The cracks occurred when continents drifted and stretched. Known as pegmatites, these formations containing large mineral crystals can include gems such as beryl, emerald, and tourmaline. Bands can range from a few inches to tens of yards thick, and Connecticut once hosted dozens of pegmatite mines of substantial commercial value.

Driving Route 9 toward Middletown, we remained in a land of metamorphic rock. But the roadcuts now revealed darker, foreboding-looking material, sometimes in a dull grayish-green. Unlike the bright rocks along I-95 that share their origin with the bedrock of West Africa (to which that part of Connecticut was once joined), these were the metamorphosed remains of ancient ocean-bottom sediments scraped and pressured into rock during the cataclysmic collisions. The muted, lusterless green was sometimes stained orange from the presence of iron that had accumulated in the air-starved ocean environment.

Between exits 3 and 4 for Deep River, striking bands of light-colored pegmatite angled across the roadcuts. But no one rock type remained in view for long, and by the time we reached exit 5 we'd started seeing yellowish, sulfur-laden rocks. Lewis explained they were once part of an ancient sea floor.

We took exit 7 toward Haddam through a long, deep roadcut. Pulling a U-turn at the bottom of the off-ramp, we parked and gazed up at a rock wall a few stories tall. The cut revealed long, regular drill marks left by road builders. Like the other metamorphic formations we'd seen, this was an eroded nub, part of once grand mountains with heights rivaling today's Himalayas. Despite the passage of millennia, the heat and violence of mountain building remained visible. Some of the rock was so tortured with twists and bends and so finely rendered as to look like intricate script. Lewis pointed out layers of rock parallel to the grain that were stretched and thinned and broken so that they resembled the French sausages, *boudinage*, that geologists named them after.

Just south of exit 8 we encountered jagged rock faces that shone saffron yellow. Stopping to collect pieces of the rock that had fallen to the pavement's edge, I found it so brittle it began falling apart as soon as I picked it up. A sulfur-rich, strongly foliated metamorphic rock called schist, it was a telltale sign of deep water and volcanism.

Even with an eighteen-wheeler in the rearview mirror, the tilt of ledges indicating the direction in which the continents crashed is relatively easy to spot. Connecticut's bedrock was generally compacted east to west, leaving a corrugated landscape of north-to-south ridges and valleys. Thus, our rivers typically flow longitudinally, and highways cutting across the grain like the Merritt Parkway provide a rollercoaster ride.

At exit 9 we crossed the Higganum Dike, a long, narrow igneous rock intrusion of basalt about a thousand feet wide that stretches from Stafford to North Branford. It formed when a large fracture in the underlying meta-morphic rock filled with molten magma and slowly solidified. Known also as traprock, it's a hard and dense stone that is a dark greenish gray, but rusts orange when exposed to air. It breaks off in long, angular pieces called columnar joints that formed from shrinkage as the material cooled. The term "traprock" derives from the Swedish word *trappa*, meaning "step," because the fracturing produces a stepped appearance on cliff faces. Quarried for building stone and walls since colonial times, traprock is by far the state's most commonly mined material. Valued for its durability, almost all of it is now crushed and used as a road base.

More obvious traprock roadcuts are visible along U.S. Route 44 on Avon Mountain and in New Britain near the junction of I-84 and State Route 72, where it is quarried and pulverized. The steep ridges that loom over the Connecticut Valley from West Rock in New Haven to the Barndoor Hills near the Massachusetts border are made of this erosion-resistant stone. The massif most notable to motorists lies between exits 18 and 19 on I-91, where a steep grade slows heavy trucks and runs hard by the cragged cliffs of Higby Mountain.

At exit 11 near Randolph Road we passed the last metamorphic road-cut of Connecticut's eastern uplands and soon began descending with a panoramic view of the Central Valley, its spacious flatlands punctuated by traprock ridges. It's a classic rift valley formed about two hundred million years ago when tectonic forces were pulling the continent apart and the land sunk.

Just beyond the southbound lanes near Walnut Street as we entered Middletown were the first small outcrops of reddish-brown sandstone, a sedimentary rock formed from fine sandlike sediments and held together by mineral glue. Hardly noticeable with the distraction of weeds and guardrails along the roadside, they heralded a whole new realm of geology with critical implications for human culture.

The relatively flat Central Valley, of which Middletown is part, was a glacial lakebed that collected sediments from rushing meltwater streams pouring off adjacent hills. Level, fertile, and well drained, it proved ideal for colonial agriculture and for the development of tract housing in the twentieth century. Rockcuts generally indicate hard rock, so there are few here because sandstone is easily eroded.

Passing northwesterly into Cromwell the road straightened, leaving behind the dip and roll of the metamorphic uplands. Large sedimentary roadcuts, sometimes overlaid with later flows of basalt, stood out at Route 9's junction with I-91 and with the Berlin Turnpike a few miles distant. Although mahogany-hued sandstone predominated in both places, the rock was variously banded in horizons of yellow and blackish sandstone, as well as gray shale formed from ancient mud or clay. The colors, Lewis noted, indicated a changing climate of alternating wet and dry cycles. Black lake deposits told of wet conditions, while red beds evidenced a drier world.

Though we usually think of highway building as destructive, the spectacular roadcuts created throughout Connecticut by blasting and bulldozing have opened intriguing avenues of beauty as well as insights into the earth's formation. Lewis and I had spent only a couple hours together, but we had covered hundreds of millions of years, all three rock types—igneous, metamorphic, and sedimentary—and witnessed evidence of forces so powerful as to be beyond normal comprehension.

Connecticut has thousands of roadcuts worth exploring. Among them are a white marble wall near the junction of U.S. Routes 202 and 7 northeast of Danbury, formed from metamorphosed limestone composed of carbonate mud and the shells of marine fossils. Far to the east there are towering sixty-foot-high cliffs of dark gray metamorphic gneiss with broad banded granite intrusions at the junction of I-395 and State Route 2 in Norwich. Near the Mobil station on State Route 32 in Willington just off exit 70 of I-84 is a slope of khaki-colored schist that sparkles like gold in the sun. They're not just beautiful and awe inspiring. Like every roadcut, they tell a story.

Though we take it for granted, bedrock shapes much of the world we encounter daily, including the sites of cities and towns, the routes our roads take, the quality of water, the productivity and location of farms and factories, and the nature of our forests. The state's incredibly complex earth history continues posing riddles to even the most learned geologists. But just a few insights can both help us better grasp how the world around us works and enliven even the dullest drive.

Painted Ledges
Roadside Rock Art

Some seemed poised to leap, startling even the calmest driver. Others stand silent sentinel, as if guarding the pavement. But roadside rock outcrops and boulders painted like huge, cartoonish animals are neither about to jump nor watchful. They merely illustrate human imagination embedded in out landscape.

A large rock orphaned by a glacier on U.S. Route 44 in Eastford depicts a bloated frog with a dour expression. Across the state, an amphibian with a bright red tongue emerges out of a ledge on U.S. Route 7 in Cornwall. A purple and blue turtle crawls toward the Hammonassett Connector in Madison, while another rests at the pavement's edge in the center of downtown Marlborough. Sparky the Dalmatian stands watch outside the Montville Firehouse, and a dog's head peers at motorists along State Route 165 in Preston. Meanwhile, a martial-looking eagle appears ready to take off from a ledge on State Route 66 in Hebron.

Though animals get much of the attention, roadside rocks have been painted with everything from frivolous smiley faces to a sedate drum lying at the wooded edge of Canton's Barbourtown Road. Since the September 11 attacks, American flags have increasingly appeared on these stone canvasses, and some, like the one high among the graffiti-scrawled ledges of Bolton Notch, follow the undulating contour of the rock, which makes them seem to wave in a breeze.

Rock art contributes a sense of identity and injects a playful spirit into the countryside. Newcomers are startled, frequent travelers see a welcome milestone that grows in affection like an old friend, and residents find a reassuring token of home. No matter how difficult my day, I cannot help but smile on passing one.

Much as a glacier carved the face of Connecticut ten thousand years ago, our painted rocks are a melding of art and nature, a conspiracy between the ice age and modern human creativity. Because most of us just see an undifferentiated series of odd-shaped boulders or uneven grayish ledges, it takes a singular way of looking to see creatures in the stone in order to free them with a bucket of paint and brush.

State archeologist Nicholas Bellantoni finds Connecticut's painted rocks akin to the pictographs found in caves and on cliffs painted by native tribes thousands of years ago. Although today we have a rainbow of colors where ancient people used a mixture of red ochre, grease, and water, the frequent use of animal images is a motif shared over millennia. Like the ancients whose work included inexplicable geometric and abstract shapes, we paint the stars and stripes, a symbol of great significance that would have puzzled them. Perhaps our penchant for contemporary rock art compensates for Connecticut's lack of ancient pictographs, which are common in some areas, such as the American Southwest. Certainly there are parallel motivations and mysteries.

The oldest object in Connecticut's roadside gallery may be Eastford's pale green frog, which squats upon the broken pavement of an abandoned roadside picnic area. Some say it was painted in 1881 by state legislator

T. J. Thurber. A few years ago I called Eastford's town historian, but didn't find out much more. Local resident Margaret Day, then enjoying her ninth decade, recalled family picnics there with her children; she was fairly certain "it's always been there."

It's not hard to imagine a state legislator of yore envisioning a giant frog as he passed the site on numerous fatiguing trips to the capitol while fretting over taxes, roads, and local agriculture. Perhaps we'd be better off if today's senators and representatives devoted as much energy to improving their routes to Hartford. Certainly the lawmakers would be more widely and endearingly remembered. Without Frog Rock, Thurber himself would be all but forgotten.

Frog Rock is undoubtedly the state's best known and most beloved roadside image in stone, probably because of the picnic area, complete with concrete tables and fireplaces built around it by the Department of Transportation. Unlike Hebron's eagle, Preston's dog, and the other roadside stone animals seen only through windshield glances, generations of adults and children have touched and even climbed on the great amphibian of Eastford. My first visit on a college jaunt with friends is indelibly seared in my memory. We marveled at the massive critter and ascended his back for goofy photographs. A quick stop for sandwiches and soda became almost magical.

Unfortunately, after U.S. Route 44 was straightened and widened late in the twentieth century, the picnic area was blocked off, and today the frog sits alone, partially obscured by trees and undergrowth. Last painted in 1997 by a cadre of T. J. Thurber's descendants, it has begun to fade and peel again. But despite falling on hard times, the frog has staunch advocates and a recent web posting on the critter drew many nostalgic memories from those who picnicked there in the 1950s and 1960s. A few years ago it received national attention when Bill Griffith featured it in his syndicated Zippy comic strip, likening the animal's stolid expression to that of former vice president Dick Cheney.

Seen as a liability and maintenance headache, transportation officials offered the property to the town and State Department of Environmental Protection, both of which rejected the derelict local landmark. In 2011 it was sold to a private party interested in building a themed coffee shop and visitor center. But problems with the land's title mean that the frog's fate remains uncertain.

The state's most carefully maintained rock animal is probably Spotty, a white dog with a black nose, ears, and eyes peering out from a brushy slope on State Route 165 not far from Preston City. Stanley Zictorac was only sixteen in 1935 when he painted the likeness of his cherished pet. An employee of Atlantic Cotton, a textile firm in the Greenville section of Norwich, Zictorac was encouraged by his boss to take some printers' ink and paint the rock-based version of the cheerful pooch, according to the Norwich Bulletin. Zictorac repainted the image for a number of years, but eventually became frustrated by vandalism. Over time, the rock has been cared for by a series of anonymous locals who seemed to have taken a liking to Spotty. Some believe that the painters are local teens who hide behind the rock when cars pass by.

Just south of where the road crosses the Housatonic River, Cornwall Bridge's frog sticks out its irreverent red tongue at cars cruising by on U.S. Route 7. Its origin is legend, and its current caretaker remains unknown, though locals revel in his stealthy brushwork, which is treated like an inside joke. Even the proprietor of Baird's General Store (now Cornwall General Store), who hears most town scuttlebutt, was at a loss when I spoke with him a few years back. Several calls to townies revealed only that imaginative highway workers created the creature in the 1930s with some free time and extra paint.

The rock with Hebron's eagle has in former lives manifested itself as a whale, a frog, and also a turtle, according to Carla Pomprowicz, the town clerk. Clearly imaginations can differ, and though stone is unchanging in human lifetimes, ways of looking at it fluctuate with the times and minds of the beholders. Today the raptor with piercing eyes—brainchild of Jason Sawyer, who first painted the bird as a high school student in 1989—seems so apt as to have been teased out of the stone rather than merely painted over it. Nevertheless, some future Picasso may find something else in the ledge's bulges and fissures.

Signatures just below the beak indicate that Sawyer repainted the raptor in 1991, 1995, and 2002, when he shared the duties with Tara Graham of East Hampton, who then took sole responsibility for the work in 2003. In 2011 yet another painter revived the image, and after a few years in a dull molt the eagle is again as vivid as the day it was first completed. Once created, roadside rock art becomes a community institution, and the brushes wielded by one party are handed down over the years to someone else. The eagle has become a community symbol, prominent on the town's website and in other civic displays.

New work still appears. Marlborough's box turtle debuted in 2003, a few miles west of the eagle on State Route 66. Boldly rendered in yellow, orange, and black, the creature was conceived by town elderly agent Vi Schwarzmann after brush-cutting revealed a hidden ledge. Searching for a whimsical way of celebrating the town's bicentennial, she brought the rock to life with the help of some enthusiastic kids. The youngsters experienced a sense of pride and a little poison ivy. The town got a new landmark.

But however gracious a gesture, the turtle has not been without controversy. Depending on whether they're traveling east or west, motorists will claim to have seen a vicious lizard, a Gila monster, or a tyrannosaurus, creatures not welcome by some townsfolk. Bare rock or finished masterpiece, it's important to remember that we don't always see something the way the artist saw it.

Today's roadside rock artists may come as close to the ancient painters of pictographs as possible. Though they share a tradition thousands of years old, the reasons why people see images in geological formations or decide to paint them remain largely an enigma. Nevertheless, these artistic endeavors are a strong reminder that we are still tied to the land in ways not fully understood, and the urge to paint animals or symbols on natural features comes to the surface almost automatically. Rock art is emblematic of everyman's need to recreate a small piece of the world as he or she sees it, for all to see.

Last Picture Shows
Drive-In Theaters

My friend Bette and I pulled into the three-screen Mansfield Drive-In Theater, located on a still rural stretch of State Route 32 just north of Willimantic. We chose *The Other Guys*, a madcap buddy cop movie featuring Will Ferrell's nutty antics, over Adam Sandler's *Grown Ups* and a horror film with fangs and fake blood, but in the end it didn't really matter which movie we saw. I focused only intermittently on the comedy, letting my attention wander as a wispy summer breeze filled the air with scents of fresh popcorn and french fries. Whenever the soundtrack momentarily quieted, I listened attentively to the bass notes of bullfrogs calling from an adjacent swamp.

Most distracting of all was a tide of memories, as I recalled sitting in my parents' huge push-button Plymouth, its back seat as big as a living room couch. Decked out in footed pajamas, I gobbled potato chips and stared wide-eyed at Disney's big-screen magic. Or fast forward a few years, and there's me as a teenager making out with my girlfriend, parked strategically away from the concession-stand lights while John Wayne chased Indians, or Fred MacMurray flew his flubber car, or Robert Redford as the Sundance Kid leaped from a cliff with Paul Newman.

Most of us born by the mid-sixties have watched a movie through a car windshield, but few have had done so recently. Connecticut had forty-two drive-ins in the early 1960s, but only three remain today (two before the old Southington Twin Drive-In was recently resurrected as a municipal venue, albeit with just a single screen).

If roadside rock art harks back to the carvings and paintings of ancient petroglyphs—symbol-laden outdoor likenesses created to tell stories—perhaps drive-ins are modern technology's version of that tradition. Though projected onto manmade canvasses and always ephemeral, they continue a like function as communal places displaying meaningful images and telling tales in the open air. But in contrast to pictured rock sites of old, outdoor theaters have themselves proved ephemeral, having been invented, grown to cultural significance, crashed, and somewhat rejuvenated all within living memory.

A widespread national phenomenon that originated in New Jersey during the 1930s, drive-ins flourished in Connecticut, which, for its size, had among the largest number of theaters anywhere. It also experienced one of the most precipitous declines, losing over 90 percent of its venues. Drive-ins penetrated all corners of the state, from Danbury to Danielson. Often built at the ragged edge of suburban development near cities like Hartford, they also appeared in rural areas like the Quinnebaug section of Thompson.

Most drive-ins have been demolished, leaving only a telltale fan-shaped lot, if that. Strip malls, golf driving ranges, or weedy lots piled with odds and ends have replaced some of them. Often they've stood desolate for years, screens staring vacantly where imaginations once roamed, becoming bill-boards of blight in even the most beautiful settings. Many motorists who traveled State Route 8 still remember the dilapidated twin screens of the Watertown Drive-In, torn down years ago, squeezed between the Naugatuck River and the highway. The Manchester Drive-In's weed-choked sign and rusting steel frame still remain in picturesque Bolton Notch, by a shallow pond clutched in low hills. Though most of these temples to the twin American juggernauts of automobiles and motion pictures are long gone, a deep traveler can sometimes still find concession-stand foundations, screen footings, broken pavement, or even a tree line once sculpted to accommodate viewing.

Ironically, drive-ins were made obsolete by the car culture that spawned them. Frequently built at the edge of cities or on vacant sites along a main road providing an easy trip to and from the movie, they were no match for increasing automobile-centric suburbanization. Rising land values caused by construction of subdivisions and shopping centers caused intense development pressure, making it impossible for a seasonal business to compete with land uses that produced income year round. It's not surprising that the remaining two commercial drive-ins are in relatively rural areas.

In the 1980s VCRs and cable television channels were additional blows. Drive-ins once offered an informal night out with some of the comforts of your own living room, but now you could easily see the same movie in that very living room. Of course, it didn't help that the smaller cars being built after the oil crisis had seats much less comfortable than an easy chair.

Perhaps severely curtailed numbers reducing competition has enabled survival of the remaining few drive-ins.

Against all odds, a handsome marquee-like wooden sign at the entrance of the Mansfield Drive-In that also advertises a flea market tells another story. The owner started the Sunday antiques market in 1975 to help make the property pay. In the nineties, he purchased fifteen acres from a nearby chicken farm and converted a coop into fifteen thousand square feet of indoor sales space open all year, rain or shine. People came to hunt for old tools, glassware, jewelry, and collectibles. Meanwhile, the three fifty-foot-wide, 110-foot-long screens advertised the movie currently playing there to a crowd that otherwise might not have realized the drive-in was still in business.

On most nights at the Mansfield Drive-In, double features play on three screens (two of which were salvaged from Waterbury's Twin Pine Drive-in in the 1980s). There's also a playground for kids and a spacious snack bar, whose black-and-white tiled floor harkens back to the operation's 1954 origin. On my recent trip, I was surprised to have to wait in line behind over twenty cars queued at the entrance just before dusk.

Inside, the vast graveled expanse was dotted with tufts of weeds and lined with posts where car speakers used to hang in the days before radio broadcast of soundtracks. Many cars had come early to stake out a favorite spot, and there seemed to be communal excitement in watching nature bring on the dark. Accommodating up to nine hundred cars, the cinema meadow was surrounded by trees with the giant screens placed at opposite ends of the perimeter.

After a warm day, the night promised cool weather and people readied pillows and sleeping bags in the back of hatchbacks and on pickup beds. Some set up chairs and blankets beside their vehicles, pulling out trays of food and cold drinks from coolers. As cars filed in, Bette and I watched the clouds in the sky change shape and color as the darkness deepened. There was a festive atmosphere as fathers played catch with their kids, teens threw around a football, and Frisbees whizzed by. Children chased each other at tag, and there were so many soccer balls in motion it seemed as if we were at a tryout.

With twilight came the films. Laughter occasionally echoed through the dark, and the sound of latecomers' tires crunching on the gravel spoke of more company. We watched as the screen framed a cinematic landscape even as the real landscape framed the screen. Stars burned brighter overhead as the sky grew dimmer, while stars of another sort performed in front of us.

Fired up by our experience in Mansfield, it wasn't long before Bette and I found ourselves at the Pleasant Valley Drive-In in Barkhamsted. Off the beaten path, this theater has changed little since it opened as one of the state's first in 1947. Situated on gently sloping, grassy ground, it's a cozy rectangle surrounded by large trees that accommodates about 250 cars. Behind the white-painted plywood screen are towering pines whose darkness enhances the vividness of the picture. The Farmington River is just across the street.

"Happy Birthday Jenna!" read a handwritten poster in the window of the tiny ticket booth. The seventeen-year-old girl and her friends were gathered on blankets and in chairs around a cluster of cars not far from the concession stand. As they munched on snacks and shared stories, people played ball around them. Before the movie began, a woman got on the radio and belted out the birthday song. After just a couple of lines, singing erupted from over a hundred vehicles.

The night's feature, *Nanny McPhee*, starred Emma Thompson as a governess who straightens out some unruly kids in wartime England. The film brought out legions of children in bright pajamas who held colorful light sticks and brought me back to those years in the backseat of my parents' Plymouth. The soundtrack was accompanied by the background hum of late summer insects. With the windows rolled down, I felt the wind and heard rustling trees. The evening smelled deliciously of soil and freshly cut grass, and the damp aroma of the river wafted across the street. Exposed to nature while watching a film might be distracting to some, but Bette and I enjoyed this serendipitous natural version of Berthold Brecht's "distancing effect" (*Verfremdungseffekt*) by which the audience is intentionally interrupted from emotional attachment to the action in order to promote critical thought.

Ultimately, drive-ins are not about the movie or a nostalgic tradition. They're about community. Emblematic of this is the resurrection of the Southington Drive-In as a municipally operated facility several years after its commercial demise. Located near the town's sewer plant and recreational fields, it lies just off State Route 322 with a view of the steep traprock cliffs of Meriden. Only one of the two original screens is left, and the speaker posts and concession building are long gone. The old ticket booths, once derelict in a corner by some trees, have been spruced up and decorated with colorful flowers. Nine films aired the first year. A local nonprofit group staffed each event and in turn received half the proceeds, with the balance going to maintain the site. Luckily, thousands attended, and the drive-in was back in business.

The value of outdoor movies to engage a community is not lost elsewhere. Recently the Shoppes at Farmington Valley in Canton used a large inflatable screen to show movies in their parking lot. The use of such screens is becoming increasingly popular for special events and promotions. In Collinsville, local groups will occasionally show films on the exterior wall of a building.

More than an emblem of car culture or a sign of nostalgia, drive-ins strike the right balance between the fantasy of cinema and the realness of place. They help us explore the distinctions between the actual and the make-believe. In a conventional theater you could be anywhere, and hence nowhere. At the drive-in, you are grounded by the world around you.

A Cool Drink of Water
Roadside Springs

Stafford Springs was once renowned throughout the country for its curative mineral waters. John Adams took a dip and drink and spent several days there in 1771. Early in the nineteenth century the village became a resort with a large hotel accommodating throngs of visitors. The springs waned in popularity with the rise of nearby textile manufacturing, and when I was there recently, only a small, domed well house memorialized this formerly grandest of Connecticut springs.

There's probably no more singular marker of place than a roadside spring, bubbling clear and cold from the ground. Flowing along bedrock fractures and percolating through sand and gravel, their waters carry the very essence of the countryside, the "pent-up energy of elemental forces," as Connecticut nature writer Hal Borland put it. Delighting every sense, they're rare phenomena that can be seen, smelled, touched, heard, and, above all, tasted.

Springs were a boon in an age when hay and water-fueled horse-powered transportation and longer travel times induced people and animals to stop for a drink. In the days when stone mile markers were a goal to get past, springs were oases at which to linger and savor refreshment. Today, they are more of a highway hazard, undermining macadam and causing winter icing. Many have disappeared, victims of road widening and development, or closed by health authorities concerned about contamination, or blocked off by landowners fearful of liability. Some springs are polluted, others simply forgotten.

Alex Cassie Spring in Windham may be the state's best-known roadside water source. It's easily accessible and picturesque, pouring into a semicircular concrete basin from a small but elegant castle-like structure of field-

stone built with Depression era money. Jim Hooper of the local water department has seen a crowded parking lot with lines of people waiting to fill their jugs at this popular site situated at the edge of its namesake park along busy State Route 195 near the Mansfield border. Flowing at about ten gallons per minute, the spring has served a thirsty public since at least the nineteenth century. Well known locally, the spring also draws people from miles around. "It's probably the last free thing left in the state," Hooper quipped. Regularly tested, it's occasionally closed for cleaning or due to elevated levels of bacteria.

Pouring from an iron pipe that rises thigh-high out of the ground in a down-turned "E," the chilled water of a spring in Salmon River State Forest in Colchester has been periodically monitored ever since a public outcry erupted when it was threatened with closure several years ago. An artesian well flowing under natural pressure, it's situated at the edge of a dirt road just off State Route 16, a little east of the Comstock covered bridge. It's best in winter when the clear, tasteless water is so cold it makes your teeth hurt, and stalagmites of ice form below the pipe.

Testing roadside springs, however, is the exception, not the rule. As a result, stern warnings about potential pollution are often posted nearby. A large blue placard stands guard next to a North Stonington spring that pours from a white PVC pipe poking out of a grassy embankment at the rural intersection of State Routes 184 and 49. But despite the admonition that "this is not an approved water source," a devoted cadre of people stop regularly to fill jugs because, as one regular noted on findaspring.com, it's "more than just getting fresh drinking water. It's really a spiritual journey into our mother earth."

Even on a remote road ascending Mount Riga in the state's far north-west corner, an alert is posted beside an iron pipe spilling clear water into a mossy basin made from a split log. The relatively new sign doesn't change my mind. I've sampled the spring in all seasons for over thirty-five years, always finding it chilled and sweet.

Despite potential hazards like road chemicals, or bacteria from septic systems or animal feces, springs have fiercely loyal constituencies. People have faith in springs, associating them with freshness, purity, and health benefits. On a sunny autumn afternoon, I met two energetic women at a spring rushing from a white plastic pipe jutting from a wooded hillside on State Route 67 in Roxbury. Water poured into a natural pool in which pebbles seemed magnified almost to glowing. The liquid sparkled in patchy sunlight, making a delicious tinkling, wind-chime sound.

Undeterred by tricky footing as they descended the bank and crossed a rickety makeshift bridge of pallets over a tiny stream, Audrey Farrow and Nancy Sears were determined to fill several old milk jugs. Longtime employees retired from Southbury Training School, they used to come here frequently on lunch or supper breaks. After more than two decades, collecting the water has become a ritual of friendship. "It's good for you and tastes better than well or city water," Farrow explained after handing me a half-gallon jug to take home.

Located on private property, the owners have removed the pipe and bridge two or three times in the last ten years, according to local sanitarian Keith Vaughn. But each time both have been anonymously reinstalled. People bring cases of bottles to the site. One woman claimed that the spring had been blessed by a priest. A man told Vaughn it was the only water he'd drink with scotch.

Spring quality can fluctuate rapidly for reasons that might not always be readily apparent. What is potable one day may be polluted the next from causes as diverse as rainstorm runoff or a dead animal. All that remains of a spring on Campville Road in Litchfield is a moss-covered concrete box, closed over a decade ago by local officials due to unpredictable and recurring high bacteria levels. Nevertheless, nearby resident Steve Watson, who drank from the spring for over twenty years, laments the loss of a cool draught on August days. A burly, muscular man in his sixties with a booming voice, he recalls how the water "ran fresh and cold from the ground all the summer. Lots of people used it. It was a real gathering place where you got to know your neighbors."

Although signs are regularly disregarded, contamination can pose real health threats. A sign warning about e-coli marks a spring on Furnace Avenue in Stafford, where a roadside pullout and a length of disconnected black pipe testify to its former use as a water source. A deep traveler can spot many such places, often without a sign, especially along back roads.

Canton spring is located in a squat, cut-stone shed, its half-rotted door permanently ajar. Inside is a rectangular basin about two feet wide and three feet long. The crystalline spring water, which can be seen percolating through the sandy bottom, was once so pure and plentiful that a soda-bottling works operated nearby. But industry came along and contaminated the groundwater with chemicals. Though findaspring.com claims the "spring house protects the water from sunlight and contamination," Department of Energy and Environmental Protection records indicate that drinking water lines had to be extended into the area because nearby wells were polluted. Health officials advise that appearances are deceptive and contamination is not always detectable. No one has tested the water's purity.

Locating some long unused roadside springs takes a bit of sleuthing. I discovered one east of State Route 22 in North Branford only after walking the shoulder back and forth several times until I heard the faint sound of trickling water. Following the tiny watercourse a couple of hundred feet up a steep, forested slope, I found a low concrete trough topped by a rusted steel gable. A slow, steady stream leaked out of the masonry box and flowed downhill toward a culvert that passed beneath the road to flat ground, where a housing development stood. I lifted a corner of the heavy lid and found a basin full of clear water. Someone had gone to a lot of trouble building the small spring house, but no one seemed to have been there in years.

Pausing momentarily, I listened to the water's soft trickle above the intermittent rush of traffic below.

Some springs once widely used are now hidden in plain sight. It took several passes before I finally found the one I was looking for on State Route 17 in Durham near the intersection with Old Washington Trail. An empty lot with a battered "No Dumping" sign in this area of rapidly suburbanizing farmland was my only clue. Water gushed from an iron pipe partly obscured by weeds at the pavement's edge and ran down a grassy swale until disappearing into the underbrush. A local jogger who had stopped just a few feet away claimed he'd never heard of a spring in the area.

For those enamored of spring water but worried about quality, there are commercial sites that dispense water, vending-machine-style, for twenty-five or fifty cents per gallon. Triple Springs lies in an established residential neighborhood and up against a wooded traprock hillside on the eastern edge of Meriden, where the hum of I-91 can be heard in the distance. A large concrete-block bottling plant stands at the edge of a pond. Out front is a self-serve station built of decorative block and plate glass below a metal mansard roof. Customers can fill their own jugs or purchase one of the company's.

A few miles north of I-84 where State Route 32 follows the twists of the Willimantic River, a roadside sign in Willington advertises "Pure Mountain Spring Water." Nestled against a steep, rugged hillside is a fairly new, squat stone building with handsome wooden doors at Schofield Spring. Despite freezing rain on a mid-December day, a middle-aged man named Doug dressed in sweatshirt and jeans filled up a five-gallon carboy at this vending machine writ large. A regular customer, he told me that "it sure beats my well water, and springs have more stuff that's good for you."

Sources of human sustenance bubbling freely from soil and stones, springs share something with miracles of old, as when Moses struck his staff against a rock. Sometimes we imagine their waters as curative or as fountains of youth. They even evoke nostalgia for lost community, as in the biblical wells of old. A diminished number of springs, once a common quick stop for refreshment, remain historical curiosities and hydrological wonders inviting discovery.

A Great Good Place
Diners

Diners are travelers' landmarks. They measure distance like milestones, share attention-grabbing design with rock art, and offer refreshment like roadside springs. But more than most roadside attractions, a diner allows you to take the pulse of a community by the condition of its structure, the food it serves, and the penumbra of activity in and around it. Even when I'm not hungry, it's hard to resist stopping.

Sandwiched between principal manufacturers in Massachusetts and New Jersey, Connecticut is fortunate to have about a hundred diners. Although many places call themselves diners, the true stainless steel models and older barrel-roof versions are usually easy to recognize. Evolved from converted horse-drawn lunch wagons that served New England mill hands in the late nineteenth century, a diner is "a prefabricated structure with counter service hauled to a remote site," according to historian Richard Gutman. Unlike most other buildings, diners began life on wheels, having been carted on flatbed trucks to their final destination. They are not only alongside the road, but *of* the road. From serving factory workers to their proliferation on the arteries of suburbia, diners reflect cultural changes over the last century.

Some of the best are in rural centers, like the gleaming, streamlined Collin's Diner adjacent to Canaan's Victorian railroad station. Going inside is like stepping into the 1940s, with its retro stainless steel accents and sky-and-cobalt-blue color scheme. Diner aficionado Randy Garbin waxes rhapsodic about its black marble countertop, hardwood booths, streamlined sconces, and sweeping lines "that inspire awe." Over the years I've feasted my eyes, but the liver and bacon with onions and a side of local gossip is to die for.

Good diners are also found in cities, like the Miss Washington in downtown New Britain, a boxy, early 1960s model with big plate-glass windows and space-age detailing. In the heart of downtown Meriden, Cassidy's is a broad, stainless, train-car-style eatery that's a bit down-at-the-heels. Sitting at the counter one cold March morning while I waited for a western omelet, I found myself plugged into the local scuttlebutt the instant I glanced up from my newspaper at the stubble-faced grill man who went on at length about another customer's views on Red Sox pitching. In the booth behind me lawyers negotiated a divorce settlement, while on the stool beside me an electrician explained a complex job to his apprentice.

Diners often beckon for attention along busy commercial routes. At the confluence of State Routes 101 and 12 and I-395 in Dayville, Zip's has a distinctive stainless tower topped with a sign that says "E-A-T" in bright red letters. On my last visit a dad bragged to me about the high school football team, and a man at the counter offered some helpful car repair advice. Zip's has been serving coffee and Yankee pot roast since 1954, but the interior gleams like it just opened last year.

Diners are America's original fast food restaurants, but unlike franchises they reflect their individual proprietor's spirit. Like siblings, they may bear common characteristics, but each has its own name and quirky personality. A chain restaurant can be set down almost anywhere, and with few exceptions the menu and building are the same. But a diner reflects its neighborhood even as it helps define it.

With their early railcar and later aerodynamic designs, diners suggest speed, efficiency, and cleanliness, while their home-style comfort food resonates with nostalgia for Mom's kitchen. No other building so involves all the senses. My eyes linger on gleaming stainless steel, my ears enjoy the hum of conversation and the sizzle of eggs on the griddle, my hands delight in cool marble counters and the heft of a porcelain mug, while my nose drinks up the scent of grilling bacon and home fries as I savor every forkful of omelet and corned-beef hash.

Diners are indoor neighborhoods with banter among patrons, waitresses, and cooks. It's easy to see why customers become regulars and in the process form an emotional attachment with the place. What else explains the outpouring of sympathy and cash to restore O'Rourke's Diner after a disastrous 2006 fire gutted this uninsured stainless gem squatting at the north end of Middletown's Main Street? Volunteers held fundraisers netting almost two hundred thousand dollars; architects, attorneys, and other professionals donated time; and some companies gave free or steeply discounted building materials to the cause. It wasn't just patrons' hunger for Brian O'Rourke's gourmet sandwiches and soups. His customers are family; he knows their tastes and what's going on in their lives.

I like taking the measure of a community in places like Plainville's Main Street Diner, where a giant coffee cup looms atop a large neon sign. Mouthwatering frying potato scents greet me on opening the door along, with the sound of family palaver. It's an ongoing town meeting where politics, interspersed with sports talk, is discussed with more vigor than at city hall. Small wonder that U.S. senator Joseph Lieberman's website lists the diners where he's shared more than the usual cup of joe with customers.

It's the kind of place where the waitress refills your coffee before you have a chance to ask and tells corny jokes that make surrounding tables groan. From the worn counter that curves around one corner of the restaurant, I become hypnotized by the short-order cook's ballet with a dozen sizzling items. And where else can you get fried bologna with eggs or peanut-butter-and-banana French toast?

Diners are among those hangouts that sociologist Ray Oldenberg calls a "great good place." More congenial than work, less sequestered than home, a great good place is a spot where people can set aside their troubles and enjoy company and conversation in an easygoing atmosphere. Such places are essential to democratic societies, Oldenberg maintains, because they encourage informal relationships among diverse people, promote sociability, encourage civic pride, and give folks a chance to unwind and blow off steam.

Prefabricated and seemingly insubstantial, diners paradoxically often outlive their grander brick-and-mortar kin. Their lighter construction enables them to adapt and to move from one place to another. The Main Street Diner, for one, got its name from its original location on Main Street in Hempstead, Long Island.

Mickey's Windham Diner, a stainless steel eatery with red porcelain enamel striping, started out in Willimantic but, forced out by urban renewal, was relocated to Waterbury, where it operated until its homecoming a few of years ago. A few miles away at the edge of Windham Airport and across from Wal-Mart is the Aero Diner, a lovingly restored rectangular structure from the late 1950s with a gleaming steel skin and large picture windows angling outward. Once known as East Hartford's Boulevard Diner, it was moved to Southbury and then to Windham, where it was the South Windham Diner until 1995, arriving at its current site ten years later. Mobility means that a diner's life need not end when its business location is no longer viable, and the ability to maintain and attract such eateries says a lot about a community.

Not all diners are successfully recycled, however. Skee's, which dates from the 1920s and first operated on the shoreline, has sat sadly vacant and deteriorating for years on a busy corner of Torrington's Main Street. Just a block from a sprawling, mostly empty factory that was once the business's lifeblood, it is "perhaps the world's oldest viable diner," according to Garbin. A recent proposal would have moved the venerable structure a mile and restored it as an information center, but plans stalled, and the diner still sits forlorn and dark. Years ago my kids treated me to a Father's Day breakfast in the tiny barrel-roof eatery. I still remember the etched glass windows, dark wood-work, elaborate tile, and, especially, a stack of buttermilk pancakes drenched in pure maple syrup that my young children loved to stick their fingers in.

While diners like Skee's await restoration, some operating establish-ments have been remodeled beyond recognition, like vinyl-sided Tony's, which sits in the shadow of elevated State Route 8 in Seymour, or Berlin Pizza on the Berlin Turnpike, whose stainless mid-fifties exterior is hidden by vertical plastic siding. On the other hand, a few, like West Hartford's 1931 Quaker, have the proportions and soul of a true diner though built on site. Many newer models, conventionally constructed with colonial revival and Mediterranean designs or even retro stainless exteriors, may be nice places to eat, but they are diners in name only, possessing the dimensions and atmosphere of family restaurants.

Diners are not just physically versatile. They also adapt to new owners and changing communities. Don't look for a burger and fries at the shiny, mid-fifties diner on Chapel Street in downtown New Haven. But if lamb korma and chicken biryani are to your taste, don't miss Tandoor, an Indian restaurant whose well-preserved diner finishes provide a truly mind-bend-ing melting-pot experience as you breathe in the scent of saffron rice and listen to sitar music.

Even places with traditional fare often serve specialties reflecting the state's cultural diversity. In addition to a grilled cheese or even a "fluffer-nutter" at Collin's Diner, you can enjoy Lebanese delights like loobi, humus, and tabouli. At the Olympia on the Berlin Turnpike I've feasted on baklava and other Greek delicacies.

"Age *plus adaptivity* is what makes a building come to be loved," writes Stewart Brand of *Whole Earth Catalog* fame. Diners serve up both in hearty helpings, where the atmosphere is as filling and satisfying as the food. Nostalgia can sell you eggs sunny-side-up, but diners nourish our land-scape—not because they hark back to a golden age of factory work and doo-wop music, but because they adapt so well to the changing neighborhoods we live in. They are not just subject to change, but barometers of change. At their best, diners herald a kind of back-to-the-future recycling writ large. When I hunger for a sense of community and place, I put a diner on my menu.

Places We Build

Streets and houses and fields and places of work, could teach us a great deal not only about American history and American society but about ourselves and how we relate to the world. It is a matter of learning how to see.

—John Brinckerhoff Jackson, *Discovering the Vernacular Landscape*

Stone is the primal building substance. Not only one of the earliest of materials used, it is often all that remains of places that have long ceased to exist, whether it lingers as the stone walls of abandoned farms, the ruins of a factory, or the cellar holes of a ghost town. If roadcuts show what the earth is made of, then stone harvested from a quarry demonstrates what can be made of that hardened crust of earth. No material bears such a strong imprint of a place, and people reserve special affection for stone structures. Connecticut, which is blessed with a wide variety of bedrock, was once home to hundreds of quarries. But the few still operating are hidden in plain sight.

It's not surprising that towers in public parks, perched on wind-swept summits and subject to brutal weather, are made of enduring native stone. High above the surrounding landscape, they are places where ordinary citizens can feel like kings surveying the world below. Of course, even in egalitarian Connecticut some people choose to build homes that look like King Arthur's castle, with towers, crenellated rooflines, and stone to convey a fortress-like sense of security and permanence.

In the mid-nineteenth century, the first houses widely using cement, sometimes called artificial stone, were built in an octagon shape. Like castles, they were buildings that not only sheltered people but that were designed to make a statement, in this case about a modern, holistic way of life that favored using native building materials, natural light, and ventilation, as well as innovations like indoor plumbing.

Also defying conventional geometry and materials are Quonset huts. First deployed as temporary buildings in World War II, they continue to be repurposed as homes, offices, garages, retail outlets, and storage units. Equally practical and versatile, barns were some of the first structures built by European colonists. Though they are among the most common buildings to be found here, they are rapidly disappearing as the agrarian life for which they were constructed fades away. They are barometers of cultural change with designs indicative of natural conditions that favored various type of farming.

Built for spiritual purposes rather than for strictly utilitarian ones are several camp meetings that sprouted in the state during the mid- to late 1800s. Beginning as tent revivals and later existing as colorful and whimsical cottages used as summertime getaways, they usually include a central green like early New England towns. Their magnetic sense of community reminds us that the built environment fulfills many purposes.

At first blush nothing could seem further from the camp meeting or hilltop castle than a car racetrack, but these cathedrals to automotive speed were erected in service to the secular religion of car culture. Like camp meetings, they are seasonal places serving an energized constituency, engrained in our culture like stone.

A Most Enduring Harvest
Quarries

🛆

Standing at the edge of the pit was dizzying. Beyond the lip of Branford's Stony Creek Quarry, with its sheer rock walls stepped in angular terraces several stories high, aeons of geologic history were visible. Steeped also in human history, stone from this area is found in the base of the Statue of Liberty, New York's Grand Central Station, and Chicago's Newberry Library. The rock harbors fabulous stories of architectural grandeur and of molten material cooling under great pressure miles beneath the earth's surface. But unlike most quarries in the state, Stony Creek still resounds with the piercing noises of drilling and sawing.

Connecticut once had hundreds of quarries producing building stone—granite, sandstone, schist, limestone, gneiss, and other rock types. Commercial operations peppered the state, including seven in Waterford and even more in Branford and Guilford, where access to Long Island Sound made transportation of this heaviest of building materials easier and cheaper than from inland sites. Small local operations were even more plentiful and were sometimes used for a single project—a house, a mill, or a dam. Many can be found in the woods today, carved out of ledges with unnaturally sharp corners, with the telltale signs of drill marks and a few squared-off blocks piled nearby.

An 1837 geological report declared that "the building stone of Connecticut, both ornamental and common, must be regarded as constituting one of the most valuable resources of the State." Today, survival of even a handful of quarries on a commercial scale is a wonder in this thickly settled place better known for insurance, financial products, and precision manufacturing. It's a tribute both to Connecticut's complex geology, which yields a wide variety of stone both durable and beautiful, and to quarriers who take pride in an enduring and singular product.

Rock from each quarry is unique, a true marker of a place and the forces that created it. Stony Creek granite has a soft, pinkish cast set off by charcoal and light-gray flecks. Rich, chocolaty sandstone is produced at Portland Brownstone Quarries, and Tower Hill Granite in Glastonbury yields a gray stone with salt-and-pepper crystals that are luminous in sunlight. Skyline Quarry in Stafford Springs harvests gray schist often laced with brown and gold; it can sparkle with mica and be freckled with garnets.

Even as they consume the bedrock, quarrying operations have distinctive characteristics that enrich the surrounding landscape, increase its complexity, and expand our understanding of the countryside by revealing what would otherwise be hidden. Similarly, quarriers themselves, by the nature of their work, have a special attachment to a place. They see their stone as a signature of their location and labor, a bit of themselves used and useful in places near and distant.

Situated on a hilltop, Skyline overlooks an ocean of ridges stretching toward the horizon. I met Bob Minor, who started the quarry in 1952, and current owner Wayne Williams in Williams's office on the lower level of his home at the base of the mountain. The building is made of neat stone blocks harvested from the quarry. A series of sledges were lined up at the door, ready to be grabbed by workers as they punched in.

Williams, a tall, silver-haired man who speaks with a soft voice, told me that he learned the trade from his father, who worked construction and ran a gravel business. Speaking of his stone as if it were a precious gem, Williams described it as "the metamorphosed remains of an old riverbed that lies in varying layers of color and texture." As a young construction worker he remembered being struck with wonder on realizing that a part of the earth could be incorporated in a person's home.

Minor got into the quarry business after his discharge from the marines. With thinning gray hair, he seemed a bit frail for someone who once hewed solid rock from the mountainside. "A quarry wears down of a lot of tools and men," he said in a gravelly voice he attributed to years of breathing stone dust.

Williams and I left for a tour of the quarry in his pickup. As the truck bobbed uphill to the pit on a gravel road arched over with trees, Williams bemoaned the widespread use of cheap, imitation stone. "Cultured stone will never take the place of the real thing for beauty or durability," he insisted, pounding his fist on the vinyl dashboard. As we emerged from thick woods at the quarry's edge, the land seemed to fall away on all sides, and I gazed into the eighty-foot-deep hollow revealing a vast moonscape prowled by huge dinosaur dump trucks, payloaders, and excavators. "This stone has been shipped from California to Maine," he said, proudly surveying his domain. "You can find it in New York, Philadelphia, and on Block Island."

Slowly descending among piles of rock and discarded soil, we passed carefully stacked chunks on pallets and large, uneven windrowed pieces. Momentarily the businessman's bluster faded just long enough for William to muse, "I love it down here, the seasons seem so amplified."

Exiting I-95, the works of local stonecutters became increasingly evident as I approached the Stony Creek Quarry. Walls, building foundations, and fence posts hewn of local pink granite were everywhere. Rough pieces edged many driveways.

Quarry Road passed through young woods, turning quickly from pavement to gravel and ending in a big treeless space, where I faced a sheer rock wall. A worker with a pickup took me up a rutted road from which I looked down into the barren excavation set among low green hills of an adjacent forest now preserved as conservation land.

We descended about a hundred feet below the quarry's rim, where I met Darrel Petit working a bright blue computer-driven trimming machine resembling a gigantic drill press. He was smoothing a large, unevenly cut block, chipping off a few bulges and rough edges. The bottom of the pit was fairly level, with a few big stone hunks and small piles of waste pieces lying around. Water pooled in a low spot where scraggly plants grew.

With a background in urban planning and architecture, Petit came to the quarry in 1989, eager to see the source of Miss Liberty's base. He fell in love with the place and soon started work as a driller and splitter. A rangy man in a thick flannel shirt, Petit flashed a warm, thin-lipped smile as he waxed rhapsodic over the variegated flow structure of the rock that, having been used since the mid-nineteenth century, can provide new buildings with historical continuity. "Stony Creek," he observed, "is not just a place, but a color and a trademark." Petit is also a critically acclaimed sculptor. I've seen his piece entitled *Kiss*—a large abstract work in which two towering rectangles of Stony Creek granite lean into one another—at the world-renowned Storm King Art Center in Mountainville, New York.

Smaller in scale than Stony Creek, Tower Hill Quarry is a family-run operation, accessed via a rough driveway that cuts through an orchard. On a bright autumn day I met Mick Schena, a gangling, muscular man who had no problem shouting over the machine-gun rattle of drilling and the clink of hand sledges splitting stone. His Italian-immigrant grandfather began working at the quarry in the 1930s, and now he operated the eight-acre site with his brother Jeff. The pit is a tiered cliff on the orchard side, inclining to woods at the far end. Sunlight sparkled on large cut blocks, heaps, windrowed slabs, piles of waste stone, and neatly stacked pieces ready for shipment. Despite the unrelenting din, Mick told me that he found the quarry peaceful.

Several years ago, Mick and Jeff's father delivered a load of stone to my house for a wall I was building. That wall is still admired by visitors, though more for its material than its craftsmanship. First used for curbing on streets in Hartford and other cities, Tower Hill stone has since been used in buildings and landscaping from coast to coast. The University of Connecticut's law library is clad in Tower Hill product.

Not far away from the din of the quarry are two peaceful-looking stone houses. One's a nineteenth-century structure with a porch and dormers that Mick and Jeff's grandfather clad in granite and where Jeff and his family now live. Next door is a stone ranch where his father resides. "They're works of art," Jeff told me, shrugging his shoulders. "I can't even understand how some of this stone was shaped."

Situated between Main Street and the Connecticut River, Portland Brownstone Quarries may be the oldest continuous-operating quarry site in the nation, the first stone having been harvested there in the 1690s. The deep-colored, dense sandstone was the most common material for row-house residences in nineteenth-century Brooklyn, Manhattan, Philadelphia, and Boston; it was also used to build New York's Cooper Union, Hartford's Soldiers and Sailors Memorial Arch, and many other iconic structures.

Today's quarry overlooks the large historic brownstone pits. Filled with emerald water beneath dramatic hundred-foot cliffs, the old quarry is now used as a recreational water park complete with slides, docks, and boats. The original operation closed after flooding by storms in the 1930s. Reopened on a much smaller scale in 1994, the business now mostly accommodates restoration projects, though some stone is used in new construction, like Middletown's police station.

Owner Mike Meehan is a stocky, ebullient man with burnished rough hands and deeply tanned skin that tells of long hours spent outdoors. He spoke of geology as if it were his personal genealogy and stone buildings as if they were relatives. As we walked around the modest pit with its working face two or three stories tall, he eagerly showed off dinosaur footprints he'd found. The ground was uneven and muddy in places. Odd chunks of stone were piled in the middle of the pit, and several pieces of battered heavy equipment lurked close by. Near the office trailer, workmen in goggles and respirators were sanding small blocks. Finished and partially completed columns, lintels, and decorative pieces were neatly laid out or stacked nearby.

A geologist by training, Meehan was in the coal-exploration business for a couple of decades. Family brought him to Connecticut, and on a visit to Yale he saw a new building going up in red sandstone imported from Germany. He knew of the old Portland quarries, needed a job, and, after doing a few back-of-the-envelope calculations, figured he could make money with nearby native stone, even accounting for the amateur mistakes he was bound to make. He leased the only piece of land available that wasn't under water, and at age forty-five he launched a new career.

He's had as many as eight employees, but he soon missed doing the hands-on work he loves, and now he toils alongside his two stonecutters. Not just a quarryman, he's a preacher on the immutable virtues, beauty, and deep history of stone. A man of contagious enthusiasm, on the warm September day I caught up with him, he was proselytizing to a rapt college sculpture class that had come to learn about the medium.

Bedrock supports everything that surrounds us—homes, offices, roads, even the soil and its vegetation. The highway roadcuts and exposed ledges we encounter are more common in the everyday landscape, but they provide only a hint of what a quarry puts on full display.

Connecticut stone has been quarried for thousands of years, in places that range from a Native American soapstone site in New Hartford where bowls were made, to the world's largest traprock quarry in North Branford that supplies crushed stone for construction. But there's a special intimacy with architectural stone. Used in a fireplace, patio, or walls of a house, it invites us to better appreciate, and inhabit, the very stuff of which our world is made.

The People's Castles
Stone Lookouts

High atop the rugged East Peak of Meriden's Hanging Hills, Castle Craig is a thirty-two-foot-tall traprock cylinder with a classic crenellated top. Like a giant chessboard rook built on the edge of a precipice, it rises just over a thousand feet above sea level, affording a commanding view of the Connecticut Valley.

Despite the ease and convenience of a drive to the top along a winding road open from April to October, I prefer the blue-blazed Metacomet Trail, whose slow-paced, steady climb amplifies the exhilaration of reaching the tower. Heading westerly from State Route 71, the path passes into Meriden's Hubbard Park and briefly joins Park Drive as it crosses the Merimere Reservoir Dam before entering woods dominated by oak and beech. The trail slabs a steep grade above the drumstick-shaped water body, providing views of nearby South Mountain's fierce cliffs. It's a breathless climb for even a well-tuned body, and the sharp, angular traprock outcrops and loose scree make for difficult footing.

My most recent trip was on a bright autumn day. From the ledges below, the tower seemed to glisten with all the magic of Oz, and despite a tiring climb, I hurried up the metal stairway inside. From the glimmering waters of Long Island Sound to the Berkshire foothills, the heart of Connecticut was laid out below me like a map. Hartford's tall buildings on the north seemed puny, while along the horizon east and west were uneven hilly highlands of tough metamorphic rock. The broad and flat Central Valley ran longitudinally, interrupted by jagged ridges of indomitable igneous basalt, like the summit on which I stood. With wind in my face, I felt as if in the crow's nest of an inland ship.

Immediately below me were the sprawling developments of Meriden, Cheshire, and Southington, facilitated by the spacious valley's level, well-

drained soils. Narrow and orderly residential streets tightly packed with houses gave way to industrial buildings. A little further distant were Broad Brook Reservoir and the runways of Meriden Markham Airport. There was a bit of everything: small farms with neatly patched cropland and pasture, utility towers, a golf course, shopping centers, and forests.

Wealthy industrialist, philanthropist, and world traveler Walter Hubbard built Castle Craig as the capstone of the 1,800-acre namesake park he donated to Meriden. It was among a number of gifts he made to the city where his Bradley and Hubbard Manufacturing Company produced clocks, bells, sewing machines, kerosene lamps, fences, and elevator enclosures.

Built by local stonemasons, the tower was likely inspired by structures Hubbard had seen in Europe. It was dedicated in October 1900 at a ceremony attended by over 250 guests that included dignitaries, speeches, and a shellfish roast over a big fire. Ever since, Castle Craig has been a destination for thousands who wish to enjoy the view from the highest summit located within twenty-five miles of the coastline between Maine and Florida.

Something about towers captures the imagination. Attached firmly to earth, they nevertheless carry the eye skyward. Through millennia they have been constructed for defense, to hold beacons and bells, and—in structures like modern skyscrapers—to maximize floor space. Some symbolize the religious or civic power of churches, governments, and other institutions, while others memorialize famous people or events.

Connecticut is blessed with hundreds of towers, varying greatly in design, function, and location. They include the granite clock tower in Sharon center, Yale's gothic Harkness Tower, Groton's 135-foot-tall Revolutionary War battle monument, and the 165-foot-tall summer residence of liquor magnate Gilbert Heublein on Talcott Mountain. Yet there are four Connecticut towers that stand distinct from all others.

Built of native rock, Castle Craig and the towers at Mount Tom, Haystack, and Sleeping Giant State Parks are all perched on inhospitable, windswept mountain summits far from any human habitation. Designed to evoke the medieval towers of Ireland, the castles of Scotland, and Norman keeps, they lend an air of human permanence to places where nature dominates. Most importantly, they were built neither for a practical purpose (though some have been used to watch for forest fires) nor as a symbol of authority (though Meriden's is on the town seal). Rather, they were erected solely for the public to enjoy a view of their state's landscape. "People's castles," they beckon every person to survey his or her domain.

The tower atop 1,325-foot Mount Tom, which straddles the boundary between Morris and Washington, was built by the state in 1921 as required in a deed from Charles Sneff, who had donated the property a decade earlier. Erected to replace a battered wooden structure built toward the end of the previous century, the tower is a round, thirty-foot shaft. Narrow, concrete-frame openings allowed in trickles of light and air as I climbed the dimly lit, rickety wooden stairway to the observation deck with its three-foot parapet. The dark, rough stone was cut from a source near the site, but cement, water, lumber, and sand had to be hauled all the way up a crude road by horse and wagon.

Mount Tom's tower had a tristate view, extending west over some of Connecticut's hilliest terrain to the rugged Taconic Mountains of New York and Massachusetts. In the foreground was sixty-acre Mount Tom Pond to the north, while a bit east the steeples of Litchfield churches rose above the surrounding trees. The view is a hubbly, thickly forested landscape belying two centuries of change marked by roads, homes, and businesses. High above my surroundings, I felt light and expansive, as if I were hovering above the summit.

The mile-long trail to the tower, beginning at the parking lot just above the pond, ascended gradually, gently winding around boulders and ledge outcrops beneath a dense canopy of mixed hardwoods. But with the pond beckoning below, I didn't mind climbing, even in August's humidity. The tower was a bit run down, but that only made it seem more ancient and mysterious. An old fire ring and some broken glass nearby evidenced late-night revels that the stone structure attracted.

Visible from Norfolk, Haystack Mountain Tower, with its stone-step entry, neatly laid masonry, and conical roof, has a rustic grandeur. A steep half-mile trail leads up to it from the state park road just off State Route 272 north of town. The round tower was quarried from a nearby gneiss ledge, and it rises thirty-four feet above the 1,680-foot summit. On a clear day, a sea of wooded hills is visible in all directions, while immediately below, sleepy Norfolk looks like a fairytale hamlet.

In 1930, Ellen Battell Stoeckel—who with her husband helped start what is now the Norfolk Chamber Music Festival and who, after her death, willed her estate for the Yale Summer School of Music—donated the land and fifty thousand dollars. The spacious tower is twenty-four feet in diameter, though its few narrow openings make it a rather dark climb to the covered observation deck above. It's a memorial to both her husband, Carl Stoeckel, and father, Robbins Battell. Known as "The Man who Measured the Mountains," Ellen's father was a prominent Norfolk citizen determined to prove wrong the Encyclopedia Britannica's assertion that no Litchfield County summit rose above one thousand feet. Employing surveyors to measure a number of local mountaintops, he demonstrated that the seemingly definitive reference work was wrong multiple times.

Battell bought the summit of Haystack and, in 1886, built a wooden tower and carriage road, to which he invited the public. A plaque embedded above the entrance of the current tower bears the same Latin phrase Battel had posted at the original structure; translated, it reads, "To thy country, state, and town be thou ever faithful."

In contrast, Sleeping Giant State Park was established not by the generosity of a wealthy individual, but due to a public outcry in the 1920s over a quarrying operation that was gnawing away at the giant's basalt head to produce crushed stone for road-making. A traprock ridge, resembling at a distance one of Gulliver's recumbent Brobdingnagians, it is perhaps fitting that the tower erected on the giant's hip—the park's highest point at 730 feet above sea level—was also not the result of largess but rather the vision of volunteers that was executed by President Franklin Roosevelt's Works Progress Administration between 1935 and 1939.

Unlike the other towers, Sleeping Giant's tower is rectangular in shape, with generous Norman-style openings on all sides of the four-story structure. It is a spacious, romantic, fortress-like building with fireplaces and a parapet, with corner towers at the top of a winding interior ramp. The wide gravel path leading up from the parking lot wound gently through a thick hardwood forest alive with birdsong the day I visited in August. I've seen deer, foxes, and even a bobcat there during less trafficked months, but even on a summer day, when the tower was busy and teeming with activity, it didn't feel crowded with its spacious view above a broad sky filled with turkey vultures and hawks.

Studded with spires and high rises, New Haven's skyline seemed impossibly close to such a wildly rugged summit. Behind the city was the broad plain of Long Island Sound, with the low coast of New York just a thin blue-green line. To the north, Connecticut's central valley stretched toward Meriden's Hanging Hills, where Castle Craig stood watch.

A 1932 report to Governor Wilbur Cross praised the Haystack Tower as "an enduring testimonial to the love and affection which the citizens of Connecticut feel for the beauty of their State." But Haystack and the other people's towers reveal much more than beauty. From their heights we can see the logic and geologic limitations of hill, valley, and stream, as well as the connections made between housing subdivisions, roads, electric lines, and shopping plazas. We get to better understand how cities relate to farms, how quarries relate to reservoirs. As in a map, patterns hidden in plain sight are revealed when seen from above. People's towers deepen the map by providing a large perspective unavailable in our daily routines, while cautioning us to be good stewards of the land below.

King of Homes
Yankee Castles

In democratic, independent-minded Connecticut, castles may seem like the stuff of fairytales, as believable as streets patrolled by knights in shining armor. Nevertheless, our state has a handful of residences to which the words of Elizabethan jurist Sir Edward Coke, "a man's house is his castle," literally apply. Well before Mark Twain's ingenious mechanic, Hank Morgan, awakened in King Arthur's court, castles have fascinated New Englanders. Ranging from stone mansions to middle-class wood-frame houses, they are sprinkled from the Gold Coast of Greenwich to the Quiet Corner of Windham County. Some date from the late nineteenth century, and one was recently completed.

Reminiscent of Europe's fortified medieval dwellings, castle-like homes often include towers, gothic windows, and parapeted walls, but their most distinctive features are castellations, the scalloped or crenellated roofline design evocative of ancient battlements. Perhaps because castles "have inspired relatively few American houses," according to Virginia and Lee McAlister's *A Field Guide to American Houses*, they get notice out of proportion to their numbers, including juicy whispers about their sometimes controversial construction and eccentric owners. Regardless, their eye-catching, imaginative style always seems to stir romantic Camelot notions.

Connecticut's best-known castle was once home to actor and playwright William Gillette. Son of a U.S. senator, he grew up in Hartford, where his neighbor Sam Clemens helped him get his first stage job. Made famous and wealthy for his iconic portrayal of Sherlock Holmes, Gillette is largely responsible for our image of the British sleuth with the deerstalker cap, Inverness cloak, and curved pipe. He coined the phrase "Elementary, my dear Watson." Perhaps playing a detective renowned for powers of observation enabled Gillette to see what is hidden in plain sight, transforming an ordinary hilltop into a theater of imagination.

Gillette erected his domestic fantasy in Hadlyme, about two hundred feet above the Connecticut River, after falling in love with the site while cruising on his yacht. Fabricated of local fieldstone on a steel framework, the twenty-four-room Rhenish structure was built between 1914 and 1919, with a tower added a few years later. The coarse stone walls seem to grow out of the ledge, tapering from about five feet thick at the base to approximately three feet thick at the top.

The castle's theatrical design is Gillette's, and after trips too numerous to count, I still see new details and find myself astonished by what amounts to a journey into the man's eccentric mind. A grand stone portico leads to a fifty-by-thirty-foot great room with a six-foot-wide fireplace and a balcony beneath a nineteen-foot ceiling lined with heavy oak beams. Gillette's sense of humor and drama are evident in a hidden room, furniture on metal tracks, a hideaway bar with a secret lock, intricate Rube Goldberg–type latches on light switches, and forty-seven heavy oak doors. Mirrors placed in strategic positions leading to his bedroom enabled him, he said, "to make great entrances in the opportune moment."

Having designed the structure and even fabricated some of the puzzle locks and latches in his own workshop, Gillette saw the mansion as an extension of himself to the extent that his will instructed executors to find a buyer who would not only appreciate "the extraordinary natural beauty of the situation and its surroundings, but more especially the mechanical features connected with it." He worried that the castle might become "the possession of some blithering saphead who had no conception of where he is or with what surrounded."

Fortunately, Connecticut's quirkiest castle is its most accessible. Acquired by the state of Connecticut in 1943, a few years after its owner's death, Gillette Castle State Park draws thousands of visitors annually from around the world. A multimillion-dollar restoration of the building at the turn of the twenty-first century provides some comfort that the "sapheads" are being kept at bay.

Though built by a wealthy merchant rather than a thespian, Greenwich's Crowley Castle has seen its fair share of acting. Silent-film superstar Mary Pickford headlined there in 1914's *Cinderella at the Castle*. A couple of years later the mansion served as the backdrop for *Romeo and Juliet*, and in 1924 the flapper comedy *Born Rich* was filmed with actors dancing the Charleston and nursing hangovers in the breakfast room. In *The April Fools*, a 1969 romantic comedy starring Jack Lemmon and Catherine Deneuve, the elaborate great hall can be glimpsed, and the bowling alley provided the setting for Lemmon's antic sword fight with Charles Boyer. Constructed around the time of Gillette and perched on a steep rise with castellated stone towers, high walls, and dramatic balconies, Crowley Castle is partially hidden by vegetation in a neighborhood of substantial homes, and I wouldn't have noticed it if I hadn't been looking.

Most Connecticut castles are more or less visible from the street, but Cornwall's Hidden Valley Castle, set on hundreds of pastoral acres overlooking a stream, pond, and waterfall, better fits the romantic European model. It's a majestic, meticulously kept private estate with a gatehouse, long access road, guesthouse, caretaker's quarters, and eight-car garage. The massive Norman-influenced stone building with steep slate roofs and a tall, slender tower rising to a conical top was built in the 1920s by a renowned New York City surgeon and his wealthy, cosmopolitan wife, who was fixated by French aristocracy. Invited there several years ago for a nonprofit fundraiser, I was able to see for myself that the imposing structure seemed more storybook than medieval fortress. Set in a lush green vale surrounded by forested hills, it transported me to childhood fairytales.

More modest castle houses are easy to spot. In Rocky Hill I found a stone, center-chimney colonial with a crenellated tower, some pointed-arch windows, and a substantial stone entryway. Built in the 1990s, it's sandwiched between a wooded ravine and a wetland in an area of newer subdivisions. Hartford's Prospect Street features a turn-of-the-twentieth-century shingle house with a castellated tower and parapeted gables, which for years was on my daily commute to the Department of Environmental Protection. Along the shore one day I was surprised to find a shingle- and brick-clad house probably dating from the 1960s on Stonington's winding Palmer Neck Road. It included crenellations and gargoyles along the roofline as well as on its towers, and a tall gothic window framed a suit of armor.

Castles evoke mystery and intrigue, and it's hard to imagine one without a story. On State Route 83 in Ellington I came across Aborn Castle, a fieldstone structure with a prominent turret sitting on a rise overlooking a suburbanizing area. Built in 1917 by a couple wanting a reminder of their European travels, it's rumored to have been a speakeasy during prohibition, with a side door that facilitated drive-up liquor sales. I remember a real estate ad heralding its "medieval touches [and] modern amenities."

Less subject to building fashion than to the imagination of their owners, castles are hardly a thing of the past. On a drive down Brickyard Road in rural Woodstock, I was struck by an elaborate twenty-three-thousand-square-foot stone-and-concrete castle with several towers, high walls, and a drawbridge over a moat. A mongrel of Scottish, Norman, Moorish, and other styles, its design owes more to Disney than history, but it's not just size and brashness that's caused controversy.

Strong willed and independent in the mode of many castle builders, the owner has tried a number of business uses that have not played well with neighbors and local officials. His attempt to operate a zoo was turned down several years ago, though he's reported to have kept emus, a zebra, and camels. He was alleged to have improperly used the building to market luxury goods, and at one time his website promoted an international modeling agency. Recently, he made an unsuccessful bid to hold weddings and other functions at the castle.

Though they convey a sense of permanence and strength, even castles are not forever. Built in 1888, a year before Twain's *A Connecticut Yankee* was published, Castle Ronald dominated a local hilltop in Newtown, and though in 1927 it was called "one of the most widely known pieces of property in New England," it was demolished twenty years later. All that remains is a street named Old Castle Drive on a hill above the center of town.

Encroached upon by woods, covered with vines, and surrounded by chain-link fence, Hearthstone Castle in Danbury's Tarrywile Park is suffering from demolition by neglect, as evidenced through its collapsed roofs and boarded windows. The three-story stone structure with its grand arched entry was built in the 1890s for a city native who made his fortune in portrait photography. It sheltered families well into the 1980s, when the city acquired the house and surrounding land as a park. Sitting sadly derelict on a wooded hillside in a quiet corner of the property, I appreciate it for the quixotic reverie it induces.

Sometimes a large building is dubbed a castle because of its sheer size and architectural hubris, even if it contains few, if any, castle-like features. On my way to visit a friend a few years ago, I slowed the car to a halt on Bristol's Federal Hill when Castle Largo came into view. Standing out in a neighborhood of handsome older houses, it gets its moniker largely because the big brick building has a flamboyant design complete with towers and steep mansard roofs. Built in 1880 by a local inventor and businessman, some gothic revival features suggest a castle, but otherwise it's just a fancy house.

Any huge, self-important home might be called a castle, as evidenced by the pejorative "starter castle" which describes the massive new houses in today's expensive subdivisions. Such homes, like true castles, evince ego, wealth, and power. Twain lampooned such pretentions through the character of Hank Morgan. After seeing a pig sty, which his Arthurian companion claimed was a castle afflicted by enchantment, Morgan mused, "to doubt that a castle could be turned into a sty, and its occupants into hogs, would have been the same as my doubting among Connecticut people the actuality of the telephone and its wonders."

Connecticut's castles bring whimsy, adventure, wonder, and nostalgia to our landscape. They evoke some of the psychological security underlying the very concept of home. And who hasn't had childlike visions of living in such a place? Castles momentarily return us to our youth and bring us back to our dreams. They enable us to refresh imaginations, which often build castles in the air.

A Thousand Uses
Quonset Huts

Looking like giant corrugated tin cans sawed in half and lying on their sides, Quonset huts are startling structures in Connecticut's tradition-bound landscape. Despite their ubiquity and almost iconic status since World War II, their defiance of our built environment's angularity starkly contrasts with the colonial houses, redbrick factories, and barns typically associated with our region. Introduced as portable, temporary, all-purpose buildings during the war, Quonsets have had remarkable staying power, attesting to their strength and adaptability. They are liable to become a permanent part of our landscape, in whatever form they may inhabit.

Like diners, with which they often share a steel skin, Quonsets are native to New England and represent the area's twentieth-century mobility and industrial prowess. They may have an unconventional shape, but they are of this place as much as white Congregational churches or old-time salt-box dwellings. In fact, they bear the shape of ancient Indian longhouses that were framed with saplings and clad in bark.

Quonset huts are sprinkled throughout the state. Some are rusting, derelict structures verging on collapse, while others shine as if fresh from the factory. They range from models fabricated to fight the Axis powers in the 1940s, like a few decaying examples at the edge of Goodspeed Airport in East Haddam, to those built for peacetime use, like the ones that until recently served at the Barkhamsted Highway garage on U.S. Route 44.

Sometimes standing alone by the roadside, but frequently clustered with other outbuildings behind a home or business, Quonsets are often passed unnoticed. But they're the kind of thing that suddenly pops out along the roadside once you start looking for them. I like the adventure of spotting ones I've never seen, even on roads I've driven hundreds of times.

Disregarded by antiquarians and historic preservationists, these blatantly industrial-looking and utilitarian structures get, in the words of Rodney Dangerfield, "no respect."

I wasn't surprised to find a Quonset garaging delivery trucks at Brooks Oil on State Route 72 in the old manufacturing city of Bristol as I made my way to see a ballgame at Muzzy Field a few years ago. But they are equally at home in rural areas like U.S. Route 202 in Litchfield, where for decades the name of well driller E. O. Phelps & Sons was emblazoned above a tall overhead door fitted into the battered bulkhead of a large Quonset. Unfortunately, the metal structure recently disappeared, evidence that their virtue of easy construction also makes them vulnerable to quick demolition, leaving little trace.

Uncompromisingly pragmatic, Quonsets often serve as barns or sheds on farms. Those used in agriculture vary widely in size. There's a huge double-arch hut at a farmstead straddling the Durham-Guilford line on State Route 177, as well as a much smaller simple half-pipe used at the edge of fields on Gallup Road in Voluntown. Like their more conventional brethren, Quonsets serve myriad purposes, including sheltering farm animals, keeping tractors, and storing hay.

Storage is perhaps their most common contemporary use. A battered green one on U.S. Route 202 in New Milford squats near a house, overflowing like an overstuffed attic. There's a white one with knee walls at the back of the North Haven Fair Grounds, and battered ones at People's and Shenipsit State Forests. I remember retrieving lumber from under a curved ceiling on several frosty mornings and then warming up around the makeshift woodstove in the shop at People's, where I'd swap tales with park maintainers in my days working for the Department of Environmental Protection.

Despite their raw functionality, Connecticut's Quonsets are used even by businesses where appearance truly matters, like bars and restaurants. The aptly named Half Keg Tavern, whose bulkhead was modified with vertical barn board and a picture window, has been a workingman's bar in a tough section of New London for many years. By contrast, a large Quonset near the Guilford Green once housed Café Grounded, an upscale eatery styling itself "the coolest little café on the CT Shoreline." Whenever I'd visit for a sandwich and a coffee, the high-arched ceiling, painted black, seemed very conducive to conversation and focused reading. The hut's original corrugated exterior was concealed beneath a standing-seam metal skin, giving it a smoother appearance that perhaps made it less obtrusive to the historic neighborhood. The space was vacant for a while, but the quirky spot must be an attractive business location because it recently reopened with yet another café.

Quonsets can also make good retail outlets. Just past the center of Portland on State Route 66, overstocked military equipment and camping gear is sold at the large, double-arch Quonset Surplus. Five Quonsets radiate from a small central hub at Southworth's Wayside Furniture on the outskirts of Torrington. Plate glass is set in the bulkhead of two of the huts for displaying tables, couches, and other goods.

In their early days, Quonsets were most commonly used as barracks and temporary postwar housing (including at prestigious universities like Yale, where a small village of them was erected near the football stadium), but Quonset living is not for everyone. A 1945 pictorial spread in House Beautiful suggested "how a Quonset could be made homelike and livable" with traditional decorating tips, even though the magazine "did not consider a Quonset an ideal house." I imagine anyone who's called a Quonset home might dread a downpour on the echoing structure, not to mention the challenge of trying to hang a picture on the curved walls.

Despite their challenges, a number of Quonsets continue as residences. Two with shed-dormer windows are close to State Route 81 in a developing area of Haddam, while another pair lies along Howd Avenue, a short and narrow street of otherwise conventional houses not far from the quarry in

Branford's Stony Creek section. Just east of the glitzy Foxwoods Casino, one of these humble abodes sits along State Route 2.

Quonset houses are often fitted with homey touches, like awnings and porches with railings, that attempt to overcome their industrial origins. Like any home, they have curtains in the windows and mailboxes out front. They sport chimneys in block, brick, or metal, and large wood-frame additions are common. Fitted with overhead doors in their bulkhead walls, Quonsets also serve as detached garages, like the one at the end of a paved driveway beside a suburban-style brick home on State Route 66 in Marlborough.

Based upon a design by Lieutenant Colonel Peter Nissen of the British Royal Engineers in World War I, the modern Quonset was developed by the U.S. Navy at Quonset Point, Rhode Island, at the outset of the nation's entry into the Second World War. Otto Brandenberger, an architect with the firm in charge of building the local naval base, improved upon the Nissen hut by adding better insulation and interior layouts as well as simplifying construction. The name "Quonset," a Native American term meaning "long place," was officially bestowed on the hut in July 1941 to avoid confusion with the British version.

Over 153,000 of the steel-ribbed sheet-metal structures were built for the conflict, shipped in pieces, and erected all over the globe. When the process was finally perfected, ten men could set one up in a day with hand tools. Light and compact, they were easier to ship than wood-framed canvas tents, and their exterior was strong enough to deflect shell fragments.

There were three original designs, ranging in size from 320 to 1,440 square feet, and more than eighty-six sanctioned uses. The military tailored them for housing, offices, barber and butcher shops, hospital wards, laundries, chapels, and mess halls. Variations included knee walls and overhangs to keep out rain and excessive sunlight. They were so versatile, in fact, that architecture professor Brian Carter has since dubbed them "weapons of mass construction" for the critical role they played in the war.

Assembling the Quonset huts around the world was the responsibility of the newly formed Navy Seabees, whose moniker was a phonetic expression of "CB," or Construction Battalion. Recruited from the building trades and also trained as fighting men, the Seabees were headquartered in Davisville, Rhode Island, not far from where the first huts were manufactured. A couple of years ago I made a pilgrimage to the once proud base, a small slice of which persists at the edge of a shopping mall on land now dedicated as a memorial and museum, where the huts are restored and cared for by a dedicated volunteer corps.

Jack Sprengel, a tall, muscular man with a full head of dark hair was one of the volunteers on duty that day. He'd been stationed at the base, and in 1994, when it closed and operations moved south, it was he who lowered the flag for the last time. An artesian well of information, his baritone voice waxed rhapsodic with recollections of distant postings, hut statistics, information on design evolution, and secrets of construction. With his stiff, military bearing I expected Sprengel to be dispassionate, but he spoke about the steel buildings with reverence, expressing by degrees both enthusiasm and affection. Like everyone else who'd spent time with Quonsets, he had a strong attachment to them despite arrangements that were sometimes inconvenient and uncomfortable.

Far from the Seabee Museum, what may be Connecticut's largest collection of Quonsets is a battered cluster of seven huts on State Route 322, in the Milldale area of Southington at the corner of Clark Street. Amid retail plazas, light industrial activity, and old houses converted to offices, they stand distinctive even as they blend into the surrounding hodgepodge. The Wright Touch, an auto-detailing shop with a bay door in the bulkhead, is separated from A & B Manufacturing by a squat building of fieldstone cobbles. Around the corner on Clark Street, a third Quonset fitted with a boxy wooden front addition is home to Steel Rule Die Corporation. Behind these businesses is a paved courtyard of sorts around which four huts in varying states of rust and disrepair appear to serve as storage. Junk vehicles and machine parts surround them, conveying simultaneously both work and decay.

After the war, used huts were sold inexpensively as surplus for about one thousand dollars apiece, some even more cheaply. Nevertheless, new ones continued to be manufactured for purposes ranging from theaters to supermarkets to garages, barns, warehouses, and airplane hangers. Furthermore, Quonset technology finds contemporary expression in a variety of more conventional-looking prefabricated metal structures that serve as factories, stores, churches, and sports arenas. Their shape has even been adopted in the form of hoop greenhouses sheathed with plastic skins.

Whatever their design merits and range of contemporary uses, Quonsets will endure as symbols of America's can-do ingenuity, industrial prowess, and victory in the worst conflict the planet has ever known. Long subject to the cleverest types of adaptive reuse, they might well serve as examples for traditional structures that have outlived their original function. We may think we've exhausted all their possible uses and configurations, but, like the Indian longhouses of old, whose shape seemed outmoded for centuries, we may be surprised to find a future where Quonsets enjoy widespread uses beyond current imagination.

The Shape of Futures Past
Octagon Houses

Several years ago I was in Middletown looking at used cars. Returning home, I crossed the Connecticut River on the Arrigoni Bridge and was heading east along State Route 66 into Portland, when from the corner of my eye I saw a couple of two-story buildings that seemed a little lopsided or slightly off-kilter. Must have been the shadows, I thought, or the distraction of traffic. But something in me demanded a second look.

Almost immediately I passed a big double-arch Quonset hut housing the appropriately named Quonset Surplus store where I'd stopped once to buy wool army trousers. Yes, I thought, looking at the half-pipe metal structure, I had just gone by a couple of buildings possessing a second unusual shape. I turned around and a minute later pulled to the side of the road to stare at two almost identical odd-shaped houses standing next to each other. I walked around them and did a quick count. They indeed had eight symmetrical sides, but, although I'd passed them numerous times, I'd never noticed their peculiarity.

A fad of the mid-nineteenth century, most octagon houses were built in New England, New York, and the Midwest. Of the few thousand that were likely constructed, only several hundred still exist. No one knows how many octagon houses were built in Connecticut, but the number surviving is probably just shy of twenty. From the earliest colonials to Phillip Johnson's iconic modernist Glass House in New Canaan, the walls of people's dwellings have largely been constructed of rectangles. With rare exceptions, this remains the geometry of houses built today.

Of course, I couldn't just look at the twin octagonal-shaped houses, which challenged my notions of domestic existence lived within ninety-degree angles, and leave it at that. I had to know more. I returned a couple days later for a few photographs, made some phone calls, and headed to the library.

Just listed on the National Register of Historic Places when I first spotted them, the Portland houses had been built of stucco-covered brownstone harvested from the nearby quarries, and they had walls eighteen inches thick. Completed in 1855, one belonged to Joseph Williams, a local grocer, and the other to his brother-in-law Gilbert Stancliff, superintendent of the quarries. Save for bracketing around the eaves, the houses had little ornamentation and projected a simple elegance. Today, one is a tired-looking multifamily house and the other is a well-maintained doctor's office that was once a convent with a cross atop the cupola. Together the houses reminded me of an old married couple.

I never know when I'm going to stumble on an octagon house. Finding one always fills me with that particular joy reserved for collectors who uncover something unusual, like a rare coin or pristine seashell. Perhaps because of their quiet defiance of norms they've become a minor obsession of mine, and over the years I've tracked them down through Internet searches, architecture books, word-of-mouth, and chance encounters. While some are in disrepair, I've never found one abandoned or on the verge of demolition, though I know of several that have met that fate in the past. None have been renovated as museums, though they serve that function elsewhere; among the several that celebrate eight-sided architecture are high-style examples in Camillus, New York, and Watertown, Wisconsin. Despite their odd shape, which presents some challenges for room function and furniture arrangements, the quirky structures in Connecticut all appear used and useful, mostly as homes, but sometimes as offices.

Portland seems near the center of the state's octangular world with a couple of octagon houses down the road in East Hampton and another in neighboring Cromwell, which was once part of a boarding school called the Mineral Springs Military Institute, but which now serves as Saint Peter's Hall at Holy Apostles College and Seminary. Otherwise, octagons are well distributed throughout the state, with only the northeastern area lacking one. They remain standing in urban areas like Bridgeport, and they preside over bucolic countryside, like the one in Washington, Connecticut.

One of the state's most gracious octagons is on Spring Street just west of downtown Danbury. It sits on a slight rise, behind a block wall topped with a handsome white metal fence. Built in 1853 with concrete walls a foot thick, it's a big three-story wedding cake of a house, painted off-white. There's a wide overhanging roof below which are verandas with cast iron railings and decorative supports that have an almost Vieux Carré vibe. It has a cupola, chimneys on both sides, and glossy wooden doors. Set back on its lot, well maintained, and divided into apartments, it stands out in the neighborhood of ordinary, mostly two-family houses that grew up around it.

In sharp contrast is a tiny two-story clapboard octagon on Hallock Street in New Haven's Hill neighborhood. Built in the 1870s, it's on a high brick foundation that sports double-hung windows and has a mansard roof with dormers. Like the Danbury house, it's also in an urban neighborhood. But in terms of materials, setback from the street, size of the lot, and other features, it resembles the houses around it and blends in well. Still, it adds an almost playful, eye-catching difference to the neighborhood, lending fascination to an ordinary place.

Octagon houses burst on the scene with the 1849 publication of *The Octagon House: A Home for All* by Orson S. Fowler of Fishkill, New York. Fowler was an energetic and multifaceted man who practiced phrenology, a precursor of psychology that determined a person's character traits by the shape of his or her skull. Described by Madeleine B. Stern in her 1973 introduction to Fowler's book as a reformer with "a luxuriant beard, high forehead and piercing eyes" who favored more relaxed dress, vegetarianism, and abstinence from alcohol, he was also a consultant on sex education and marriage.

It was as an amateur architect and builder that Fowler earned lasting renown. For him, building was not just a matter of shelter; it was a mode of living. "Improving home facilitates [and] aids every other end and pleasure of life," he wrote. A great do-it-yourselfer, Fowler believed every person might be his own architect and that people of modest means could construct spacious octagon houses using his designs and poured concrete "gravel walls," which took advantage of cheap and enduring native gravel and lime. In the octagon, Fowler saw a shape most approximating nature's ideal of a sphere, which "incloses more space for its wall than the square," reducing building costs and heat loss, improving ventilation and sunlight, facilitating communication between rooms, and eliminating "dark and useless corners." Fowler was also a champion of modernity, advocating indoor plumbing, central heat, and other improvements.

Fowler's own octagon home was an elaborate sixty-room structure on a hill overlooking the Hudson River in Fishkill. Known as Fowler's Folly, it was rented when its builder fell on hard times, then went through a series of owners, and in 1897 was dynamited by the city as a public hazard.

Built in 1856, the Leete-Griswold House sits among eighteenth-century homes on Guilford's leafy Fair Street, which is remarkably quiet given its proximity to the Post Road, U.S. Route 1. I arrived there after visiting the 1639 Henry Whitfield House, Connecticut's oldest home, and having had lunch in a renovated Quonset hut. The contrast of the house with the two other structures, all within about a mile of each other, heightened my interest in the octagon, which had vertical board siding, a cupola, and an Italianate-entry porch that added a touch of grandeur. And at the end of the driveway was a matching octagon garage!

I like dropping in on the two octagons on New Place Street in Yalesville—one painted white, the other in a natural-concrete color—separated by a conventional home on the lot between. Though both are two-story "gravel wall" structures with a cupola, they nevertheless exhibit many differences in design, renovation, and upkeep, which emphasize how structures occupy time as well as space. The white octagon looks like it has always been neatly maintained. It has a brick foundation and brick accents over the doors and windows. Two narrow entrances are on either side of the wall directly facing the street, and a large boxy addition is to the rear and side.

The tannish-gray house has cracked and spalling walls. It's hard to tell whether the porch, which shelters a large front door, is old and falling into disrepair, or half built, perhaps never to be completed. Despite its infirmities, this house retains more of its valuable original features, such as divided-light windows and decorative, exposed rafter tails under the eaves (a detail covered by siding on the white house). Clearly, generations of families have adapted their homes differently according to their needs, wherewithal, and interests. Standing close together, the homes speak not only to their architecture but to the lives lived within. They remind me that deep travelers look not just at styles and construction techniques to take the pulse of a place, but at how buildings adapt and grow into the world around them.

On my way to the beach a couple years ago, I almost missed the octagon house fronting Old Saybrook's wide and heavily trafficked Main Street, and I was reminded that looking cannot be formulaic, but must always anticipate something a little different. As was the case with my first octagons in Portland, I hit the brakes and turned around. Once I got out and walked around the building, it was easy to see why I hadn't noticed this house before—it wasn't symmetrical. Some of the eight sides were longer than others, and its steep pyramidal roof was dormered with a finial at its apex, making it the state's most unusual eight-sided structure. It had a handsome front porch above which was second-floor gallery with a crossbuck railing. Now the home of Saybrook Family Dental Care, I was half tempted to feign a cracked filling just for an excuse to step inside.

Our homes typically project personal statements, but octagon houses were also the physical manifestation of an entire social philosophy. In that regard they are, perhaps, not much different from other radical houses of the next century, like Buckminster Fuller's Dynamaxion House or the prefabricated, enameled-steel Lustron houses built after World War II. Their geometry and innovative use of materials may get all the attention when they're built, but it's the stories behind their unusual design that are often more enduring than the architecture.

Practical, Adaptable, and Disappearing
Barns

I find few close-to-home roadside views as soothing and reassuring as the Perry Farm's three red barns clustered with a silo on Barbourtown Road in Canton Center. Nestled at the base of a wooded ridge and seen from across a verdant field they suggest hard work, closeness to the soil, and connection to the past. Perhaps most inspiring and simultaneously unusual is that this remains a working dairy farm in a time when so many barns continue to be lost to development or converted to other uses. It's a bucolic scene belying the gritty, unending toil of a farmer's life.

Every Connecticut town has barns of some type, from urban areas like Hartford, New London, and Meriden to the rural precincts of the state, where we expect to see them. Many of the barns in these rural precincts are local icons. They range from cow palaces like Suffield's twenty-thousand-square-foot Hilltop Farm barn displaying multiple gables, silos, and cupolas to much smaller but equally quirky structures like Gallup barn on State Route 14 in Scotland, with its weathered shingles, gambrel roof, and curious twin pedimented dormers projecting above wide doors.

Some barns become standouts as the world in which they played center stage slowly fades. Situated next to a broad hayfield on West Avon Road, the weathered gray Sunrise Farm barn in Avon, with its crossbuck doors, handsomely windowed cupola, and rising-sun image in the gable, is an enduring symbol in a town that has a rich agricultural heritage but is now 85 percent built out. Patrons come to Tulmeadow Farm's store in West Simsbury from miles around to enjoy ice cream and find a brief refuge from suburbia by soaking up the calming view of its large, classic red barn with a transom window over the door and silvery vent stacks along the roof ridge. But the cows that were once here are long gone.

Agriculture is far from the dominant occupation it once was, but Connecticut's landscape is still peppered with barns. They may be set back from the street, hidden behind houses, or located in fields where they seem so natural a part of the landscape as to barely merit notice. But despite their ubiquity, barns are rapidly disappearing. After all, they are working buildings, and when there is no work available they slowly fall prey to weathering and eventual collapse, like the swayback tobacco barns at the Windsor landfill or the abandoned dairy barn along South Main Street in East Granby. Many are razed to make way for new shopping centers and subdivisions. According to Todd Levine of the Connecticut Trust for Historic Preservation, there were at least twenty-five thousand barns in the state in 1920, and there could be as many as nine thousand remaining today. The trust recently completed a multiyear survey that documents around eight thousand barns in what might be the most comprehensive inventory of agricultural structures in the country. A thematic State Register of Historic Places nomination of the most significant barns is being prepared, and the trust hopes their work will have "an impact on federal and state policy and funding for farms and barns."

I like counting numbers and species of barns from behind the wheel. Starting in urban areas usually provides more variety but a bigger challenge because, like the Kenyon Carriage Barn on Kenyon Street in Hartford with its louvered cupola, they are often tucked behind other structures. Although more farm buildings are in outlying towns, as expected, the count and types in the cities can still be startling.

Connecticut barns have housed farm animals, equipment, or crops for centuries. Their architecture expresses practical solutions to agricultural issues of their day. Once I started recognizing a few general barn types, I began to better understand why they were built, their design sense, and a little of their builders' outlook. I began to see beyond their exterior sheathing, few decorative details, and current state of repair and started uncovering clues to their age, uses, and the nature of the surrounding landscape.

The oldest barns, dating to colonial times, are simple gable structures with large side doors. Known as English barns because they are based on those that early colonists knew from their homeland, they are traditionally divided into three bays sheltering animals, hay, and grain. Common and easy to find, they have never ceased being built for both practical and aesthetic reasons. In an agrarian mood after the Harwinton Fair in early October, I found over twenty of them in a random forty-five-minute drive. Some dwarfed the adjacent house while others were little more than tool sheds. A few seemed near collapse.

By the 1830s New England–style barns were built with doors beneath the gable to keep the entry free of water running off the roof and to simplify expansion through the addition of parallel bays. They're widespread throughout the state, and I chanced to spot four along U.S. Route 44 in Coventry on my way to the Mansfield Drive-In last summer. Surrounded by hilltop fields, a large modern dairy barn at Hytone Farm was among those to catch my eye for its pastoral setting at the edge of cornfields. A few miles east, I saw an 1870s barn converted to a garage that stands beside Brigham's Tavern, where George Washington once breakfasted.

Another nineteenth-century innovation were basements created by building "bank barns" fitted into a hillside or raised on a foundation. Originally used to collect manure, lower levels were later adapted for additional animals. By the Civil War, extra windows as well as cupolas eased ventilation.

Gambrel-roof barns include both English and New England entries. Their storybook appearance stirs childhood nostalgia, but they were built for the practical purpose of providing more loft storage. My favorite is the handsome old UConn dairy barn with twin tile silos on State Route 195. The slate roof provides an air of elegance and permanence. It's an icon revealing the school's origins, but it has not always been well maintained, thus also expressing the university's distance from its beginnings.

Mostly found in northeastern Connecticut, connected farmsteads where home, workshops, and animal barns are joined together for efficiency may be the most intriguing farm construction. A good example of this "big house, little house, back house, barn" style is on Union's Rindge Road, where a one-and-a-half-story barn with its gable end to the street is connected to a center-chimney house by a long single-story structure. Another is on West Stafford Road in Stafford, where a three-story white clapboard bank barn is joined to the house by a lower connecting building.

I'm always on the lookout for unusual and specialized farm structures, like chicken coops and corncribs. One of my favorites is the clay-tile mushroom barn topped by a monitor roof at the 4-H Education Center in Bloomfield. There are also a few octagon barns, and Quonset huts, too, have been pressed into agricultural service. Perhaps Connecticut's most distinctive specialized barns are tobacco sheds. Typically long structures, they're fitted with hinged siding that can open for ventilation when the crop is drying late in the year. It's hard to drive through the Connecticut Valley north of Hartford without finding them either abandoned, converted to other purposes, or still in use. Seen by thousands of people daily from the Bradley Connector, which funnels traffic between I-91 and the airport in Windsor Locks, is a cluster of these gabled forms that seems to define the flatness of the fields around it.

Grown under gauzy tenting that billows in a summer breeze like sails, Connecticut shade-grown tobacco has a reputation as the world's finest cigar wrapper and is the highest value-per-acre crop produced in the state. Tobacco growing is both a seasonal and cultural phenomenon, and generations of teenagers and migrants have spent their summers toiling in the hot fields. As a young man, Martin Luther King Jr. was one of numerous Southern black youth sent north to work in tobacco, and today many West Indians are thus employed during the season.

Barns are among the most beloved structures, a kind of architectural comfort food. Their functional simplicity gives them a rough elegance, an elemental and timeless beauty. Offering a whiff of happy nostalgia, they provide hope that amid suburbanization our communities can retain some connection to the land. Fortunately, simplicity has also rendered them adaptable, because as agriculture fades, new uses are necessary for survival.

Old barns have always seemed like a natural fit for antique sellers. Similarly, at least three used-book businesses—in Colebrook, Niantic, and Bethany—are in old farm buildings and use "barn" in their business names. The Hartford Children's Theater is in the Storrs Family Carriage

Barn on Farmington Avenue, and the Westport Country Playhouse—which has featured Richard Dreyfus, Jill Clayburgh, and Paul Newman—got its start in a now extensively renovated barn that once sat in an apple orchard. Acclaimed restaurants like the Still River Café in Eastford, renowned for serving locally grown foods, and the gambrel Red Barn just off the Merritt Parkway in Westport have thrived in buildings that once sheltered livestock and crops. Houses have long offered a second life to barns, like the "Dutch Colonial" on Bushy Hill Road in Simsbury, which was built for dairy cows in the 1890s and converted to a home in 1951.

Especially in more developed areas, barns that may once have sheltered hay and horses or served other farm purposes are today often used to house vehicles or have become workshops and tool sheds. A good place to find them is ensconced behind the eighteenth- and nineteenth-century homes on Main Street in Farmington Village. Some are simple structures clearly built for function, like the blue barn behind 107 Main Street. Others are more elaborate, like the carriage house–style barn a few blocks away with its fancy cupola, slate shingles, gothic windows, and decorative accents.

As their numbers dwindle, many new buildings pay barns homage. The Department of Transportation's salt sheds are built with an exaggerated barnlike gambrel and sheathed in shingles. Many newer firehouses have a barn aesthetic, like the one on State Route 154 in Higganum and North Canton's red metal building on State Route 179. Commercial buildings often take on agricultural affectations, such as cupolas and crossbuck doors, and some, like a relatively new frame structure on State Route 10 near U.S. Route 44 in Avon, even have faux silos. Occasionally, houses are also built in barn fashion.

More than other antique structures, barns offer insight into the past by recalling not just architectural styles but a way of life. They're a reminder of Connecticut's varied agricultural history dating back to colonial times, when it was nicknamed the "Provisions State" for the plentiful food and fiber it supplied to General Washington's army. Furthermore, barns often reflect their location in the state. Tobacco sheds generally indicate the rich soils of the Central Valley, while large chicken coops betoken eastern Connecticut. Smaller, rough-hewn barns are more widespread in the rocky uplands, while large barns are typically located in bottomlands or on hilltops, where the soil is thick and fertile.

Most barns date to an age when local agriculture supplied our cities with vegetables, dairy products, meat, and the hay that fueled horse-borne transportation. In the twentieth century, barn building slowed, and by the 1950s, "other than tobacco sheds, 'hobby' barns, and barnlike storage buildings, barn building virtually stopped," according to the Connecticut Trust's Levine. Of course, there are exceptions, such as the spacious modern barn in Avon, built for the Governor's Horse Guard (a ceremonial military unit that began in 1788), or the open-sided pole barns (foundationless structures supported by poles set in the ground) built for dairy cows at Graywall Farms in Lebanon.

Barns are hot subjects for tourism posters and postcards, and they're a favored sight in residential picture windows. But their meaning goes beyond nostalgic longing. They suggest intriguing possibilities for our future landscape, provided that our farms and farm buildings will continue to be put to good use.

The Spirit of Community
Camp Meetings

I'd crossed the Connecticut River from East Haddam hundreds of times without ever noticing the tiny houses blending into the trees along the ridge on the opposite shore. Perched on a forty-foot bluff above the water with a view of the Goodspeed Opera House and the silvery swing bridge, my first visit to Camp Bethel in the Tylerville section of Haddam was startling. On behalf of the state's Department of Environmental Protection I had come to review plans by cottage owners to preserve their views of the river, partially obscured by overgrown brush on adjacent state-owned property. I couldn't get over the brightly painted, steep-gabled summer cottages clustered beneath tall trees. I felt as if I'd discovered a lost world.

My business completed, I wandered among the little fairytale homes set close together with their gingerbread brackets, scroll-sawn bargeboard, and fancy lathe-turned spindles and columns. Almost every cottage had a porch with worn and weathered chairs, suggesting easy conversation. Most were stretched along the bluff, but several were horseshoed around a central wooden pavilion known as the Preacher's Stand. Others were sprinkled about the forty-six-acre grounds, which included a white steepled chapel, a dining hall, and athletic facilities. More remarkable than the architecture, however, was the way in which the cottages were connected without a road.

Camp Bethel began as a meeting place for a religious revival in 1878, during one of several periods of renewed religious zeal that has swept New England since colonial times. Apparently there was sufficient religious fervor to warrant permanent structures a couple of decades later, according to Steve Gephard, a fourth-generation Bethelite whose great grandfather built his shingled cottage in 1918. Reminiscent of the original tents, most of the houses are a story and a half, with steep roofs and vertical board siding. An authority on migratory riverine fish, Steve attributes his professional interests to childhood summers on the river.

Today the Land of Steady Habits hardly seems a hotbed of religious ferment, but New England's first camp meeting—which kindled the flame of the Methodist movement—was held in Bolton, Connecticut, when thousands gathered in 1805 to hear the fiery Lorenzo Dow preach in a natural-ledge-bound amphitheater now deep in the woods. The spot is currently owned by the local land trust, and the only sermon I've ever heard near those rocks is wind sough and birdsong.

Camp Bethel was built by the Life and Advent Union, an evangelizing millenarianist denomination established in 1863. The layout of the grounds, especially the circle of homes around the Preacher's Stand, is emblematic of camp meetings and among the features that distinguishes the community from an old-time secular resort. Today it retains its evangelical Christian mission through the interdenominational nonprofit Camp Bethel Association. There's lots of impromptu communal activity, Gephard told me, as well as Sunday services in the chapel. A camp meeting is held annually with prayer, lectures, music, Bible school, and family activities.

Beyond worship, Camp Bethel also represents an attachment to community. I could see it in the layout of the grounds and the proximity of cottages, between which you could almost pass a cup of coffee through your window to your neighbor's next door. One recent autumn I met resident Heidi Mach as she raked leaves around her shingled cottage, remarking on how difficult it was to maintain, like other summer places that are built without durability in mind. Possessing a warm smile and long brown hair finely streaked gray, Mach said she came to Bethel with a youth group over twenty years ago, "fell in love with the place," eventually got married there, and is raising her kids in "a neighborhood where people watch out for one another. It's a magical spot," she said, and with "cars corralled in a lot near the entrance, at moments the modern world disappears."

Community is what it's all about at the Methodist Campground on Camp Street in the west end of Plainville. Beginning in 1865 as a tent colony hosting lively Methodist revival meetings, the site was sold in 1957 to a nondenominational religious organization that has morphed into "a seasonal residential community committed to preserving its place in America's architectural history with limited connections to its own religious and cultural history," according to a book by resident Arthur K. Pope. Most owners of the more than eighty homes situated on seventeen acres are retirees who winter in Florida.

With their whimsical designs and vibrant colors, these houses exude a Hansel-and-Gretel quality. A circle of nineteen larger cottages with two-story porches surround a rectangular outdoor pavilion where the gospel is still preached on summer Sundays. Smaller cottages line five gravel streets not much wider than big-city sidewalks, which radiate northerly from the hub. Almost every house has a welcoming porch, and the cottages are lively with elfin decorative bracketing, quirky windows, spindles, and arches. An island surrounded by postwar housing and modern brick schools, the inward-facing campground has an insular, calming quality I found soothing.

The days when thousands flocked to the site for religious reawakening are long over, and Cliff Cote, a slight, bespectacled man with a mustache and soft silvery hair, told me that he had lived in the area many years before discovering the cluster of houses tucked away beneath the trees "like an open secret." Though summer visitors are fewer now, it remains a tight-knit community, with Sunday chapel, bus trips, Friday pizza dinners, an Independence Day parade, and card nights.

Despite its beauty and vibrant community life, if not for a dedicated cadre of residents, the place would have been bulldozed more than a generation ago. By the mid-1960s its structures and facilities had suffered years of neglect, and the neighborhood was officially labeled a "pocket of deterioration" and threatened with condemnation for poor wiring; city planners floated an urban renewal proposal that would have brought modern housing for the elderly to the site instead. Meanwhile, the historic preservation movement emerged in the mid-1960s in reaction to urban renewal's wholesale destruction of neighborhoods like Hartford's Front Street, where Constitution Plaza stands, and demolition of landmarks like New York's Penn Station. The renewed esteem given historic structures bred community pride and gave impetus to protecting the grounds, which eventually succeeded; the Plainville Campground was listed on the National Register of Historic Places in 1980.

Tucked on a hill just off State Route 32 about a mile from the Frog Bridge in downtown Willimantic are the grounds of one of the nation's oldest continuous camp meetings. "Shouting Methodists" founded a tent community in 1860 there; today's Willimantic Camp Meeting Association continues under church auspices. I visited the village on a recent, unusually warm November day when many residents were outdoors tinkering with their homes or walking about, eager to greet a stranger with a nod, a smile, or quiet hello.

"These Holy Grounds are Set Apart for the Worship of God," read a sign near the entrance, which led to narrow streets of bumpy asphalt winding through an eccentric collection of tiny houses. Some, like the lemon-yellow board-and-batten Barrows Cottage, were brightly painted and in high Victorian style, while others were plain and more conventional. Unfortunately, many of the oldest, most elaborately designed homes were lost to the 1938 hurricane.

Nevertheless, this congregation of homes was a delicious riot of gables, oddly shaped windows, and intriguing doorways. About half of the ninety cottages are occupied year-round and many seemed like fixer-uppers, lending the grounds a down-at-the-heels fairyland quality. Flags, whirligigs, small statues, and gimcracks distinguished many of the cottages. Near the middle of the community an arc of cottages, including a library and chapel, faced a large outdoor pavilion, still the focal point for annual camp meetings where, according to the association's website, people come for "refreshment, renewal, and evangelism."

There's a more mystical vibe at the Pine Grove Spiritualist Camp on Niantic Bay in East Lyme, which proclaims on its website that "it is not unusual for visitors to say they have seen, heard, or felt spirits." Indeed, I walked the quiet, narrow streets near the uneven shore with my senses on high alert and a slight foreboding. Established in 1882 as a resort for Spiritualists, who believe in "communication, by means of mediumship, with those who live in the Spirit World," Pine Grove hosts events throughout the year, including workshops, visiting mediums, regular services, and ceremonies for healing and animal blessings.

Despite my initial discomfort, it was hard to remain gloomy on a sunny, tranquil day. Strolling beneath tall trees I peeked into the many gardens ensconced in tiny front yards or in the narrow spaces between houses, very at ease—that is, until I passed a mailbox with the image of a raven perched on top. I glanced at the house, painted in dark red; a witch on a broomstick—a weathervane—hovered above. I took a longer look at the house, noticing now that witches had been carved into the shutters. Yet despite the spooky ambience of this place and other houses like it, people greeted me cheerfully and without reservation, projecting the same communal, welcoming feeling that I had experienced at the other meeting grounds.

I wandered along the streets where some of the tightly packed houses had elaborate porches or decorative bracketing, but most were plainer structures with a simple gable or shed roof. Few had driveways or garages. I then came upon the long, low Temple, a white clapboard building with tall, divided-light windows set in a grove of trees along the water. A nearby gazebo faced wooden benches intended for outdoor gatherings. It seemed a quiet, contemplative place where spirits might commune.

Camp meeting grounds are communities within communities, not just

of buildings but of belief. In some ways they hark back to early ecclesi-
astically centered colonial settlements. In other ways they presaged early
suburbs, with houses on small lots in quiet precincts with one road serving
as entrance and outlet. Whether in rural areas, like Methodist Pine Grove
in Canaan, or in busier places, like Camp Faithful, squeezed between I-84
and the commercial-shopping complexes of Queen Street in Southington,
camp meeting places are oases of brightly painted, sociable cottages in a
world where alienation from the neighborhoods we live in is increasingly
the norm.

Exploring Gasoline Alley
Racetracks

I forget whether I was searching for a roadside spring, on the trail of yet another Quonset hut, or on my way back from Aborn Castle in nearby Ellington when I passed the crowded parking lot of a building that looked like a huge gambrel-roof barn with a grandstand beside it. I stopped and rolled down my window; a loud, whining buzz filled the air. Looking up at a large sign, I realized I'd found the Stafford Motor Speedway, a place I heard about and read about in the newspaper sports section, but had never seen.

Heading west along State Route 190, I passed through forest and small-town crossroads before getting mired in the stop-and-go stretch of traffic lights in Enfield's commercial district, with its big-box stores, gas stations, and fast food outlets. Continuing home, I passed auto dealerships, shopping centers, and vast parking lots dotted with brightly colored vehicles. It was obvious that car culture had transformed Connecticut's landscape and that we increasingly experienced the world from behind a windshield. And while we may revel in driving, turn our heads for a good-looking car, and enjoy their ever-increasing living-room comforts, few of us pause to admire them as working machines. Sure, car shows and cruise nights featuring old-time autos keep growing in popularity, but they tend to be static art openings with the vehicles gussied up like girls in prom dresses. Until the battery dies on a frigid morning or a radiator hose bursts, we take their existence as mechanical beasts for granted. But with cars ever present in our lives, why wasn't love for automotive muscle more widespread?

Determined to find out, a couple weeks later I found myself sitting in the 8,700-seat aluminum grandstand at Stafford, a raging buzz vibrating in my chest as cars sped down the straightaway jockeying, bouncing, and squiggling for position. It sounded like a full-throated roar fading to angry bees

or the whine of giant mosquitoes as the vehicles hit the oval and headed for the backstretch. Sound and movement together were hypnotic, the smell of tire friction and exhaust like a pheromone for an audience mesmerized by the action.

Connecticut's oldest operating racetrack was built in 1892 for running horses at the Stafford Springs Fairgrounds, a venue for agricultural events. Although an auto race was held during the Depression, not until 1948 did weekly stockcar races begin. The half-mile banked, oval track wasn't paved until 1967.

Gradually thinning out after the pack's release from behind the pace car, the racecars wobbled and twisted for advantage on a track enclosed by metal guardrails, concrete barriers, seventeen-foot-high tire walls, and chain-link fence. Not long into the third race, a black sedan suddenly spun into the cement wall and ricocheted into another car as speeding vehicles slalomed around them, just as a red flag was dropped, stopping the action. The crowd gasped as smoke rose from one vehicle and debris littered the pavement. Strobe lights flashing, a fire truck, ambulance, and wrecker rapidly responded from their station on the infield, while the speeding cars came to an abrupt halt just short of the accident. Crews in orange jumpsuits ministered to what was broken and rumpled, and the crowd slowly relaxed under the patter of the announcer reassuring them that everything was okay. Fortunately, no one was seriously injured, and after the battered car was towed away the race quickly resumed.

Since the dawn of the automobile age, Connecticut has hosted mechanized races. Branford Park, a dirt track for horse racing in New Haven, held the state's first automobile race in 1899, with the winner behind the wheel of a Columbia Special, a car made in Hartford by Pope Manufacturing Company. By some accounts, Albert Pope was just one of nearly two hundred carmakers, including New Britain's Corbin, New London's Cameron, and Bridgeport's Locomobile and Trumbull, calling Connecticut home in the twentieth century's early years. Many Nutmeg State cars proved world class, and in 1908 a Locomobile became the first American vehicle to win an international road race, Long Island's Vanderbilt Cup. With a long heritage of precision manufacturing of guns, machine tools, typewriters, locks, sewing machines, bicycles, and clocks, it was only natural that for a few short years, at least, Connecticut would become a center of automotive development and manufacture.

Connecticut now has four tracks, but during the last century there were more than thirty. Some succumbed for business reasons or owing to changes in racing fashion, but development pressure caused by rising land values spurred, ironically, by increasing automobile access to the countryside has been a major cause of their demise. Danbury's Racearena was among those bulldozed into oblivion by the onslaught of suburbia. Built in the 1980s on the outskirts of the city, the Danbury Fair Mall now occupies the site of the Danbury Fair Grounds, which for decades held races on what started as a half-mile dirt horse track. One of the most beloved racing sites in the state, it was shortened, lengthened, paved, converted back to dirt, and paved again depending on the type of car and racing style popular at the time. Watching the brightly colored machines whiz around the oval was a highlight of my visits to the fair as a young child.

Built in 1951, Waterford Speedbowl is a high-banked, oval track. A row of pennants flaps at the top of a barn-red, wooden grandstand. Across the infield, billboard advertisements hawk radio stations, newspapers, doughnuts, and automotive products. Somewhat tired, the facility has a bygone, homey feel, like an old-fashioned minor league ballpark.

The Speedbowl has been "a family tradition for many racers," Brian Darling, a member of the track's board of directors, told me after a prerace meeting with drivers and pit crews. "It's a tight-knit community, with some third-generation participants," he added, removing a pair of sunglasses and perching them on his head. "This is a grassroots, blue-collar, grind-it-out kind of place where many drivers get their start. Folks here don't have a lot of money, but they pour whatever they've got into their cars."

Waterford is the home track of twenty-five-year-old Keith Rocco, a slender young man with dark hair and penetrating brown eyes. His father raced at Waterford during the 1980s. A 2010 NASCAR national champion, Rocco has had 53 wins, 123 top fives, and 151 top tens in 189 starts over the past four years. "It's an awesome track," he crowed, adding, "The short straightaways keep it very competitive, and there's lots of side-by-side racing, keeping things exciting." Although he enjoys the camaraderie of a local track, it does have its disadvantages. "A lot depends on what happened in the race a week earlier," he said.

The pace car that night was a souped-up Subaru Valenti. Before the first race I took a spin around the track with Bob, a burly man with bushy shoulder-length hair sprawling from beneath a baseball cap. A former racer, he looked almost clownlike squeezing into the tiny driver's seat. Bob took us to about sixty-five miles per hour, and the road seemed close enough to scrape the windshield as we banked into the turns. With such short straights it was a white-knuckled ride during which I was sure I could hear my heart pounding even over the engine's roar. It felt like we were constantly turning left on the track, which measures a mere three-eighths of a mile roundtrip. "Racers travel twenty to forty miles per hour faster," Bob said matter of factly.

Racecars come in a number of categories, but are generally classed in two types. "Modified" cars are open-wheeled vehicles that anyone would recognize as a racecar. Stockcars, often raced as "late models," resemble regular cars, though they are in fact specialized machines crafted to tight specifications. Each vehicle class has a distinctive feel to it as it flies around the track, and drivers jockey among each other differently in each type of car. Modified cars feel like thunder in your chest, while late models emit a deep, piercing scream as they bank.

Thompson International Speedway is situated in an area of low, forested ridges dotted with clusters of deep-green pines. A relatively large five-eighths-mile track built in 1940, it was the first in the country to be paved from the outset. Its size and high-banked turns keep competition keen.

The main event might be on the track, but during my visit there was plenty of action in the paddocks. Crews alternated between relaxing conversation and frenetic activity, prepping the cars and making repairs. They crawled under vehicles, changed tires, or bent over engine compartments. The whine and pop of air-powered tools was a constant soundtrack among tall metal toolboxes, stacks of tires, car trailers, and tow vehicles. Tattooed up with numbers and logos, the cars were flower gardens of color.

Standing in the infield, the cars zoomed around me, engulfing me in a continuous rhythm of sound and vibration. Pit crews had ferried in rolling steel boxes, jacks on wheels, and carts with pneumatic tools and tires. During the race they yelled encouragement and advice to the drivers. "Dial some brake into that freaking thing!" a slight, bearded man screamed. "Keep the bottom covered!" yelled another. Suddenly a car spun and crashed against the first turn wall. A yellow flag was down. "They'll cool off now!" a big tattooed guy shouted. But it was only a matter of seconds before the cars began aggressively chasing each other again.

Opened in 1957, Lime Rock Park is a one-and-a-half mile, paved-road course with eight turns that winds through rolling countryside. Ensconced in a natural amphitheater of forested hills, it felt as much a park as a racetrack. There's no seating at Lime Rock, so fans spread blankets and pitched lawn chairs on grassy slopes under shade trees. Surely this was the Tanglewood of racing.

Here in the self-proclaimed "Road Racing Capital of the East," where Westporter Paul Newman used to take the wheel, the track rises and falls, bends and twists with the grace of our New England country roads. The roar and whine of the cars coming and passing has a Doppler rhythm of high pitched and suddenly lowered sound.

At Lime Rock's Historic Festival held every Labor Day weekend, there are cigar-shaped prewar cars and 1950s competition vehicles, a race for classic Porches and British-production cars like MG, Jaguar, Sunbeam Alpine, and Austen Healy. There are Minis, formula cars, and others. Canoe shaped with an open cockpit, a black John Fray Special on display was made in Bridgeport in the 1960s. Truly, Lime Rock is not just a race event but also a beauty pageant, where car bodies are polished to perfection and chrome glows for the admiration of milling crowds. Loud and engaging, the majestic cars seemed a mechanical analog to the exotic chickens in the poultry building of the Durham fair.

Located in the well-to-do Litchfield Hills, Lime Rock has the distinction of no racing on Sunday and no events after 6:00 p.m. But what was once seen as an economic disadvantage is now "an eccentric signature that gives the track a special cachet," according to media liaison Rick Roso. Harkening back to our Blue Laws, the restrictions seem very Connecticut.

Auto racing may not be for everyone. Indeed, racetracks are physically and demographically invisible to large segments of the population. But with Connecticut so steeped in car culture, this phenomenon of summer is not to be missed.

Seeing Green
Trees, Culture, and Agriculture

In speaking of community, then, we are speaking of a complex connection not only among human beings ... but also between the human economy and nature, between forest or prairie and field or orchard.

—Wendell Berry, *The Art of the Common Place*

Among the first spaces carved out of the wilderness by European colonists, town greens were envisioned as the core of settlement and the center of civic and religious life. Remaining among the last islands of nature in increasingly urban areas, they've always served as a bridge between the built and natural environments. Whether formal parks, mere slices of grass, or reverted to forest, greens continue to reveal much about their communities. They are perhaps the last physical vestiges of a world envisioned by our Puritan forebears.

While it may seem quixotic in a place as densely settled as Connecticut, I determined to find the state's most remote place, the kind of space that confronted the original settlers as they established greens. Canaan Mountain in the northwest corner is wild and rugged without habitation, marked trails, or roads. But its wilderness character is as much a function of time as it is of space since for more than a century it was heavily exploited for agriculture, timber, and charcoal. With neglect over the last hundred years, it has slowly grown wilder.

Unique among states, Connecticut has both a highest peak and a highest point (on a mountain whose summit is just over the border in Massachusetts). Inaccessible by road, they partake of remote, wild places. But like a town green, they also serve as public focal points for the curious and intrepid who like to climb them.

Big trees capture the imagination in settled or wild places, and while Connecticut no longer has large tracts of virgin forest, there are a few remote, remnant patches of trees that were seedlings when the pilgrims landed and are the oldest living things in the state today. There are also several groves of big trees close to roads that feature pines and hemlocks towering well over a hundred feet tall.

Called the perfect forest tree, chestnuts accounted for half of our woodlands before blight struck around World War I, yet shrub-sized remnants of these forest giants continue to sprout with persistent hope from old stumps. Elms were known as the perfect urban tree for their columnar trunks and gracefully spreading branches that formed arcades along streets. Dutch elm disease radically changed the look of cities and towns, but outlier elms can still be found.

Nothing seems more quintessentially New England than autumn's forest colors, yet the changing foliage was not a widely celebrated seasonal event until about a century ago, when it was practically invented to attract tourists. An ephemeral season of sorts, Indian summer may be the rarest and most prized time of year. It's marked by witch hazel trees, which perversely bloom as leaves fall and the first snows arrive.

For a real taste of our most renowned season, nothing beats a glass of fresh-pressed cider in a state that features both the nation's oldest mill and its only steam-powered press. And when cider is ready to drink, the time of agricultural fairs has arrived, the true confluence of culture, seasonal change, and nature. Here, at the intersection of food and entertainment, we find a last manifestation of the yeoman community the first settlers envisioned when they established town greens.

A Place for Common Ground
Town Greens

Perhaps there's nothing more quintessentially New England than the town green. Beloved by natives and visitors alike, it conjures images of a white clapboard church and colonial houses around a neat rectangle of grass studded with tall trees and sometimes a granite Civil War soldier standing sentry atop a pedestal. Having lived on the Collinsville Green for almost three decades, I'm among those with a deep affection for these oases of lawn and shade. But greens vary greatly, and the view from my windows isn't exactly typical of what one might expect.

The focal point of an old mill village, Collinsville Green appears more functional than idyllic. Laid out in the 1840s by a paternalistic axe-factory owner who wanted to inject some beauty and order into the community he created, it features a rectangular greensward crossed diagonally by two carriage paths. Now widened and paved, the village green is actually more street than green. At each end, triangular traffic islands are planted with a single crab apple tree, grass, and flowers. There's an elongated curve of lawn on either side in front of nineteenth-century houses, where several Kousa dogwoods bloom each May. It's a postcard-worthy image, and artists occasionally set up their easels there, but it's not the idealized notion of a village green.

Connecticut has about 170 town greens, no two of which are alike. Sometimes they aren't even recognized as such because they are small, out of the way, or look more like parks than the town commons of our imaginations. Thousands of people drive by town greens each day, yet it's remarkable how few take time to stop to explore their paths, gaze at their monuments, or enjoy the shade provided by mature trees. There are towns blessed with more than one green, like Norwich (which has four), and others in which a traditional green is absent, such as Avon and Rocky Hill. Greens exist in rural hamlets, like Colebrook, and in cities the size of Waterbury. They may be just a tiny slice of land, like Plainfield's Memorial Park, or a vast expanse well suited for today's dog walkers and joggers, like the historic green in Lebanon.

At over a mile in length, the Lebanon Green is the nation's longest. Lacking parklike amenities, it remains almost all meadow and is as near to the eighteenth century as any public open space in the state. Located in the heart of a community still largely agricultural, the green sits on elevated ground surrounded by well-spaced eighteenth- and nineteenth-century houses, behind which the land slopes away to open farmland.

On a late, cumulus-studded summer day I parked in front of the Governor Jonathan Trumbull House, built in the 1730s and featuring a large central chimney. Now a museum, it was once home to the only colonial governor who supported the Revolution. Situated in the center of town, the green seemed vast, filled with light and the scent of newly mown hay. It is Connecticut's last town green still used for farming, and a large patch of its hayfield had been cut to golden stubble and was dotted by bales. I felt moved in its presence, as near to the pastoral ideal of the nation's founders as I would ever come.

Walking along the edge, I spied a small, gambrel-roof building across the street. Once Trumbull's store, it is known as the "War Office," where he met with Washington, Lafayette, General Henry Knox, and Rochambeau, whose troops camped on the green during their march through Connecticut. Looking across the grass to the opposite side of the green, I spied a big colonial house where General Washington spent the night in March 1781. It was home to Jonathan Trumbull Jr., second speaker of the U.S. House of Representatives and, like his father, a governor of Connecticut. At the far end was the former residence of William Williams, signer of the Declaration of Independence.

Greens were often established at the outset of New England settlements since common ownership of land was a tradition dating to medieval England, where freeman shared pasture and woodland. Although such property might be at the outskirts of a community, a small central plot was typically set aside for a Congregational meetinghouse, and this slice of land would become the green. These were places that "allowed the militia space in which to exercise and provided an area for hangings, outdoor religious assemblies, and—most importantly—livestock collection," according to Harvard professor of landscape John Stilgoe.

Although too small for widespread grazing, families pastured cows or horses on greens, commonly turning them into "wide, muddy paddocks."

Not until the advent of the village improvement and colonial revival movements in the latter part of the nineteenth and beginning of the twentieth centuries did greens take on their current appearance, complete with shade trees, monuments, carefully maintained walkways, and fences. Thus, the idyllic, grassy, leafy, well-tended green as a center of community pride is a relatively recent evolution, part of calculated efforts to beautify communities and connect them to their past.

Today, greens are prized as tranquil oases of history in rural areas and precious open spaces in the hearts of cities. They've become largely parks with a past. Sometimes they are the only physical remnant of a world envisioned by the original Puritan settlers. Their maintenance, varieties of trees, types of monuments, and the activities on and surrounding them, as well as their nexus to civic and commercial life, speaks volumes about a town.

I've encountered many of Connecticut's greens in my years of driving around, looking for abandoned roads, cider mills, roadside springs, old graveyards, and other places hidden in plain sight. Because they all offer something different, I almost always stop at an unfamiliar one, and some, like the Lebanon Green, are so beautiful or intriguing that I make a point of visiting them whenever I'm nearby.

Of my favorite greens in Connecticut, none could be further from Lebanon in spirit than the sixteen-acre New Haven Green. Considerably older (it was laid out in 1641), New Haven's green is located downtown and serves as the "lungs of the city," It's a bustling green space rich with traffic sounds and voices where I've enjoyed many a day people watching from a shaded park bench. Sometimes there's entertainment, guitar players, or mimes, but mainly it's the invigorating diversity of life that draws me— businessmen, Yale students, shoppers, and locals. Especially during performances for the annual Festival of Arts and Ideas, it can feel like an open-air assembly hall walled in by three centuries' worth of architecture, ranging from colonial to Greek revival, gothic to modern skyscrapers. Despite the city's hurried pace, a row of three early nineteenth-century churches along Temple Street provide a sense of timelessness.

Notwithstanding the green's urbanity there are only two monuments, one with a flagstaff and radiating walkways in a sea of lawn near city hall, and a fountain at the corner of Chapel and Church Streets. But perhaps the arcades of statuesque elms still lining the paths are the greatest monuments to a place known as the Elm City. Though its namesake tree has all but disappeared from municipal streets since the scourge of Dutch elm disease in the 1930s, the trees' survival (and occasional replacement) is itself a monument to the diligence and care lavished on this ancient ground by the city, volunteers, and the private proprietors that have owned and maintained it for generations. Such efforts have been fueled by contemporary environmental, historic preservation, and urban revival concerns. The self-perpetuating committee of proprietors consisting of prominent citizens has ensured that the green remains relevant to the times while maintaining its heritage.

I especially remember walking one winter beneath the high branches as dusk settled; I was on my way to a poetry reading at the Institute Library, which has the distinction of being one of the oldest, as well as one of the last, membership libraries in the country. The gravel path crunched underfoot while arcing above me was a shadowy, irregular lattice of uncommon grace. I remember thinking that I was as close as a person can come to the living architecture that was the glory of most New England towns at the beginning of the twentieth century.

The Lebanon and New Haven Greens, despite vastly different appearances and functions, are an essential part of community identity and pride. In contrast, the ten-acre Ashford Green is hardly noticed, though it sits along a busy rural stretch of U.S. Route 44. I'd passed it many times before a friend tipped me off to its significance. Pulling on to narrow Fitts Road, which divides the plot, I walked onto a weedy lawn where a few shade trees stood near a dilapidated gazebo and the elegant Ashford Academy, an early nineteenth-century two-story schoolhouse with a belfry and twin doors. Nearby was the original outhouse, and just beyond was Babcock Cemetery. But most of my walk was through sloping woods because two-thirds of the green has reverted to forest.

It was hard to believe that this was once a bustling community center with a meetinghouse, blacksmith, and several homes, including that of a doctor. Nearby were sawmills, tanneries, a cotton mill, and a glass factory. I headed down Fitts Road to Goss Brook, where I found old cellar holes, a mill structure, a breached earthen dam, and an abandoned cemetery surrounded by a stone wall with an iron gate. The onetime center of Ashford was now largely a ghost town.

Like Ashford, Glastonbury has also seen the locus of civic and commercial activity move away from its once central green, which is located at the intersection of Hubbard and Main Streets. But Hubbard Green, surrounded by colonial revival houses and a cemetery, is given loving care. The old town hall at the west end is now a museum, and the lawn is meticulously groomed and soft. When I was last there on a warm day in early October, three barefoot boys were playing catch, and a young couple had spread out a blanket and picnic. Large trees shifted with the wind, and a huge, commanding pin oak stood near the center, not far from a modest bluestone plaza where a Civil War soldier stood guard on a pedestal, flanked by slab monuments remembering other conflicts.

Clearly, a green no longer at the center of community life has lost some of its original purpose. But at the other end of the spectrum, a busy location amid sprawling development can sometimes damage a green's communal value. Sixteen miles west of Hartford, Canton Green abuts heavily trafficked U.S. Route 44. The green's small triangle of grass lies in front of a nineteenth-century schoolhouse that's now home to Gallery on the Green, Connecticut's oldest surviving art guild. Nearby are other old buildings intermixed with a hodgepodge of modern commercial structures. Once the center of a small community, the Canton Green is now just another node on a long retail corridor increasingly consisting of big-box stores and strip malls. For years I attended concerts performed in a gazebo there, but they're no longer held due to noise and traffic safety concerns. I pass by several times each week, and although the green provides two benches, I can't recall the last time I've seen anyone sit on them.

Perhaps no green functions more as a community hub than the one in Guilford. It's a true town square, with the town hall, library, and three churches located around its rectangular twelve acres, planted with well over a hundred trees. Although the bulk of commercial activity has shifted to the nearby Boston Post Road, the streets surrounding the green are vibrant with restaurants, boutiques, clothiers, galleries, a bookstore, hardware, and other retailers that occupy neatly kept colonial and Victorian buildings. High on a pink-granite pedestal near the grassy center is a Civil War soldier leaning on his gun, and around the edge of the green are small memorials commemorating not only past wars but fallen firefighters.

True to its original purpose, Guilford Green remains a gathering place for the community, with events such as the Harvest Fest, Little Folks Fair, Jewish Festival, and the chamber's Taste of the Shoreline. It has also hosted political demonstrations, from support of the American hostages in Iran to world-peace gatherings. In good weather there are always people about, sunning themselves on blankets, reading a newspaper, playing ball, or enjoying lunch on a park bench.

Whether in actuality or imagination, few landscape elements tie us to our place and history as well as town greens. Established as sites for churches, graveyards, pasturage, schools, meetinghouses, and military-parade grounds, these commonly held lands, where trash was sometimes dumped or gravel extracted, in the past were often messy, discordant places. Created for purposes light years from today's world, they continue to serve the critical role of providing much-needed green space in an increasingly crowded environment.

Heart of Nowhere
Connecticut's Most Remote Place

It was a week before the solstice in December. The ground was frosted with a couple of inches of snow under a sky of hammered pewter. My thermometer registered in the low teens, while stiff, gusty blasts plunged the wind chill deep into single digits. As if the weather wasn't inhospitable enough, I found myself climbing a craggy slope through an unyielding thicket of mountain laurel. No person in his right mind should have been there. But that was just the point. I was tramping through Connecticut's most remote place.

Sandwiched between New York and Boston, finding a place even vaguely remote in Connecticut seems odd, if not impossible. At 726 people per square mile, Connecticut is the fourth most densely populated state in a country in which eighty-seven people per square mile is the average.

But paradoxically, even after the mid-twentieth century, when the state became increasingly thickly settled, it was nevertheless valued for rural seclusion and proximity to the natural world. Some of the nation's leading nature writers sought refuge here, like Pulitzer Prize winner Edwin Way Teale, who settled on a farm in Hampton. Playwright Arthur Miller, novelist Philip Roth, and poet James Merrill, some of the nation's most highly regarded and prizewinning authors, are among those who have found sufficient solitude in Connecticut to do their work. Despite the state's small size and burgeoning population, perhaps the Yankee taciturnity of neighbors as well as a patchwork landscape of villages, fields, and forest felt sufficiently remote to those seeking quiet. Proximity to the writing capital of New York probably rendered the state ideal.

Clearly the common conception of remote places as wildernesses on the scale of Alaska's Brooks Range or the heart of Amazonia is nonsense in a place like Connecticut. Given its geography and population, maybe the concept of remoteness in this state had to be translated to something other than a matter of open spaces. Perhaps in order to find Connecticut's most remote place, I needed to examine places remote in time, like Dudleytown in Cornwall or Gay City in Hebron, once small but busy communities with schools, churches, farms, and factories, which are now ghost towns with only cellar holes and old stone waterpower structures as epitaphs. What could be more remote from today's reality than once settled places reverting back to forest? After all, time itself provides a kind of distance. Even this wooded mountainside where I struggled through thick brush hid the remains of fieldstone cellar holes on its lower slopes as well as leveled circles of blackened soil where colliers had once made charcoal for a booming nineteenth-century iron industry.

Or perhaps there were other species of remoteness more suitable to a populated state. Connecticut has long wrestled over the concept of social remoteness, and though many people find a home outside of town desirable today, living beyond the pale of settlement was not only frowned upon, but could be a punishable offense in colonial times. In 1665, for example, the colonial legislature chastised smithy William Cheessbrooke for living in what is now Stonington because, according to the public records of the colony of Conneticut, "by his solitary living [he] advantaged to carry on a mischeivous trade with the Indians" and 'it seemed more than uncomely for a man professing Godliness so to withdraw from all publique ordinances and Xtian society."

During the eighteenth and nineteenth centuries, social remoteness sometimes took the form of rural outsider communities composed of people of African, Indian, or mixed descent in places like Negrotown in New Hartford, Little Egypt in Redding, and the Barkhamsted Lighthouse in Barkhamsted. There were also "pest houses" at the edges of some communities to isolate those with communicable diseases. Later waves of immigration resulted in urban ethnic immigrant enclaves with their own forms of isolation.

Such experiences continue today. Even though they are just a few miles apart, the impoverished north end of Hartford may seem remote to those in well-to-do suburbs, and vice versa. Throughout the state, self-isolating gated communities for those with higher incomes are increasingly common, as are "active adult" developments requiring residents to be at least fifty-five years old. Perhaps, in an area rife with human activity, remoteness had less to do with geography than with differing lifestyles. No doubt, this is the type of remoteness that most of us experience.

Still, I wasn't ready to give up on the idea of a physically remote Connecticut, so I continued my hunt for the spot most uninhabited, as far from manmade structures, roads, and trails as it was possible to get in a place known more for its human history and culture than its wide-open spaces. You might think identifying such a place would be relatively easy. Instead, it became a puzzle.

Since most of us experience the landscape from behind the windshield of a vehicle, the principal measure of remoteness might logically be the place furthest from accessibility on four wheels powered by an internal-combustion engine. But that raised the question of trails. An ATV can certainly go beyond maintained roads, and mountain bikes and footpaths can provide regular access even to places deep in the woods. Seasons matter also. Winter road closures may isolate places, like Mount Riga in Salisbury, that during the rest of the year are relatively accessible. And did logging and fire roads count, even if they were temporary?

Certainly, a remote place shouldn't have any permanent habitations. But a hunting cabin or summer-camp buildings also seemed inappropriate, even if they were used only a few weeks or days a year. Uninhabited places that drew visitors because they had a view, interesting ruins, or some unusual natural feature also didn't seem a good candidate for isolation, no matter their distance from roads and habitations.

Islands were also a conundrum. An island in Candlewood Lake—the state's largest, which lies in Fairfield and Litchfield Counties—might lack trails or buildings, and it certainly cannot be reached by wheeled vehicles, but it might lie in shouting distance of houses or be a picnic site for fishermen and water skiers. Connecticut's coastal islands' maritime location makes them remote by most standards, yet vessels frequently glide by. Some have substantial uninhabited structures, like the Falkner Island and Stratford Shoal lighthouses.

Finally, after deciding that the most remote place should be accessible only on foot, I enlisted the help of Bill Keegan of Newington, a whiz with geographic information systems, who examined several databases on large land holdings as well as road networks. He found over fifty candidates, ranging from eight hundred to eight thousand acres, spread throughout the state. Many were state forests, but there were also water-company lands in Madison, Wolcott, and North Branford, a Boy Scout reservation in Ashford, and a few large private-forest holdings like Yale-Meyers forest in the northeastern part of the state and the Great Mountain Forest in Norfolk and Canaan. The data revealed a cat's cradle of roads crisscrossing many large blocks of raw land, including forty-eight roads within a 7,700-acre tract in

Voluntown's Pachaug State Forest. Roads did not traverse only two areas.

One roadless area was Sleeping Giant State Park. But, proximate to New Haven, Sleeping Giant is laced with heavily trafficked hiking trails and can be as busy as a downtown corner, especially when leaf peepers climb to the top of its ridge for an autumn view. The second area, however, seemed about as remote as Connecticut could get.

Canaan Mountain is a vast, rock-strewn, and brooding presence looming over its namesake small town in northwest Connecticut. Now totaling over two thousand acres, the largest portion of the mountain is a state forest first designated by Governor Thomas J. Meskill as a wilderness natural-area preserve in 1972, during the first flush of the environmental movement. A 2003 management plan developed by the Connecticut Department of Environmental Protection that outlines appropriate activities on the property and approaches to protecting it described its "rugged and seemingly remote character [as] most suited to relatively 'primitive and contemplative' uses." Rising from a lowland area underlain by marble, the mountain, with its indomitable cliffs, looks like the prow of a huge ship towering over the surrounding countryside.

Inasmuch as the mountain is situated in the acknowledged "icebox of Connecticut," the cold this day seemed fitting, amplifying the sense of isolation. As I slowly climbed through oak and beech, I paused often to catch my breath. Gray, lichen-crusted ledges leered from above, and so sharp was the ascent and so various the angles of nearby slopes that I felt as if the entire world was canted. At the top, the wind was brutal, and I sought shelter behind rocks and in groves of evergreens. Stunted oaks and bare ledges spotted with leafless blueberry plants were raked with blowing snow. A few twisty roads, farms, and houses were visible far below, but the overwhelming impression was of a world of dense hardwoods interspersed with pine, spruce, and hemlock.

A vast forest studded with wetlands, vernal pools, talus slopes, and streams, Canaan Mountain is one of the state's most diverse natural places. Testament to its remoteness from human activity is the presence of over twenty animal and plant species of concern to scientists for their rarity, including rattlesnakes, various sedges, flowers like Canada violet and three-toothed cinquefoil, and insects, especially several unusual moths.

More than just a high point, Canaan Mountain is a huge massif of uneven, stony land with rises, steep declivities, and cliffs. Rocky bald spots are interspersed with dense thickets, and the only trails are those left by deer and other animals.

This is a wilderness befitting a densely populated state. Hardly primeval, Canaan Mountain has supported centuries of hunter-gatherer, farming, and heavy-industrial culture. Native peoples hunted on the mountain for thousands of years, sometimes setting fires to drive game. When European colonists arrived in the early 1700s, they began subsistence farming and lumbering on the lower slopes. By the latter part of that century, sheep and cattle were grazing. Around this time, nearby discovery of iron ore led to the manufacture of everything from cannons to chains in myriad furnaces and forges, which required charcoal for fuel. The mountain's trees were continuously cut in a regular cycle to make charcoal, a process of slowly charring mounds of moss-covered cordwood with damped-down, flameless fires. This not only left the mountain denuded, but it clouded the air with acrid smoke. Left to its own devices in the twentieth century, though, the forest slowly recovered.

The mountain now stands as a monument to the resiliency of Connecticut's landscape. Wandering the vast plateau for about five hours, I saw no other soul, save two young deer. It was a place of both physical and social isolation. There were no footprints in the snow and frozen mud, only the markings of small rodents and birds. As evidence of humanity, I encountered a few unsteady stone cairns and found a fire ring on a windswept ledge and another secreted among hemlocks. Neither had been used in a long time.

The Measure of a State
Connecticut's Highest Point(s)

One might well expect that Connecticut's highest peak is a windswept summit with a panoramic view. After all, state high points bring to mind the bare rocky top of Colorado's Mount Elbert, the rugged heights of New York's Mount Marcy, or the majesty of snow-capped Rainier in Washington. Crossing the crest of Salisbury's Bear Mountain in the state's far north-west corner, hikers on the Appalachian Trail may understandably conclude that the 360-degree vista is just such a site. In fact, the stone tablet embedded in a large cairn there unambiguously refers to it as "the highest ground in Connecticut, 2,354 feet above the sea." Unfortunately, words carved in stone, though long lasting, are sometimes no more reliable than a penciled note on a swatch of scrap paper. Simply put, both assertions are false. Bear Mountain is not the roof of Connecticut, and it measures only 2,323 feet high.

My most recent trip to Bear Mountain was last summer, beginning on the blue-blazed Undermountain Trail at State Route 41, just north of the village of Salisbury. It's one of a network of more than eight-hundred miles of trails threading throughout the state and maintained by the volunteers of the nonprofit Connecticut Forest and Park Association, the state's oldest conservation organization.

The path first climbed gradually but soon made a steady ascent up an escarpment decorated with lichen-splotched ledges. The woods were dense with a towering hardwood canopy that created cooling, deep shade on even a torrid day. After reaching the top of the wooded cliff, the trail continued to climb, crossing Brassie Brook and reaching the Appalachian Trail at Riga Junction, a clearing surrounded by mountain laurel. Heading north on the mother road of footpaths, the trail rose slowly and then more steeply through oaky forest until it burst suddenly onto open ledges. The view grew increasingly spectacular as I gained elevation, climbing from one rock outcrop to another, and a steady, cooling breeze quickly licked away the sweat of a humid afternoon.

Bear Mountain's summit is fairly broad. Unmarked trails leading to viewpoints wind through scrub oak and pitch pines. The mountain is capped with a somewhat trapezoidal-shaped fieldstone platform, providing unobstructed views in all directions. To the north, west, and south, I saw forested terrain punctuated by lakes and hills, reminding me of the grand Hudson River School paintings by Hartford native Frederick Church. On the east were the sparkling sheets of Twin Lakes, some bucolic farmland, swamp, and dense woods stretching miles toward the hulking presence of Canaan Mountain.

The fieldstone platform was once a low tower marking the top of Connecticut. Like the tower on Haystack Mountain in nearby Norfolk, it is the fruit of Robbins Battell's successful challenge to the *Encyclopedia Britannica's* declaration that no place in the state was over one thousand feet above sea level. The incensed Battell declared Bear's summit the state's highest ground, and in 1885 he secured a 999-year lease of the peak and hired local mason Owen Travis to erect a monument. Travis's name is inscribed on the slab marking the elevation, providing a humble tradesman with a modicum of dubious immortality.

It took Travis three years to haul 350 tons of stone to the summit, with only the help of oxen. Using no mortar, in the manner of Yankee farm walls, he built a slightly pyramidal tower that was twenty-by-twenty feet at its base and ten-by-ten feet at its top. It stood just over twenty-two feet tall (thirty-nine feet if you include the lightning rod topped wth a metal ball). There weren't many trees on the hills in those days, so the stone pile, visible from the valley below, provided Bear Mountain with a crowning distinction.

By the 1960s, Travis's monument had suffered decades of harsh winters and vandalism from visitors who liked to pull out rocks and toss them down the sheer slopes. Eventually it experienced partial collapse. But in 1972 a private benefactor's contributions and helicopter-delivered supplies enabled restoration of the monument, including a poured-cement cap.

A few years later, new damage was repaired by a group of Scouts. The fix was short lived, however, and in 1978 the monument's east corner gave way. It sagged and toppled, the cement cap slid to the ground, and the inscribed marble slab lay in the rubble. Pocked with bullet holes, the ball on the lightning rod became an armored, buzzing hornets' nest. The tower would never again be rebuilt to full height.

It took a 1982 visit from commissioner of environmental protection Stanley J. Pac, along with some behind-the-scenes political muscle, before state funds were allocated the next year to stabilize what was left. That ruin now provides the modest viewing platform. Given what modern instruments have recorded about the height of the state's hills, it is perhaps more appropriate that the once proud tower, dethroned from the superlative glory of being Connecticut's high point, be swapped for a humbler crown.

Regardless of what surveys dictate, Bear Mountain—with its blueberry-covered ledges and nearly wild panorama—is the state's emotional high point for me, even if it's an unsuccessful topographical one. To the north I spied ridge after ridge of uneven hills all the way to Mount Greylock, Massachusetts's high point about fifty miles distant. To the south, the route of the Appalachian Trail headed toward the rocky prominence of Lion's Head and the wooded sides of Prospect Mountain. The jagged Catskills formed a distant silhouette on the western horizon, and the grassy summit of Brace Mountain stood in the foreground, just over the border with New York. A bit northeast of Brace was an unremarkable wooded peak—Mount Frissell.

About a mile and a third west and a bit north of Bear Mountain's errant stone marker, a hiking trail crosses an easy-to-miss spot on the south shoulder of Mount Frissell, a mountain whose 2,453-foot peak lies in Massachusetts. At 2,380 feet, Connecticut's highest point is unassumingly commemorated by a small green metal stake drilled into the ledge.

This "high point without a summit" is unique among the states, according to Peakbagger.com, a website that caters to hikers seeking high places. Of course, it's a distinction to which most Connecticut residents would rather not draw attention. After all, to have a state's grandest height be a climb down from a higher location in a neighboring jurisdiction seems, well, a little undignified.

On the north side of Bear Mountain, the Appalachian Trail becomes precipitous and bouldery with uncertain footing. On the day I visited, I moved slowly, measuring each step. Rarely have I made it down without slipping at least once. The forest was thick with beech, hemlock, maple, and birch. After about three-quarters of a mile the trail began to flatten, and I took an old-woods road leading west as it angled gently downward, passing nineteenth-century charcoal hearths and paralleling a boisterous brook. In little less than a mile the path reached unpaved Mount Washington Road, not far from the Massachusetts border.

After crossing the road, I took the red-blazed Mount Frissell Trail, which soon climbed steeply to Round Mountain, whose open summit is marked by glacially scratched ledges and low brush. From the top of Round,

I followed the trail directly down into a narrow col and then rose quickly to the forested top of Mountain Frissell, where visitors can sign a logbook fitted into a battered metal box attached to a tree. Curious about those who preceded me, I paused to read a few pages. As "highpointing" has gained in popularity in recent years, hikers have come from increasingly far places to what would be a low-priority climb for most. Thus, while our highest ground may be underwhelming by usual standards, people from around the country and even the world have stood here. Descending the mountain's south ledges, I soon reached the unceremonious high point of Connecticut, eighty vertical feet below the summit and fifty-seven feet above the acme of Bear Mountain.

Despite its subpeak location, the view was exhilarating. Huddled among forested hills with no visible sign of civilization, Mount Frissel provided an unusual and refreshing sense of remoteness. Below was a wooded valley cradled by steep slopes. Riga Lake and the longer, narrower Forge Pond rippled in the wind, reflecting the clouds above. The land looked uninhabited, though I knew the trees hid a few summer homes and unpaved roads. Yet, like Canaan Mountain, Mount Frissel's wild countenance belied its history.

Once a busy center of iron making, the mountain's forests were cut repeatedly for the charcoal that fueled furnaces. At the turn of the nineteenth century, the area was an incipient Pittsburg, with smoky fires and gangs of workmen. The hills were tangled with slash and pole timber. Near the outlet of Forge Pond, a large fieldstone iron furnace still stands where cannon, chains, and other matériel were forged for the American Revolution. One of the original anchors for the USS *Constitution*, "Old Ironsides," was reportedly made there.

As usual, I couldn't resist continuing along the trail another quarter mile to the tristate monument, where Massachusetts, New York, and Connecticut converge in a wooded saddle between Frissell and Brace Mountains. Although it's not a grand elevation, for some visitors the notion of being in three states at once is the real high point of a hike here. Set by a New York–Massachusetts commission in the summer of 1899, the granite shaft reads "Mass." on the northeast and "N.Y." on the southwest face. The Connecticut portion was unlettered, perhaps because the state was too parsimonious to contribute to the post's cost. However, someone has etched "Conn." on the appropriate side with a stone or knife.

Connecticut's high point may be a lower spot on a neighbor's mountain, but the view is inspiring, and the trip there is an adventure that is neither overly arduous nor so easily attained that the spot will be unappreciated. Unlike fabled New England high points to the north, there is no road to the top of Mount Frissel as there is to Vermont's Mount Mansfield, New Hampshire's Mount Washington, or Massachusetts's Mount Greylock. There are no buildings or communications towers. If getting away from the world is an essential joy of climbing above it, Connecticut's highest elevations can be measured in more than just feet above sea level.

Big Trees
Old-Growth Forests

Connecticut has no large stands of towering virgin forest, which is hardly surprising after 350 years of clearing land for agriculture; harvesting wood for heating, railroads, the iron and other industries; and the inexorable spread of development. The last substantial plot of ancient big trees was three hundred acres in Colebrook that fell to lumbermen in 1912. Most of Connecticut's truly old-growth forests are startlingly different than what most people imagine, bearing absolutely no resemblance to the archetypal California redwood groves or stands of giant Douglas fir found in the Pacific Northwest.

Some of Connecticut's oldest trees are growing in the most inaccessible places along the traprock ridges that stretch from New Haven's West Rock to the Barndoor Hills of Simsbury and Granby. In these high, wind-bitten places are stands of oak, hickory, and ash that may be well over two centuries in age because poor soils discouraged agriculture, and their gnarly shapes left them unusable as saw timber. Although some have been cut for fuel wood over the years, difficult locations have kept harvesting to a minimum.

But rather than grand, magisterial groves usually associated with old-growth forests, these are pockets of shrunken, wizened trees typically no more than thirty to forty feet tall. They are tenacious, surviving extreme temperatures, drought, thin soils, and the wind, which shapes some of them into forms that are the envy of bonsai aficionados. I find their presence as good a reason as the spectacular vistas to make one of my favorite climbs to Lamentation Mountain just north of Meriden on the blue-blazed Metacomet Trail. Persistent under the harshest circumstances, I can't help but admire these stunted, twisted ancients growing at the edge of steep cliffs and lean-

ing over the precipice with roots wedged into rock fractures. Thousands of people pass them every year, but hidden in plain sight, few realize the hoary age of these diminutive, misshapen trees. Today they face their biggest threat as houses sprout on fragile ridgelines where they are cut to improve the view.

Native Americans set fires to clear brush and drive game, so the first European settlers found parklike old-growth forests covering most of the state. For colonists, the forest was an impediment to agriculture, and clearing for pasture and cropland by girdling and burning was widespread. Timber was harvested for houses, barns, fuel, furniture, and other domestic uses. After initial settlement and into the first decades of the nineteenth century, small water-powered sawmills were established to supply local products, and in 1820 only 25 percent of the state remained forested.

By the middle of the nineteenth century large-scale lumbering catering to outside markets was under way. Most of the wood went into general construction lumber, but cheese boxes, oars, turned bowls, and tool handles were the among specialty products that relied on Connecticut wood. Trees were also felled to produce charcoal for iron making, brick kilns, and other uses. Chestnut and hemlock were cut for tannins used in curing leather. Resisting rot, chestnut was also used almost exclusively for utility poles. During the early twentieth century second-growth pine was turned into crates, containers, pails, and barrels. But as forests became exhausted, coal and oil became popular, and agriculture faded, Connecticut's forests began a slow process of change and regrowth. Today, forests cover about 60 percent of the state, and lumber is harvested for structural framing, cabinets and furniture, architectural millwork, flooring, and doors.

Connecticut does have some last stands of large virgin trees. In the shadow of Canaan Mountain, they are all in inaccessible parcels of just a few acres. I recently visited the largest of these plots, where hemlocks dating to the early 1600s grow in excess of 110 feet tall, with some trunks measuring up to three feet thick. Just above Norfolk's Bigelow Pond, they stood on steep hummocky ground in thin soils strewn with boulders. Whether isolation, difficult terrain, or unsuitability for charcoal saved them remains a mystery. The oldest living things in Connecticut, they have survived centuries of hurricanes, ice storms, and insect pests. Their majesty recalled Henry Wadsworth Longfellow's "forest primeval," where "murmuring pines and the hemlocks, bearded with moss, and in garments green, indistinct in the twilight, stand like Druids of eld, with voices sad and prophetic." I lingered among them in order to absorb their staid, calming influences. Though centuries of hard-won survival has left many with twisted and broken crowns, the dense canopy left little understory, "giving the stands a grand gloomy aspect," as forest scientist Herbert Winer wrote in 1955.

Canaan Mountain may have the oldest trees, but, due to less than ideal growing conditions, they are not as tall as some that have grown up in other areas previously cut. These "secondary old-growth" trees are bigger, notwithstanding that most are only about 150 years old. But just because they are tall doesn't mean they're easy to spot, even though most are a short walk from a road.

Tucked behind the West Cornwall firehouse on State Route 128 are a few magical acres that contain Connecticut's best stand of large second-growth trees, some of which may be almost two centuries old. This grove of sylvan giants—known as Gold's Pines—contains the state's tallest tree. Rising almost 145 feet, it is thirty-two inches in diameter at breast height. Even more impressive is a massive forty-three-inch-diameter pine more than 134 feet tall. Although the area was probably timbered about 1740, it likely grew trees again by 1820, a time when many small, infertile patches of farmland were being abandoned.

By 1870, when T. S. Gold purchased the site, it was ready again for harvest. Only a change from wood to coal prevented the big trees from being felled, cut up, and tossed into locomotive boilers. But their value for purposes other than lumber or cordwood grew as they did, and in 1932 a slice of the pines was designated a scientific research plot still maintained today by the Connecticut Agricultural Experiment Station. In 1941, when the pines were again threatened with sale to lumbermen in settlement of an estate, the Connecticut General Assembly purchased the property for five thousand dollars at the urging of the Connecticut Forest and Park Association. Within recent years, the grove joined Canaan Mountain as a state natural-area preserve, ensuring that it will be managed to protect the big trees in perpetuity.

From the road, a typically dense tangle of mixed hardwoods hides the majestic trees, which are only a five-minute walk up a broad path. On the day of my visit, I suddenly found myself among lofty pines and hemlocks standing like massive pillars, their first branches growing about two stories above the ground. No brush deigned to grow beneath them, and the forest floor was carpeted in orange needles amid an eternal twilight. I put a hand on deeply furrowed bark and looked up the arrow-straight trunk to a dizzying height. Stretching my arms around the trees, I barely encompassed a third of the girth. I felt tiny among them, comparatively possessed of so little time.

In a case of wilderness regained, remote stands of tall trees can be found in small pockets on the slopes of Bear Mountain. They are easily accessible by trail. En route to Connecticut's high points, slight detours will take you to some of the tallest. Less than a mile from State Route 41, the blue-blazed Undermountain Trail swings left toward Brassie Brook as it begins climbing more steeply among mixed hardwoods. Last time I was there, I took a short bushwhack into the ravine, which revealed a stand of stately hemlock rising skyward along the slope to over 110 feet. In little more than half a mile, the trail crossed the stream, and I followed its course uphill into another tiny hemlock grove. With my heart thumping from the climb and my eyes turned upward along the trunks, I felt practically giddy in their presence.

It's another seven hundred or eight hundred vertical feet and little more than a mile and three-quarters to the fieldstone monument atop Bear Mountain, where, in addition to ridgelines, you can look north down into the narrow gash of Sages Ravine, which is marked by a line of evergreens starting in Massachusetts and descending into Connecticut. I've always found hiking along the ravine's brook to be steep and treacherous, but the giant hemlocks—some probably over two hundred years old—rise straight up and cast an ethereal gloaming, like an outdoor version of a dimly lit cathedral.

While inaccessibility and benign neglect has left groves of large trees on the slopes of Bear Mountain, cultivation and careful management by foresters has fostered the big pines in Meshomasic State Forest in Portland, New England's first, and the nation's second, state forest. On an autumn day I found myself wandering Meshomasic's rough, winding gravel roads past old cellar holes, colonial mines, and remains of a Nike missile base. Dry ledges supported contorted pitch pine not far from swamps, ponds, and brooks. Large deer are hunted in this forest, and the state's most extensive rattlesnake population persists here, despite development nearby.

I stopped my pickup near the junction of North Mulford and Mulford Roads and walked among the towering trees. The forest floor was plush with fallen orange needles. Ferns and princess-pine clubmoss grew in patches among fallen branches and standing snags. Protected in a valley where clear Buck Brook moves swiftly, the big pines have survived for over a century. They seem as ancient as the Bible, but they were in fact planted by the state in the first decade of the twentieth century—a time when scrubby brush is what passed for forest in Connecticut. The plantation has been thinned twice in the last thirty years, but it remains dense, a refuge for birds like the white-throated sparrows and chickadees I heard that day.

On the other side of Cornwall from Gold's Pines is Cathedral Pines. Designated a National Natural Landmark by the U.S. Department of the Interior, it was the best-known ancient forest in New England until a July 1989 tornado quickly flattened all but a token remnant of what had taken hundreds of years to grow. Cleared for agriculture in the eighteenth century, some of the trees that had grown since then were about three hundred years old and as tall as 172 feet. In what is perhaps Connecticut's longest legacy of purposeful land conservation, the Calhoun family, who had been protecting the trees from logging since 1883, donated the site in 1967 to the Nature Conservancy.

From among the columnar trunks of the few towering giants that remain, I peered through to the devastated hillside. Several misshapen and weathered trees stood over downed logs and branches now woven with a tangle of sun-loving honeysuckle and raspberry. The forest was alive with the sounds of blue jays, chickadees, gold finches, and red-winged blackbirds. A pileated woodpecker banging away at a long-dead trunk sent a drumbeat through the woods. Young hardwoods, taking advantage of the light available in the wake of the fallen giants, were growing rapidly. Cherry, oak, birch, ash, and maple will come to dominate this site, growing on the rich organic layer left by the pines. But the pines themselves—which require exposed mineral soil and a lack of competition to flourish—are unlikely to ever grow back.

It's sobering that such seeming permanence can be eternally disrupted in just a few seconds. Yet such catastrophic disturbance is an essential part of nature's rubric of forest succession. A small grove of large trees is vulnerable, and it is possible that a similar fate awaits Gold's Pines as well. Perhaps next time it will be disease, invasive insects, or ice. I felt awe for both the grand trees and the overwhelming power that destroyed them.

Ensconced in river valleys and dotting Connecticut hillsides are other groves of big trees. Cornwall's fifty-five-acre Ballyhack Preserve hosts giant white pines and hemlocks, including a 143-foot pine, the state's second-tallest tree. Sandwiched between the Farmington River and East River Road in Barkhamsted is Matties Grove, a two-acre plot of pines, some of which are about 130 feet tall. Catlin Woods at White Memorial Foundation in Litchfield features large hemlocks and pines where there was once colonial pasture and woodlot.

The value of these remaining big trees is neither in the commercial potential for wide, knot-free boards nor in their old-growth ecological characteristics. Rather, their real worth lies in their ability to capture our imaginations and stir curiosity about Connecticut's forests. Such incalculable benefits cannot be measured—not even in units as large as centuries.

A *Sacred Grove*
Hope for the Chestnut Forest

In the northeast corner of Hamden lie a few acres unlike those found anywhere else on the planet. When I first stepped into the Connecticut Agricultural Experiment Station's chestnut plantation, it was like finding a lost world. Sandwiched among suburban-style homes and unkempt woods is a few acres' worth of medium-sized trees, whose wizened appearance, gnarled limbs, and lichen-crusted bark convey a feeling of great age. The grassy ground beneath them is littered with nuts and spiny burrs. Though the trees include all chestnut species and many hybrids not native to the state, it is the closest a person can come to experiencing, if somewhat imperfectly, a significant aspect of Connecticut's forests that existed before the bark-shattering chestnut blight ripped through the state just before World War I.

Though it's a singular place, it's not hard to get to. Located along either side of Chestnut Avenue on the east end of Sleeping Giant State Park, I've stopped there many times to wander through this living file of scientific specimens.

My favorite way of reaching the grove is the long, rough hike along the blue-blazed Quinnipiac Trail from the stone tower on the giant's hip. After enjoying the 360-degree vista, I head northeasterly, descending steeply over sharp traprock. The trail then rises and falls over a series of bumps where ash, hickory, red cedar, scrub and chestnut oak, and white pine compete for soil and sun. From a viewpoint known as Heze-Kiah's Knob, the way down is by switchbacks through a forest of red oak, hickory, and maple, with red cedar, witch hazel, and tall thickets of thriving mountain laurel crowding the understory. As the trail levels out, beech, white oak, and sassafras become increasingly plentiful. It's an area rich in sylvan variety, but you won't see any chestnut trees—at least not the ones that used to stand one hundred feet tall and ten feet in diameter. Once a dominant feature of forests throughout the state, they are long gone.

In 1904, when the fungal infection was first detected in sickly trees at what is now the Bronx Zoo, half of Connecticut's standing timber was American chestnut, an estimated 130 million mature trees. Fast growing, tall, and columnar, American chestnut frequently occurred in pure stands. But in less than a generation the state lost a devastating 50 percent of its forest canopy. With spores carried on the wind, the blight quickly infected trees through cracks in the bark, often at the crotches of limbs or where insects had been boring. Killing the living cambium layer just beneath the bark and cutting off nutrients, it essentially girdled them. Catching a ride on Chinese chestnuts that were imported for ornamental purposes, the fungus was only the first and most devastating of nonnative invasive species to attack our forests. Dutch elm disease came soon after. Emerald ash borer, hemlock wooly adelgid, and Asian longhorned beetles, which attack sugar maple, are among the latest threats.

Fortunately, blight did not kill the roots of these once majestic trees. Today they persist as an understory shrub, sprouting from old stumps to a height of as much as fifteen feet before succumbing to disease, typically before flowering. It's hard to walk a mile in the woods without seeing them, sometimes in fairly thick stands. Nearby you might find fallen limbs of the one-time forest giant littering the ground. The dark, deeply furrowed wood survives because it is rich in rot-resistant tannin. In fact, just under a century ago two-thirds of the tannic acid (used primarily in leather tanning) produced in the United States came from chestnut bark and wood. The leaves are distinctively large, narrow, and toothed. Several stems generally grow from old stumps, and the largest ones have cankered and shattered bark.

One of the easiest places to see chestnut is in Farmington's Memorial Town Forest off State Route 177, where they sprout right beside trails running along relatively flat ground. In a few places around the state, I've found standing hulks of once majestic trees. My favorite is on the blue-blazed Natchaug Trail in Eastford, a little more than a mile north of General Nathaniel Lyon Memorial Park. It's over fifteen feet tall and, if hollowed out, could shelter several standing hikers. When I first saw it thirty years ago, its main trunk was taller than a house, and three massive dead limbs radiated from the top. Though much diminished today, it remains impressive, a fossilized forest dinosaur.

From northern Georgia to southern Maine, this forest giant—with "value and versatility unmatched by any other hardwood"—was often considered the "perfect tree," according to Susan Freinkel in her book *American Chestnut*. Its bountiful, nutritious nuts—as many as six thousand from a single specimen— were a tasty treat in many homes and an important food for wildlife, including bears, deer, turkeys, squirrels, and the now-extinct passenger pigeon. The wood—light, straight, strong, rot resistant—was used for railroad ties and utility poles. It framed and sheathed many Connecticut houses. Easy to split with an axe and long lasting, it was ideal for fence rails. "Chestnut found its way into nearly anything made of wood," Freinkel notes, "from pianos to packing crates."

At just over eight acres, the Sleeping Giant Plantation was once the homestead of Dr. Arthur Graves, who taught at Yale and worked for New York's Brooklyn Botanic Garden. He began the longest-running chestnut-breeding project in the nation when, in 1930, he planted over a hundred trees. He soon commenced crossing blight-resistant Asian trees with American chestnut, planting new trees, and keeping detailed records until his death in 1963.

A few years after Graves began his endeavor, the Connecticut Agricultural Experiment Station became involved; when Graves sold his land in 1949 for inclusion in Sleeping Giant State Park, the plantation acres were set aside for tree-breeding purposes. With all seven species of chestnut represented— along with a plethora of hybrids—this Lilliputian arboretum has become the world's finest grouping of chestnut trees.

Regardless of its renown, the plantation is not merely a tree museum or a memorial orchard. It is also a critical part of ongoing research by the Experiment Station's Dr. Sandra Anagnostakis, a bespectacled, round-faced woman with an impish grin and a quiet passion for the trees that have been her responsibility since the mid-sixties. On a gray mid-March morning, she took me on a tour of the site, as she has done for scientists and other pilgrims from as far away as Spain and China.

Despite decades of familiarity with the chestnuts, she entered the plantation with a kind of quiet reverence, as if stepping into a church. In her eyes, the trees, with their dark furrowed bark, have distinct personalities indicated by varying trunk lengths and diameters as well as by their contorted limbs, some bearing cankers and scars from years of fighting disease and weather. She knew their names, where they had come from (whether it was a site in Japan or a roadside in Connecticut), who had planted them, and when. Each tree bore a little aluminum dog tag. Anagnostakis bridled at the popular notion that the American chestnut is extinct, and, even though it's now just a shrubby shadow of its former glory, she's confident that with continued scientific work it can regain its rightful place in the forest.

A few of the trees have interesting names like Tiger Paw or Mahogany; some come with colorful stories like the ones grown from the seeds of trees planted by Mao Tse-tung in 1929. The most famous tree is an early Japanese cultivar (a variety cultivated for its particular properties) planted by Dr. Graves himself, which won a contest in the 1940s for the flavor and size of its chestnuts. Today it's down to just one angled branch rising from a chest-high stump. Anagnostakis refused to pick a favorite. "It would be like a mother choosing among her children," she said.

As we wandered among the bare, wizened trees, Anagnostakis glowed with enthusiasm for all things chestnut, regardless of species. She's traveled around the world looking at specimens, and she regaled me with tales of tracking down ancient monsters in England. "Some of the trees," she said with a smile, "were planted by the Romans."

The Sleeping Giant grove is filled with mature trees that are like a genetic warehouse, a living library. Most of the breeding and testing, however, takes place out in the fields or in the greenhouses of a nearby farm. Ideally, the chestnut program will produce both short, spreading trees with large tasty nuts for orchards, and tall, straight ones for forest timber. The Experiment Station's program calls for breeding American trees with Asian ones to produce partially resistant specimens, backcrossing them with American chestnuts to maximize native genes, and then recrossing two partially resistant trees to obtain a small percentage that are fully resistant.

Anagnostakis has become a Johnny Appleseed for the species, planting resistant chestnuts across Connecticut where native stump sprouts persist, including Goodwin State Forest in Hampton, Sessions Woods Wildlife Management Area in Burlington, and Connecticut Water Company–managed land in Prospect. These sprouts are then inoculated with a viral biological control, which enables them to live long enough to flower and produce nuts by cross-pollinating with planted resistant trees. The resulting offspring hold the promise of becoming a naturally reproducing native population of blight free chestnuts.

During this visit in late winter the grove is stark, the trees revealing a skeletal beauty that showed years of battling ice, snow, insects, and infection. During the heart of spring, I've found the trees adorned with slender catkins bearing small, greenish-yellow flowers that smelled vaguely sweet, though not necessarily pleasant. In summer, the leafy canopy hid many imperfections, and a short stroll was edenic. With the leaves shriveling to yellow and brown, the site wasn't much on fall color. But the spiny green burs, which were turning brown, hung like sea-urchin Christmas ornaments. Frosts had already cracked a few open, revealing glossy, mahogany-brown nuts inside.

For almost a century, Connecticut's chestnuts have been sprouting hopefully from the roots of long-gone forest titans; during much of that time, work at the Sleeping Giant Plantation has matched that hope. Its pivotal role as ground zero in the effort to restore the species has made the plantation a kind of sacred grove, not unlike those hallowed by the gods of ancient myth. With lots of science and a little luck, the stewards of these trees will bring renewed meaning to Connecticut's motto, Qui Transtulit Sustinet, or "He Who Transplanted Still Sustains."

The Perfect Street Tree
A Few Good Elms

The rumors of their demise are only slightly exaggerated. Although rarely seen in colonnades anymore, single elm trees or small clusters still stand along roadsides, in parks, yards, and on the grounds of institutions. There's a big one on State Route 30, across from the South Windsor firehouse; there's a huge umbrella of a tree, which I've admired while waiting in line for tickets, near the main gate of the Woodstock Fair; and there's yet another, which I frequently drive by, close to U.S. Route 44 in Pine Meadow. I've encountered elms while walking the Wesleyan University campus in Middletown or the lawn of the Hill-Stead Museum in Farmington, which had fifteen in 1992 and has only three today. Despite popular notions that Dutch elm disease has rendered the tree virtually extinct, you can still find quite a few that have survived the scourge once you start looking.

Elms once seemed the perfect urban tree. They grew fast, tolerated drought, their high crowns didn't obstruct building facades, and their broken shade allowed enough light for a lawn. Elms have architecture of unrivaled sylvan elegance, their tall trunks of deeply furrowed bark rising to a fountain of pendant leaves. Antiquarian Wallace Nutting asserted there were "no more perfect curves than those assumed by elm branches." Their beautiful profile makes them easy to spot, and they remain a reminder of once grand urban forests, whose arcades of branches ornamented many New England roads.

Today, Elm Streets are ubiquitous, but, though I always look for them, I find few if any namesake trees. Connecticut was once at the center of an elm-dominated urban landscape. In the late 1940s, the American naturalist and tree connoisseur Donald Culross Peattie wrote that "there are no New England villages so beautifully shaded by this species as Fairfield and Litchfield, Woodstock and Windsor, Woodbury and Wethersfield." Love of

the tree was evident in place names like Elm Hill in Newington, Elmville in Killingly, and Elmwood in West Hartford and Bethel. The elm capital was New Haven, to this day known as the Elm City.

Elms were planted in New Haven as early as 1685, but it became an obsession and source of civic pride in the late eighteenth century. By 1842, Charles Dickens could write that "these groups of well-grown trees, clustering among the busy streets and houses of a thriving city, have a very quaint appearance: seeming to bring about a kind of compromise between town and country." Along streets and on the green the trees rose to leafy loggia, arboreal cathedrals softening the effects of urban growth. New Haven was "the apotheosis of urban pastoralism in antebellum New England, and the pinnacle of elm culture in America," writes Thomas J. Campanella in his book Republic of Shade.

Forest elms favor moist, rich bottomlands and prefer growing along rivers and lakes, where they can reach towering heights of eighty to one hundred feet. The thick bark is grayish and heavily ridged, sometimes with a corky quality. The deep green, elliptical leaves are doubly toothed and usually sandpapery. Although the wood has been used for flooring, railroad ties, furniture, plywood, barrel staves, and wagon-wheel hubs, it is not an easy wood to work with. It is tough and fibrous and dries slowly. It's also difficult to split for firewood, as I found out one day while trying to stoke a wood stove. In colonial times the wood had low commercial value, which, combined with the fact that elm shade isn't too dense, led many farmers to spare the axe and let the trees grow. With a chance to flourish in the open, their beauty became widely recognized.

Before European settlement, Native Americans commonly used elms. Some tribes used the bark to cover longhouses, make rope, and build canoes, while limbs were used to create bowls and cups. Infusions of bark, roots, and twigs served a variety of medicinal purposes including treatment of internal bleeding. Connecticut's Mohegan found in the inner bark a cure for coughs and colds.

Elms were not just valued for their streetside elegance. In many towns, large individual trees became venerated civic landmarks with names and stories. "They were among the first symbols of collective remembrance to occasion the landscape," Campanella writes, "'repositories of memory' that endowed quotidian space with historical depth and richness."

A local eccentric poet, in exchange for some rum, planted New Haven's long-gone Benjamin Franklin Elm on the day of the great man's death in 1790. Until 1815, Litchfield's Whipping Post Elm was a place of public punishment. East Hartford had a row of elms, planted in 1778 by Rochambeau's troops, and a single large one attributed to a German soldier captured at Trenton during the Revolutionary War, according to an 1891 *New York Times* article. The grandmother of Civil War general George B. McClellan reputedly planted the McClellan Elms of Woodstock. Hartford's Ledyard Elm was attributed to John Ledyard, a friend of Thomas Jefferson who sailed with Captain Cook and later died in an attempt to walk around the world. It grew near Arch Street, along the Little River (now the subterranean Park River), on the property of Lincoln Iron Works, where a deed restriction forbade cutting down the tree.

Like many big trees of the species, the Great Elm at Wethersfield reportedly sheltered General Washington. About 102 feet tall and forty-one feet around at breast height, it was reputed to be the nation's largest when, in 1945, it was infected with Dutch elm disease. It succumbed in 1953, and its thirty-five-ton stump was carted away on a flatbed truck.

Although street widening and modern utility systems had damaged elm roots and canopies in many communities, Dutch elm disease wiped out two centuries of trees in a single generation, leaving barren-looking neighborhoods. An unforgiving landscape of angular buildings, hard pavement, utility poles, and wires was suddenly, for the first time, deprived of the soft-ening effect of arcing branches and soothing shade. The bleached hulks of dead trees marked an environmental and civic catastrophe. Familiar places were changed suddenly and forever.

Dutch elm disease is caused by a parasitic fungus carried by burrowing bark beetles that invade a tree's vascular system, preventing nutrients and water from reaching the crown, and leaving it to wilt and die. Originating on imported logs, it was discovered in Ohio in 1930, and the first New England tree to succumb was in Greenwich's Glenville section. The beautiful urban monoculture of row upon row of elms, once an asset, had now become the cause of the tree's quick undoing.

With the disease spreading rapidly, the quarantine, removal, and burn-ing of damaged trees was ineffective. By 1951, over sixty Connecticut towns were spraying DDT, which, though it killed the beetles and slowed the disease's spread, managed to cure nothing after all. By poisoning benefi-cial insects, birds, and other creatures as well, the deadly chemical became instrumental in inspiring Rachel Carson's *Silent Spring*, sparking the envi-ronmental revolution.

The Connecticut Botanical Society lists about fifty elms on its Big Tree inventory, though none are as large as yesteryear's monsters. They exist largely due to isolation and, perhaps, some modest disease resistance. As recently as 2010, the town of Suffield boasted on its website that it had the state's largest living elm, but it's now dead. Greenwich hosts the current state champion, which is 106 feet tall and just shy of eighteen feet in circum-ference. No more than 2 percent of elms with girth measuring at least three feet remain from before the disease's onset, according to photographer and elm enthusiast Tom Zetterstrom, who lives in Canaan.

I try finding big elms wherever I go. It's a kind of treasure hunt in which the reward is a heart-lifting beauty and sense of grandeur. There's an element of nostalgia, as well as the bittersweet excitement of pending doom, like seeing the last dinosaurs. But their continued survival also feeds hope that one of these big trees might be uniquely disease resistant, especially when it's found in an unlikely location. There's a towering giant in Durham, squeezed between a store called the Country Barn and its parking lot, and another along U.S. Route 1 in front of the McDonald's in Old Saybrook. Hartford's High Street Elm, which looms over cracked parking lots, brush, and a billboard in an area just north of I-84, may be the most visible elm in New England.

Although many elms have died, cultural memory runs deep, and passionate advocates have worked hard to protect existing trees and promote resistant cultivars. Consistent with the elm's cultural identity, many new varieties bear patriotic names like Liberty, Valley Forge, Independence, and Washington. Zetterstrom has been among the most tireless crusaders, not only by creating compelling photographic images of trees, but also as the founder of Elm Watch and the Adopt-an-Elm program, which inventories trees in the region, sponsors life-saving injections of preventative fungicide, and promotes the planting of resistant varieties.

Replanting with new cultivars is increasingly common in many communities, like West Hartford's Elmwood, where thirteen trees (representing the thirteen colonies) were first planted in 1777 to celebrate the American victory at Saratoga, New York. Since 2007, several good-sized trees have been set in the ground. I drive by periodically to check their progress, imagining mature branches hanging over roads, walkways, restaurants, and shops. As in the past, commemorative elms continue to be planted. In 2002, a tree was dedicated in Salisbury to memorialize a woman killed in the World Trade Center.

Though the majestic green arcades that were once the signature of New England cities and towns will never return, Connecticut still harbors a couple of places where an inkling of that past can be experienced. A stroll beneath the arching elms of the New Haven Green can be a truly awe-inspiring experience. Rising like the columns of a grand public building, branches reach out gracefully above the path, just as Dickens described. Walking among them I feel an inexplicable elation. The city assumes a renewed grandeur, buildings seem more elegant, and the flow of traffic appears as logical as a river's current. The trees somehow bring the past into the present. Of course, the trip back in time is no accident, but rather the result of careful planning and maintenance.

When I first entered the grounds of the Hotchkiss School in Lakeville, I was instantly struck by an alley of elms that lent gravity to the institution's bucolic main drive. Nearby, old elms overtopped three-story redbrick classroom buildings and dorms, spreading their limbs high above lawns. For a moment, I could imagine a world without the deadly fungus, feeling the grandeur and grace that once clothed many Connecticut towns.

Not just trees, elms are icons of culture. They are a lens through which we can see history: Native American ingenuity, colonial land clearing, nineteenth-century municipal beautification, the development of urban infrastructure, the natural consequences of global commerce, the birth of the environmental movement, and the social transformation of cities in the late twentieth century. As long as elms grow among us, they will remind us of a heritage now past, even as remaining trees continue to shape the places we live.

Inventing New England Autumn
Leaf Peeping

On a cloudless day in mid-October, I hiked up a blue-blazed trail from State Route 341, in Kent, to Numeral Rock. Once part of the Appalachian Trail, the path rose steeply through oak, birch, maple, and other hardwoods, creating a dizzying kaleidoscope of color against a sky tinted like a pair of faded jeans. In little less than half a mile, I reached a brightly painted ledge, where generations of Kent School seniors have gone to paint class numerals and sometimes images and slogans. Worn from decades of student celebrations, the site isn't particularly pretty, the victim of erosion and bits of foil, broken glass, and other litter. But, layered over the years, I found sloppily applied paint in every color of the rainbow and then some.

Though bright and garish, the colors of the rock paled in comparison to nature's vivid display of sylvan hues, which turned the view into an impressionist painting of monumental scale. At almost seven hundred feet, Numeral Rock is well situated for leaf peeping. I looked out over a hardwood forest, afire with the season, alongside patches of still-verdant pasture and the wide Housatonic River. Across the road, sunlit Schaghticoke Mountain's irregular ledges were aglow with russets and yellows, amplified by oases of dark evergreens. Beyond the river, and largely hidden in trees, was the quaint village of Kent, recently anointed the "Foliage Capital of New England" by Yankee magazine, self-styled arbiter of all things New England. Not a bad change for a place the Reverend Benjamin Wadsworth, in 1694, called a "hideous, howling wilderness."

Kent was honored as the top foliage town the year *Yankee* was celebrating its seventy-fifth anniversary. The periodical issued its "first ever" list of twenty-five top foliage communities and, consequentially, stunned a public that usually associates Vermont and other northern destinations with the height of fall color. Of course, to a publication fixated on tourism, the vibrancy of autumn is not just about trees, but is part of a total excursion package. "The heart of the New England leaf-peeping experience lies in the details: the farmstands and covered bridges, the water falls and antique stores that provide the eye candy, framed by the colors of our most glorious season," the article crowed. *Yankee*, it seemed, was reinventing a natural phenomena as merely a bright backdrop to upscale sightseeing. But this was just one step in a long evolution.

As days grow ever shorter following the autumnal equinox, and frosty mornings signal the advent of October, trees in our woods and neighborhoods are slowly transformed from a calming green to an electric palette of striking colors. Elms become lemony, sumacs turn fiery red, and maples burn bright orange and yellow. Millions of tourists flock to New England destinations and clog our two-lane blacktops to gawk at gaudy hillsides. Radios, televisions, and newspapers enlist meteorologists and foresters as prognosticators, hanging on their oracular words about temperature, rainfall, and wind velocities in an effort to divine "peak color." State tourism machinery is revved to a frenzy with foliage-oriented telephone hotlines, advertisements, and websites.

Scientists have wildly estimated that the average wooded Connecticut acre produces 2,748 pounds of dry leaves annually. These leaves, which we break our backs removing from lawns and gardens—and on which we spend millions of dollars carting, composting, and burying—are, for a few short weeks, a critical engine of commerce as well as a cultural symbol.

Even though, in the course of a generation, the soft rasping sound of rakes and the sweet pungency of smoldering fires has been replaced by the whine of blowers and roar of suction trucks, the fall of leaves remains a natural event that provides many people with a connection to the seasonal cycle. Working at his Salisbury home along the Housatonic River in the 1960s, *New York Times* editor Hal Borland wrote that "the more I raked and the more I lugged, the more certain I became that I was participating in Autumn's affirmation. In that simple task I was affirming my belief … in a tomorrow, a future." Though the work can be both tiring and tedious, I find an elemental truth in that old-school sentiment, even as my back aches while I rake.

According to another authority, *The Encyclopedia of New England*, Connecticut and other states are "world renowned" for their "brilliant autumn foliage." Such understatement is almost laughable. After all, fall color is the very axis of our regional identity. Lifelong residents find that familiarity does not dim their wonder, and it's the first (and sometimes the only) thing outsiders know about New England. Thus, it may come as a surprise to native and visitor alike that our continuing infatuation with leaf peeping is not an ancient rite but a phenomenon developed little more than a century ago.

It isn't that autumn leaves went unnoticed before the twentieth century. Artists and poets have long been inspired by fall color. But until a few generations ago, most people saw the leaves as just a part of the background of daily life, and few visitors came solely to experience such an ephemeral occurrence. Ahead of his time, as usual, Henry David Thoreau wrote a paean to these seasonal hues. Delivered as a lecture during his lifetime, including the last one he ever gave, which was in Waterbury, "Autumnal Tints" was published shortly after his death in 1862, and it not only evokes the bright crayon colors of October, but also chides the pragmatic people of his era for failing to appreciate the radiant display. "Not only many in our towns have never witnessed it," he writes, "but it is scarcely remembered by the majority from year to year. Most appear to confound changed leaves with withered ones, as if they were to confound ripe apples with rotten ones."

Thoreau's contemporaries are not alone in failing to notice what *really* happens in fall. Given the annual cultural craze, it's easy to forget that autumnal change is a natural phenomenon. Some northeastern Indian customs attribute red leaves to the spilled blood of the celestial Great Bear slain by hunters in October, and the yellows to its splattering fat as it cooked. In British folktales, the elfish Jack Frost paints fall leaves. Science, on the other hand, explains that the colors manifest as the green chlorophyll, used in capturing energy from the sun and producing food, fades away as trees prepare for winter. When chlorophyll breaks down, yellow and orange carotenoids (a pigment) hidden by summer's green grow dominant, and remnant sugars trapped in the leaves form red anthocyanins (another pigment).

Beginning with the tourism practices of grand resort hotels in the late nineteenth century, the mass fascination with leaf peeping took off with transportation improvements about a hundred years ago and came to fruition following the Second World War, especially with development of the interstate highway system, which made motor vehicle trips easier and faster, according to *The Encyclopedia of New England*. The foremost reason for this relatively recent interest in fall leaves may also lie, perhaps, in the regrowth of our woodlands. Before, there wasn't much forest to see in New England, the land having largely been plowed over for cropland and pasture, fuel wood, and charcoal. The forests that remained were appreciated less for their aesthetic value than for practical uses. The advent of color photography, too, was probably a factor, bringing the allure of New England autumn to mass audiences around the world. Certainly increased leisure time has played a role, especially as interest in the outdoors has grown. Most of the region's hiking trails, state parks, and campgrounds were developed over the last hundred years.

The rise of automobile tourism is no doubt "an important factor in the creation and maintenance of fall foliage as a New England icon," according to Kent Ryden, an American studies professor at the University of Southern Maine. He maintains that by the mid-twentieth century it may even have been culturally valuable to celebrate the forest at its peak. Increasing urbanization and suburbanization, Ryden notes, spiked interest in "a timeless natural tableau" that satisfies a need to experience beauty and nature, as distinct from daily existence with its pressures and commitments.

A more jaundiced view might see the huzzahs and hosannas over fall color as just the latest example of Yankee ingenuity, exploiting limited natural resources for economic benefit and regional bragging rights. Regardless, interest in our flashy autumns is evidence not only of a changing landscape, but also of our evolving relationship with the natural phenomena around us.

Whatever its origins, the fall-foliage marketing machine is likely to remain with us. Any year in which the color is less spectacular than one would wish is followed by a string of doomsday articles. In October 2005, there was a public uproar when environmental factors—including drought, warm temperatures, and days of driving rain—produced a less-than-stellar season. "Where's the Foliage?" lamented one *Hartford Courant* headline. "Wind, Rain Takes Its Toll on Connecticut's Peak Colors," read another. From these and other media reports one might have thought that Connecticut was experiencing an economic disaster and identity crisis over how orange the maples had turned.

With so many tourism dollars at stake, worry over autumnal intensity has become as dependable as the fall of leaves themselves. In 2006, "Columbus Day No Longer the Peak" was the banner for a *Courant* article. In 2007, it was "For Foliage It's Wait till Next Year." "Fall Color: Muted," lamented the above-the-fold front-page story in September 2011. But annual variability is just part of nature's cycle. "Every October is different, strange with new beauty," wrote Connecticut author and nature lover Gladys Taber in *The Book of Stillmeadow*, a volume about her home in Southbury. "There should be new words every October for the colors gold and scarlet and bronze and russet."

Well-watered trees produce larger leaves, which tends to amp the brilliance of their hues. Some years drought, or prolonged abnormally cool or hot temperatures, mutes the display. High humidity and long wet periods can also foster diseases or insects, dulling the color. Regardless of media-hyped superlatives or the vagaries of the weather, fall colors are intoxicating year in and year out. As former Connecticut state forester Donald Smith told me, after years of giving interviews to overanxious reporters, "the intensity may vary from one season to the next, but the leaves never disappoint."

From my perch on Numeral Rock, I didn't need the people at Yankee magazine to tell me how stunning Kent is in October. After all, I could get an equally high-definition view from the Heublein Tower at Talcott Mountain State Park, the Saville Dam at the Barkhamsted Reservoir, the Lebanon Green, or out my own window at home in Collinsville. Autumn's show may sometimes lack incandescence from behind a windshield, but whenever I get into the woods and walk under the canopy of color or climb a ridge to look down at a world ablaze in leaves, I'm never disappointed.

A Most Useful Tree
Season of the Witch Hazel

In late October or early November, as the radiant hues of maples subside and ferns are bronzed by frost, come days of azure sky and unremittingly brilliant sunshine, when nothing can keep me indoors. Just as I've become acclimated to icy mornings and chill winds that have me hunkered into a coat, the air again becomes soft and warm. A light haze hangs in the distance. On the cusp of bitter winter is a remembrance of June, and I succumb to the charms of Indian summer. A prized and most ephemeral season acclaimed by all who have had the experience, cultural historian Adam Sweeting has called it the time when "New England seems most New England."

Plenty of newly fallen leaves crunched underfoot as I made my way along the blue-blazed Tunxis Trail in Barkhamsted to the jumble of glacial boulders known as the Indian Council Caves. Though well past peak, color still hung in the branches, especially the deep scarlet and burnished copper of oaks, but the most enchanting thing in the woods were the delicate blooms of a small and irregular understory tree. Up to twenty-five feet tall, but more often a shrub reaching but a dozen feet in height, witch hazel bucks nature's trend, blooming in crinkled golden stars even as its leaves are falling. I paused a few moments, and over the low whoosh of the wind I could hear the occasional snap of the plant's fruit pods firing their seeds like bullets, ten feet or more from the branch. Though witch hazel grows throughout the state, sometimes in thick stands, few people notice it among fall's gaudy hues.

The flowers are emblematic of Indian summer, with its enticing nostalgia for warmer times, and they hold the promise of spring blossoms, just a few months away. Even after this short season within a season has yielded to arctic blasts, and the leaves have all fallen, witch hazel flowers persist on

bare limbs, bringing color into the gray woods of early winter.

Connecticut is the witch hazel capital of the world. Not only does this resilient plant grow profusely here, but Connecticut has long been the top producer of the aromatic essence extracted and distilled from witch hazel twigs and bark.

The secret of witch hazel extract was handed down from Native Americans, who, believing that a plant that blooms in winter must have magical healing properties, boiled the twigs to create a clear liquid that was both fragrant and astringent. Having found that the extract contained therapeutic qualities, they applied it to cuts, bruises, scratches, sore eyes, and a variety of external inflammations. A publication of the Rhode Island Department of Environmental Management and other sources say they also sipped it like a bitter tea for coughs, diarrhea, colds, and other maladies.

Once they learned the recipe, missionaries and settlers made it in small batches and used it as a folk medicine until, just after the Civil War, Connecticut's Thomas Newton Dickinson perfected the product's commercial manufacture. His sons ran rival witch hazel distilleries in the lower Connecticut Valley, and the state has been the center of witch hazel production ever since. In the late 1990s, the two Dickinson brands were consolidated at American Distilling of East Hampton, a company that got its start in the nineteenth century producing birch bark extract, a product it no longer makes. It now produces a whopping 98 percent of the world's witch hazel distillates.

Sitting on State Route 66, not far from town hall and the tavern where Governor William O'Neill once stood behind the bar, the factory looks like a nondescript office building, with darkly tinted ribbon windows along its stucco exterior. On an icy day in early March, a few witch hazel stems rose out of the snow near a glassy atrium. The reception area was vaguely scented with the same sweet pungency I remembered from the witch hazel I'd applied to a burn a few months earlier. The woman at the desk had an array of products in colorful packaging in front of her.

With a contagious enthusiasm for both the process and the product, Bryan Jackowitz, vice president for marketing, took me on a tour of the plant, where we crossed concrete floors below high ceilings and walked across catwalks among a maze of pipes and conduits. The place was well lit and looked antiseptically clean, like a hospital, and the workers wore light-blue hairnets.

Raw material comes into the plant as woodchips, and it is chopped even finer before being placed into squat, cone-shaped silos where it's regularly aerated. Distillation begins when purified well water is heated to steam and then fed through pipes into tubby stainless kettles filled with witch-hazel pulp. Essential oils are extracted in the steam, which is then piped away and chilled in condensers, returning to liquid form before it is mixed with 14 percent alcohol, which acts as a preservative. The liquid is then pumped into tall stainless steel holding tanks. About 70 percent is shipped out in bulk containers or tanker trucks; the rest is bottled as Dickinson products. Bottles are filled, capped, and labeled on an automated line and then hand-packed into boxes. The used chips are recycled for landscaping mulch.

Jackowitz's father, Edward, bought the antiquated plant in the early 1970s, when pulp was still forked by hand and every bottle was individually filled and labeled. Combining an engineering background and entrepreneurial zeal, he built a new plant around the still-running old one, automating the entire process and, at the same time, bringing the advantages of modern chemistry and quality control to an old-fashioned operation. It was a stroke of Yankee business acumen and practical sense that would have made old T. E. Dickinson proud.

American Distilling's witch hazel is cut on thirty thousand to fifty thousand organic-certified acres each year, with as much as half of it coming from Connecticut, where the plant grows with a wild luxuriance. Rhode

Island, Massachusetts, and Vermont are also major supply sources.

Several years ago, while working for the state Department of Environmental Protection, I walked through a stand of witch hazel being harvested in Cockaponset State Forest in Haddam. The ground was rocky and uneven, and brush cutters were slicing the stems close to the ground with chainsaws. The air was filled with the saws' roar and the scent of wood-chips and bar oil. The branches were piled up neatly for a tractor to haul them away and deposit them at a landing near the main road, where work-ers were feeding them into a woodchipper. Harvested in the cold months when the plant is dormant and the ground is mostly frozen, witch hazel sprouts again in spring from the cutting, and it can be harvested continually about every seven years. The brush cutters were burly, woods-hardy charac-ters who seemed a singular breed as they moved quickly from one trunk to another. It was clearly strenuous work, requiring endurance and subjecting the cutters to all manner of harsh weather.

Except for the use of chainsaws, the process is not much different than the one Edwin Way Teale observed almost fifty years ago when he saw a longtime cutter "move from clump to clump," watching "his short handled axe rise and fall. A downward gash into the yellow-green wood on one side near the base is followed by a reversal of the implement and a blow with the head of the axe that knocks the trunk free. In this way nicking the cutting edge on . . . the woodland floor is avoided."

American Distilling bottles two products: its Blue Label is for first aid uses like cuts, bruises, burns, and insect bites; the Yellow Label formulation is milder and serves as a gentle skin toner. But in addition to these clear liquids splashed on the skin, witch hazel has become the most widely used natural botanical ingredient in cosmetics and pharmaceuticals. For this reason it is shipped in bulk to manufacturers around the world. "It's the Swiss Army knife of the medicine cabinet," quipped Jackowitz, "good from nose to toes."

After leaving American Distilling I headed home, making what I thought would be a quick stop at my local Shop Rite for something to throw on the grill for dinner. But I wound up spending an hour reading product labels in the cosmetic and medication aisles. I found witch hazel in sham-poos and conditioners, in shaving creams, depilatories, sunscreens, clari-fying lotions, face creams, and bath splashes. It was in acne preparations, psoriasis and hemorrhoid creams, topical antibacterial lotions, foot sprays, deodorants, and insect-bite formulas. Toothpastes and mouthwashes also included witch hazel. Products with brand names like Neutrogena, Olay, Noxzema, Suave, Clinique, Estée Lauder, Stridex, Clearasil, Toms of Maine,

Preparation H, L'Oreal, Johnson & Johnson, and Avon all contained a small amount of Connecticut's landscape.

Despite its venerable history as a remedy, no one is exactly sure why witch hazel works. The distillate contains flavonoids, volatile oils, and other constituents, none of which fully explains its healing properties.

The origin of its curious name also remains a mystery, though folklorists and philologists have their theories. Teale surmised that "early travelers mistook it for the witch-elm, or 'wyche-hasill,' of Old England." Twentieth-century naturalist Donald Culross Peattie agreed with Teale, but also thought the name might come from the word "wych which has nothing to do with witches but is related ... to Anglo-Saxon wicken, meaning to bend, or Old English wick, meaning quick or living, or possibly even to the modern word, switch." The Royal Botanic Garden in Edinburgh, Scotland, traces the origin of "wych" to an elm known as wicken in part of England or to the Anglo Saxon wice, meaning "flexible." We may never know the true etymology of witch hazel, but that just adds to its intrigue. Valued for its flexible, forked branches, witch hazel was commonly used as divining rods to detect groundwater or precious metals, thus water witchery may be the closest it comes to the supernatural. The plant's flowering around Halloween, when witches are said to abound, is only a coincidence, alas. Colloquial monikers like "winter-bloom" or "snapping alder" relating to its odd time of blossom and means of distributing seeds may be more suitable, albeit practical and prosaic, names.

Blooming witch hazel is both prologue and afterword to Indian summer. "I lie on my back with joy under its boughs," Thoreau wrote in October 1851. "While its leaves fall—its blossoms spring." Perhaps witch hazel epitomizes a season that is merely a cruel tease before winter inevitably resumes. Older residents in Grace Metalious's *Peyton Place* "know sorrowfully that Indian summer is a sham to be met with hard-eyed cynicism."

While Indian summer is fleeting and fickle, the sustainable values of witch hazel, its truest symbol, are at once enduring and contemporary. It bewitches us with a healthy juxtaposition of skepticism and hope—exactly what we need to get through winter.

Tasting the Landscape
Cider Mills

On a crisp October Sunday, a huge crowd spilled from the doors of B. F. Clyde's Cider Mill in Old Mystic. I wormed my way inside the cupolated two story barn as chopped apples slid down a chute onto a cheesecloth-covered rack where a couple of young men spread mash with short-handled hoes. Seniors and teenagers leaned over for a glimpse, and parents lifted up young children. A festive atmosphere held sway, alive with anticipation as if for a celebrity's arrival. The air was sweet with the scent of macerated apples and pungent with a hint of the building's old wood and the press's machine oil. The racks were stacked several high, and the motor started with a hiss of steam, the clank of gears, and slapping leather belts overhead.

A slight hush swept the crowd, followed by a kind of wide-eyed approval, as if it were watching a circus. When America's only steam-operated cider mill goes into action, it's as much performance as food production. The cogs slowly cranked on the venerable mechanical press with threaded posts at the corners, gradually bringing down two brawny I-beams whose tons of pressure against the racks caused juice to pour into a basin beneath. Like few things today, the entire process is an experience you can see, hear, smell, taste, and touch.

"Spectacle is a big part of the business," according to soft-spoken Harold Miner, who at fifteen began working at his wife's family's mill, which was started in 1881. But as old timey as the operation appears, modern enterprising savvy has meant survival. In recent years a new building was erected as a gift and food specialty shop with a bakery. Clyde's also installed a state-of-the-art pasteurization system (a process that remains contentious among both cider producers and drinkers).

Cider making is a signature of autumn, a cultural tradition tied to nature and the very taste of our landscape. From mid-September to a few weeks beyond Thanksgiving I find it hard to resist stopping at cider mills, not just to slake my thirst but also for the people, process, and places.

Cider makers are passionate about their labor and delight in telling stories about customers with odd preferences, botched batches, and the science and lore of their product. The mills are often quirky, bearing the stamp of time and the eccentricities of their proprietors. They range from old dairy barns to modern structures. The machines themselves are fascinating: some are century-old marvels and others are contemporary models of stainless steel wizardry. For those who crave more than just a quick stop at a grocery store, cider is an experience that reveals much about the places we live.

Cider mills used to be a common adjunct to farms, but their number has dwindled with the leveling of orchards for development, economies of scale, and the cost of pasteurization. You can still buy a gallon of cider at Silverman's, in Easton, but they don't make it there like they did back when my father would take our family for a country drive on Sunday. The orchard rises on a hill behind the spacious farm store with its knotty pine paneling, but the old cider press has long been retired and now serves as a decorative display among fancy jams, condiments, and tchotchkes. The old machine with its giraffe-neck conveyor, small motor, and stack of pallets looked tiny, a toy compared with how I remembered it.

A family operation since its founding in the 1920s, Silverman's ceased pressing cider in 2004 "because of new processing standards." The same is true at the Old Cider Mill in Glastonbury, which has made cider since the early 1800s and claims to be the nation's longest continuously operating cider mill. Now owned by the town, the weathered, unpainted barn and surrounding acreage are leased to farmers. Once a year the old press is put into service, but the resulting juice is thrown away because the facility isn't sanitary. Mill operator George Purtill, a local lawyer, worked at the farm as a kid in the 1960s and 1970s, when he drank "gallons of the stuff." It "hurts to toss it off, but you'd have to be crazy to sell it unpasteurized," he said. Cider sold at the farm store there is made elsewhere.

In 1996, several people fell ill from a new strain of *E. coli* bacteria, which was traced to cider that was likely pressed from "drops" (apples picked off the ground) contaminated with animal feces. As a result, unpasteurized cider can only be sold at the mill with a warning label. Producers selling to supermarkets and other offsite accounts must pasteurize. Many small mills decided that the risk, however small, was not worth taking and shut down in the face of additional costs.

Many producers and consumers argue that pasteurization changes the flavor and structure of cider. Using dairy-style heat and procedures surely will do so, but newer techniques, with lower temperatures tailored to cider, ostensibly do not change taste or mouth feel. While those who favor pasteurization claim that not treating cider plays Russian roulette with customers' health, partisans of untreated cider say that good sanitation and fruit selection enable them to safely produce the traditional drink.

This controversy involving government regulation, technology, health, and personal choice continues cider's role as a barometer of social conditions. First brought to this country with European colonists, cider became the national beverage in a world where water often had off tastes and could be contaminated. In those days cider meant hard cider with an alcohol content of 6 to 12 percent. When mills like Clyde's started, they made only hard cider and vinegar. Considered a healthy, body-strengthening drink, hard cider was consumed daily by men, women, and children. But it lost its popularity with the rise of the temperance movement in the late nineteenth century, an era when even orchards got the axe in the name of teetotalism. Not until the 1960s and the widespread adoption of refrigeration did sweet cider rocket into vogue.

Sloping fields and orchards of apples, berries, and other fruit rise to forested ridges around Sharon's Ellsworth Cider Mill, a boxy brown building with vertical siding and a tall gable. In this idyllically pastoral setting, I entered the mill's second-floor sales room and looked down through a window at the small stainless steel press. Cider maker Mike Bozzi is a tall, dark haired man who doesn't pasteurize because he feels safe using only his own apples right off the tree. He gave up a lucrative wholesale account to keep it that way.

A couple of towns over is Park Lane Cider Mill, which, like Ellsworth, doesn't pasteurize, but it's worlds apart in appearance, history, and process. The small racecar-red building is perched at a busy intersection on U.S. Route 202, just outside the center of downtown New Milford, where there's no orchard in sight. Greg Jajer had just finished pressing when I arrived, and the building was filled with a sweet apple smell. Built in 1924, the press is a hulking machine with a central piston rising from below. There's a whir, squeaking, and the *whap, whap* of slapping leather when the belt-driven machine is running. (Once powered by a Chevy motor, it now operates on electricity.) Jajer is a strong, burly man with a generous, open manner. His grandfather started the business over eighty years ago, and his father moved it to the current site and built the mill. Pictures of his grandparents and parents hang on the wall.

Good cider requires a mixture of apples, and flavor changes as varieties ripen. Cider starts sweeter and later gains complexity and astringency. A cider maker's efforts to balance aroma, tartness, and flavor gives each mill its own distinctive flavor. Usually six to eight apple varieties go into a batch, including Red Delicious, McIntosh, Cortland, and Baldwin, as well as more unusual varieties like Roxbury Russet, Rhode Island Greening, and Newtown Pippin.

As hard cider regains popularity and apple wine sales increase, more and more cider makers are producing these value-added products that help stretch their season and sweeten the balance sheet. Clyde's makes them, as does Bishop's in Guilford and Holmberg's in Gales Ferry. The latter two are multigenerational orchards with big retail operations and a tradition of science-based entrepreneurship. Russell Holmberg and Keith Bishop might not fit the popular image of the arch Yankee cider maker, but their dedication and knowledge of craft is evident in any conversation on the subject.

Favorite ciders are often closest to home, and Hogan's on State Route 4, in Burlington, is luckily just a few miles from my house. I'd bought cider from Morris Hogan, a sturdy octogenarian, for a number of years, but I got to know him better when I started buying apples from him for a small home press I'd purchased. Hogan's father opened the mill in 1912 and Hogan ran it until his death in 1989. A burly, grizzled farmer typically dressed in an old ball cap, baggy work pants, and suspenders, Morris was a fount of small-town wisdom, had served in the legislature for twenty-two years, wrote poetry (which he sometimes read on the floor of the state House of Representatives), and was well known for his generosity to local causes.

After Hogan's death the mill continued operating under his elderly but energetic assistants, Martin and Wendell. When golf pro Chet Dunlop, a tall wiry man with glasses, purchased part of the property for a golf school and practice center in 1992, he inherited the mill and, under the tutelage of the two men, "just kind of fell into it." He's made improvements, like replacing wooden storage casks with stainless steel, but the 1950s-era press with a big hydraulic piston remains. "Cider making works well for me," he said, as he ladled a draught for me right off the press, "since it starts as golf slows down in the fall." Strange as it seems, a modern putting green, driving range, and miniature golf course saved Hogan's old-timey mill. Dunlop's wife, Theresa Clifford, has learned to make hard cider and runs the gift shop. "We're never alone here," she told me. "I feel Morris's presence every day."

A Community Harvest
Agricultural Fairs

Fairs conjure images of teeming crowds, noise, and bright lights. But I've returned, year after year, to the Goshen Fair for the relative quiet and soothing atmosphere of the spacious dairy barn. Located on a grassy, breeze-swept ridge, as far from the dust and whir of the carnival rides as possible, there's something intoxicating in the sweet smell of fresh straw and manure. Teenagers groom iconic black-and-white Holsteins and stately Brown Swiss. A boy may be asleep with his back resting against one of the cows. There's no jostling among the suburbanites, who lift their children up to pat a Jersey or watch as a man milks a cow.

When I crave a little time travel I head to the Hamburg Fair in Lyme, which recently celebrated its 110th year. The tiny three-acre site is off State Route 156, on a pasturelike hillside dotted with large oaks and wizened cedars. From among the small cluster of carnival rides at the top, there's a view of Hamburg Cove, which drains to the Connecticut River. On the other side of the hill, there's amphitheater seating—old boards terraced into the ground—looking out upon an oval-shaped ring, where oxen are yanking at sledges piled with large concrete blocks. I sat next to Donna, a middle-aged woman with dark hair who'd spent some years in California. She has attended the annual fair since childhood. "It's a refuge from the world," she told me while munching french fries, "because it changes so little. The oxen are great, but people are the most interesting animals."

At the south end of the grounds in a long two-story grange hall, flowers, baked goods, fruits, and vegetables were on display, along with canned items and crafts ranging from photography to embroidery. I was especially drawn to the "Friendly Critter" vegetables—squashes, tomatoes, and cabbages decorated with fanciful faces, like backyard Mr. Potato Heads. On my way out, I bought a coffee and slice of homemade blueberry pie from a

clutch of older women who'd spent the past few days baking.

Just beyond the hall were antique tractors and vendors who sat under nylon awnings, hawking cosmetics, kitchenware, houseplants, and replacement windows. In a nod to modernity, an ATM sat inside a small yellow tent. Food stands sprinkled throughout the grounds scented the humid air with fried potatoes and grilled sausages.

A long, rectangular tent with a few dozen chickens, rabbits, geese, and turkeys stood near the entrance of the fair. People asked simple questions that revealed their suburban upbringing, like how many eggs do hens lay, and do they need a rooster? Though the farmer had probably heard these questions hundreds of time, he seemed nonetheless delighted to repeat answers, as if he'd been waiting all year to do so.

I've often wondered whether the size of a fair is directly proportional to the diameter of its Ferris wheel. If so, the Woodstock Fair, which recently celebrated its 150th anniversary, is one of the largest. During my visit, the fair was congested and, with its paved paths and many permanent structures, it had a harried, almost urban feel. There was as much agriculture as you'd find at any other fair, but sometimes agrarian life felt hidden among all the attractions and distractions.

Rows of antique tractors—Farmalls in red, Fords in blue, and John Deeres in green—were parked near where one-lung engines with power takeoffs were sputtering and backfiring. There was a Civil War encampment, Go-Kart racing, vintage cars, and ceremonial Indian dancing. Along the busy paths and in the Better Living Building, filled, I supposed, with products and ideas to make one's life better, were hucksters selling medical magnets, leather apparel, vacuums, smokeless cigarettes, windows, woodstoves, beef jerky, steam mops, T-shirts, and velvet Elvises. Itinerant food vendors were everywhere, but I was drawn to the wooden shacks where the Lions Club sold chili, Killingly High School cheerleaders offered sandwiches, and the Putnam Congregational Church made icy frappes.

From an agricultural perspective, the fair's frenetic activity and garish contrasts were best expressed in the large barn where rows of chickens were stacked high in wire cages. Roosters crowed shrilly to a background of constant hen clucking. Animated with busy, nervous movements, the birds appeared in a startling array of sizes and shapes, feather and comb arrangements, and colors and patterns whose eye-popping variety grabbed for attention as surely as the midway's lights. With salt-and-pepper speckles; iridescent browns, greens, and reds; and compact and wildly fluffy feathers, their designs could have challenged the imagination of the most whimsical artist. "Don't eat that in front of the birds," a woman chided her husband as he munched a smoked turkey leg.

There was a much different vibe at Meriden's stately redbrick grange hall, not far from downtown. The fair was located in a quiet, old-fashioned auditorium, with a stage and hardwood floors, where only a few people gazed at a small selection of baked items, canned goods, needle and thread crafts, and houseplants. While the century-old building indicated a once well-to-do farm community, the fair spoke of decline. A similar quietude prevailed in semirural North Canton. At the Cherry Brook Grange Fair, I was the only visitor at mid-afternoon viewing fruits, vegetables, and baked goods. The judging having just concluded, I purchased three prize-winning apples for only a dollar. Such fairs are precious but unfortunate reminders of fading agriculture near urban areas and in small suburbanizing towns.

Held on a flat field sandwiched between I-91 and busy U.S. Route 5, with its strip malls, fast food joints, and gas stations, the North Haven Fair brings a taste of rural life to a heavily developed area. Although the atmosphere is more midway than farm, there are cows, sheep, poultry, rabbits, and other animals housed in brightly painted sheds. There's also a children's zoo, a few circus barkers, elephant and camel rides, and a psychic. Its combination of farm animals and suburban surroundings make palpable the significant changes in Connecticut's landscape since the mid-twentieth century, when the first fair was held there.

The Durham Fair is literally at the center of its community, since the main gate and some of the exhibits are located on the town green facing town hall and the library, with the grounds sloping down behind it on a vast field. As the state's biggest agricultural fair, and North America's largest without paid staff, Durham's fair remains more than physically at the community's heart. Despite its large size and contemporary amenities, it harks back to the small-town, volunteer origins of these autumnal events.

Eccentric collections are among my favorite fair exhibits, and Durham's has included Dalmatian figurines, playing cards, vintage pins, brooches, Red Sox memorabilia, frog figurines, old medicine bottles, and purses. The fair also often has the largest giant pumpkins, with two, in a recent year, weighing over one thousand pounds. The attraction of these Brobdingnagian squash remains a mystery to me, but at every fair I've attended, people stop to gawk and jockey to have their photograph taken with them. Here they sat in a tent just beyond the llama barn looking like military heroes with their bright ribbons. A gray-haired man at a table told me that the precocious vegetables could grow as much as forty pounds a day.

From onion rings to clam fritters, funnel cakes to steak bombs, food is always a fair highlight. At Haddam Neck, food booths concentrated in a shady area with picnic tables function as a kind of outdoor food court. Pulled pork, baked potatoes, and fried dough are among the culinary delights to be had there. "Where There's Smoke There's Chicken," read the sign in front of the big grills that the Covenant Church hauls in for the occasion. A crew-cut fellow in a sauce-stained apron said the church sells around three thousand pounds of chicken each year. Nearby, the fire department dispensed sausage grinders and pizza from a red trailer with black and gold stripes. In a sign of changing tastes and ethnicities, there was Thai, Indian, and Middle Eastern food in addition to pirogues and calzones.

First held in 1838, and one of Connecticut's oldest, the Four Town Fair in Somers was a friendly, relaxed affair at which the crowd ambled slowly. The main promenade—a road of packed dirt—passed by food booths, a board-and-batten bingo hall run by the fire department, and vendors offering everything from tractors for sale to panning for gold. Republicans and Democrats each occupied small booths of T-111 plywood tattooed with bright signs and bumper stickers, but at a safe and civil distance.

Four Town sponsors a corn-eating competition, a women's skillet throw, and a frog-jumping contest. The corn-eating contestants line up at a long table and are judged in three categories: time it takes to eat two ears of corn, neatness, and cleanliness of the cob. Like boxers before a match, entrants talk up their prowess, debating the merits of "spiral" versus "typewriter" technique, strategic swallowing, and their training regimens. During the contest that I observed, loud cheers erupted from a surprisingly large crowd, and winners shouted and pumped their fists in the air.

In the skillet throw—a kind of kitchen shot put—women were often dressed in colorful skirts or aprons. As one contestant explained to me, the grip, wind-up, and release point all make a difference. They stepped to the line like batters to the plate, making adjustments, surveying the field, and taking a stretch before making a toss. Men and children watching were fierce partisans with loud, encouraging screams. "Her poor husband," someone yelled after a particularly long throw.

Frog jumping, open only to youngsters, is always an epicenter of serendipitous fun because the lively amphibians are unpredictable. Each frog gets three jumps, and first prize is a trophy and seven dollars, but the event seemed to generate more laughs than jumps. Angie Sandberg has been volunteering at the fair for forty years, and she likes it for its neighborly, easygoing atmosphere. She never tires of frog jumping, which keeps her young. "One entrant had a record eighteen-ounce green frog," she said with childlike amazement.

Agricultural fairs are agrarian, commercial, and recreational kaleidoscopes. They mix science, politics, art, and entertainment from rock bands and magic shows to Noodles the Clown. At a fair I know exactly what I'll get—rides, games, fried food, cows nested in straw, barkers hawking new-fangled gimcracks, and prize-winning fruits and vegetables. But although I know what I'll get, I never know quite what I'll find because in all the hubbub and distraction it's easy to miss the reflections of incremental cultural change, whether through new foods, products, music, or demonstrations.

As farms continue to dwindle, the number of fairs has declined. Yet they remain indelible and resilient institutions annually drawing large crowds as summer fades into autumn. Fairs were once conceived as a way for farmers to celebrate harvest, display their skill, and learn about scientific innovations and new equipment, but the vast majority of people who attend them today have little more farming experience than growing a backyard tomato patch. Nevertheless, we seem to need agricultural fairs more than ever because they remind us where food comes from, provide farmers with consumer contacts, and connect us to our agrarian roots. With so much packed into a few crowded days of alluring noise and clamor, it's hard to see the grounds and buildings stand forlornly vacant most of the year, leaving us nothing to do but anticipate.

Ghost Towns and Graveyards

The built environment is a sort of palimpsest, a document in which one layer of writing has been scraped off, and another one applied.

—John R. Stilgoe, *Outside Lies Magic*

Everyone loves a ghost story, and some are embedded in the landscape. Though you won't find old-time movie tumbleweeds rolling through them, Connecticut has its share of once thriving farming and even manufacturing communities that have disappeared into the woods, leaving no more than cellar holes, stone walls, dams, and faded streets. These streets are part of a network of ghost roads bypassed by newer, straighter stretches of pavement or routes heading toward more significant destinations. These ghost roads evidence bygone needs and technologies. Such abandoned routes may once have been trod by Native Americans, some saw the passage of George Washington, and others are modern creations, like the unused levels of the "stack" that cross over I-84 in Farmington. All are hidden in plain sight, beckoning to the wandering eyes and feet of deep travelers.

Sometimes these abandoned roads threading through the woods lead to reservoirs where ghost towns were purposefully established by demolishing whole communities so that valleys could be filled with water to slake city thirsts. In drought years, old roads, bridges, cellar holes, and stone walls are occasionally revealed in shallow water or on the dry lakebed. Many lakes and pond are themselves ghosts, the legacy of past industrial activity from an age when water powered machinery to make practical products like knives and cloth. A little sleuthing reveals that most of these lakes and ponds, beloved for their beauty and ecological value, are the work of man, created or enhanced by a dam.

Perhaps the ultimate ghostly mystery place is Groton's Gungywamp with its underground stone chambers, standing stones, and ledges chiseled with symbols. Archeologists see an early colonial farmstead, while others claim it was a Viking landing or a settlement of ancient Irish monks. But ghost places are not limited to sites beyond the reach of memory. Cold War–era, space-age Nike missile control and launch sites dot the state with ruined buildings and rusting wire, fences, and piping. Like abandoned farming and manufacturing communities, they tell of a change in culture and technology. Some sit derelict in the woods, while others have been demolished for new uses or have survived by being reused for another purpose.

While graveyards give rise to notions of perpetual care, many lie abandoned in the woods or even at roadside. Little is more eerie than an overgrown graveyard where tree roots and vandals have broken headstones and no one remembers the dead. Some exist in ghost towns, while others are passed by traffic daily, speaking volumes about remembrance and local budgets. At many such sites and in well-maintained cemeteries as well, I've found headstones that glow with a ghostly pearly-blue luster. If you tap them they sound with a hollow ping because they are made of metal manufactured in Bridgeport between the Civil War and World War I.

Of all ignored graveyards, those we build to entomb the stuff we no longer want are the most easily forgotten, even though these landfills and dumps are now grassy mountains alongside highways and at the edges of communities. From some you can retrieve forty-year-old newspapers that can still be read, nineteenth-century bottles, eighteenth-century pipes, old cans, ceramics, combs, shoes, and almost anything else that might survive burial. A scrounging deep traveler's delight, dumps are libraries of the consumer culture.

Forgotten but Not Gone
Ghost Towns

Along the Blackledge River in Hebron just off State Route 85 lies a village existing only in legend and ruin. Now a place where chirping birds, hikers' footsteps, and swimmers' shouts dominate, Gay City State Park was at one time bustling with mills, homes, and a church. But despite a once promising future, no one has lived there for many decades. Walking through the old cemetery or past collapsing basement walls half lost in the woods can give me the chills.

No dust devils whirl down abandoned streets as in classic Hollywood iconography, but Connecticut has its ghost towns. In a densely populated state with incorporated municipalities occupying every square inch and even rural villages no more than a few miles apart, the notion that whole communities have disappeared from maps and their remains lay moldering in the woods seems the stuff of fables. Yet such places persist and offer a refreshing perspective in a world where we see progress as linear and our settlements as permanent and growing inevitably larger.

Because our moist climate rapidly corrodes metals, rots wood into humus, and erodes even the strongest masonry, the remains of Connecticut's ghost villages are generally little more than stonework and excavations. Evoking a disappeared past, the tangible remains sometimes stir imaginings of long-gone lives and can conjure phantasmic ectoplasms where real people once stood.

These places typically feature old roads that are still detectable because they are often lined with stone walls or sunken into the ground from hard use by horse- and oxen-drawn wagons. Also common are house foundations whose size, use of field or cut stone, and location of chimneys and doorways may indicate their age and the status of their owners. Although the physical vestiges of these abandoned hamlets bear many similarities, the distinctive characteristics of their landscape and the stories surrounding them can be strikingly different.

Sometimes houses are adjacent to the remnants of barns, animal pens, wells, and root cellars, indicating a farming life. Others are focused along brooks with dams, stone culverts, sluiceways, and the remains of small mills that might have produced products as diverse as textiles, lumber, and furniture. Occasionally there are small graveyards, ordinarily bounded by a stone wall, containing a few faded, lichen-encrusted headstones.

Many of Connecticut's ghost villages are on private land accessible only by permission, but Gay City welcomes visitors, and it's one of the best. It includes a cemetery with burials between 1808 and 1848, cellar holes, mill ruins, canals, dams, and abandoned roads, including one to Glastonbury that is now a blue-blazed trail. Armed with stories gleaned from books, the Internet, and chat with locals, my wanderings among the quiet old structures and excavations have become lively with discoveries.

Gay City was settled at the turn of the nineteenth century by Methodists seeking religious freedom. A textile mill was established by 1811, and within twenty years there were also three sawmills, a blacksmith shop, and a distillery. The textile mill burned in 1830, and the small village never fully recovered. Although a paper mill was established years later, yet another fire in the 1880s was the death knell for the community. Today, the mill's long, narrow foundation casts an uncanny spell in thick woods.

Along with stone ruins, Gay City is rife with tales of drunken revels, a couple of murders, feuding families, superstitious inhabitants, and fiercely competitive personalities. In the early days it's said that hard liquor was served to men at church services, perhaps to encourage attendance or move them to the spirit. A laborer constructing the first mill reputedly fled because he thought the canals were "the devil's work" since they appeared to move water uphill. Like many of our ghost villages, Gay City has become a kind of spectral Peyton Place, some of whose legends may be apocryphal no matter how much we yearn to believe.

On a warm April morning I walked in the woods down a wide road lined with stone walls that has long inspired ghost stories. Deep among the trees is Pomfret's Lost Village, a nineteenth-century community where people farmed and made spinning wheels and looms at a mill powered by a small brook. Once the Main Street of a bustling community, crumbling house basements were hidden in ferns and brush and sometimes had large trees growing in them.

On a rise sat a huge cellar hole with the stub of a massive center chimney. There was a well and a flat rectangular area, where a kitchen garden may have grown thyme, chives, and rosemary. Across the road was the impressive foundation of a large barn with a tall standing stone in its midst. Sitting down on a big slab of what was once a house step, I gazed into woods of pine, oak, hemlock and hickory, intently listening. Unfortunately, wind sough, bird song, and a squirrel darting through last year's leaf litter were all I heard.

Since at least the 1920s, when Odell Shepard, a literature scholar who would later become lieutenant governor of Connecticut, relayed others' reports of hearing "the laughter of children at play in dooryards ... the voices of mothers who have long been dust calling their children ... and a hum of harp strings in the air, and the rumble of wagons along an obliterated road," visitors have heard voices and sounds here. Sometimes called the Village of Voices, Pomfret's Lost Village has inspired recent Internet commentators to report not only having heard people speaking, but also footsteps, strange rapping, a feeling of being watched, or the sensation of being shoved or punched.

I was disappointed at having heard only noises of nature, so I bushwhacked down to the river, which I crossed on a large flat stone serving as a culvert deck. Although some people have commented that animals are strangely absent here, I saw a doe with two fauns just above a low fieldstone dam that created a small, irregular pool backing up to a marsh, letting light into in an otherwise dark forest. Water surged toward the remnants of a small mill.

Cornwall's Dudleytown, sometimes bearing the sobriquets "Cursed Village" or "Village of the Dammed," is perhaps Connecticut's most notorious ghost town. Located near Coltsfoot Mountain, I hiked there as a teenager in the days when the Appalachian Trail ran right by the abandoned community's main street near the foundation of an old schoolhouse. But the village's snowballing reputation as a haunted place drew ghost hunters, aficionados of the paranormal, Halloween revelers, and devil worshipers who disturbed neighbors, left trash, and damaged the ruins. As a result, the privately owned site has been closed for many years.

Dudleytown was settled in the mid-1700s, and people made a difficult living by farming, charcoaling, and working at small mills on nearby streams. By the late nineteenth century, few people remained. Whatever their origins and truths, bizarre tales out of the past seem amplified in Dudleytown. There are stories of disease epidemics, madness, a person struck by lightning, murders, and people and animals gone missing under mysterious circumstances.

I felt no ghostly presences on the cool spring day I recently revisited Dudleytown with state archaeologist Nicholas Bellantoni. There were only prosaic cellar holes along an ancient road roughly paved in rock, dirt, grass, and moss. The presiding spirit was that of entropy, epitomized by tree roots and harsh weather that were slowly obliterating the site. "How does a place like this get a haunted reputation?" I asked the thin, bespectacled scientist. All he could do was shrug. "These things take on a life of their own," he said.

Remains of hardscrabble farming communities and small mill villages of the late eighteenth and nineteenth centuries are found throughout the state. The Trowbridge Mill site in Ashford has an impressive breached field-stone dam, house foundations, and a tidy walled-in cemetery a short walk from busy U.S. Route 44, where the town green sits. Unpaved Den Road in Easton follows the landscape's contours through a lost community of cellar holes hidden in an oak, ash, and maple forest. Waterford's nearly impassible Pember Road includes the fieldstone remnants of homes and farmsteads, wells, sawmills, and root cellars. Danbury Quarter in Winchester was once between 150 and two hundred families strong, but today its most prominent marker is a lonely cemetery. Simsbury's Pilfershire is another tract of forest-land cut through with abandoned roads and pocked with rundown stone foundations. Once it had about fifty homes, a dye house, cider mill, school-house, distillery, buckle shop, and rubber shop.

Though they are quiet now save for rustling trees or purling streams, these were once lively places where laughing youngsters and lowing cows could be heard, cooking odors and freshly turned soil wafted on the breeze, and people labored at water-driven machinery or tended their gardens. There is an eerie quality to standing in dense woods where men, women, and children once worked and played and faced the daily joys and tragedies of life, just as we do now.

Although the specifics vary, people abandoned these settlements largely for the same reasons they pull up stakes today. New technologies made small water-powered mills obsolete, economic opportunity in cities beck-oned, and distant places, often where the soil was deeper and less stony, lured people away.

In the twentieth century, rural ghost towns were created in service to big-city water systems and hydroelectric facilities. Valley Forge in Weston and Hartland Hollow in Hartland are but two examples of communities demolished and submerged beneath reservoirs. Churches, stores, homes, and schools disappeared in the wake of inundation. When the water recedes in drought years, their long-ago flooded roads and building foundations are occasionally revealed.

However silent the stones and soil are today, the presence of these abandoned communities can be read like volumes of text. To a person who actively looks, they tell stories as vivid and intriguing as any book. They divulge little to the casual glance, but to an individual who pieces together the fragments of what they see with what they've read and heard old-timers tell, whole worlds long gone and hidden in plain sight are revealed. Lilac bushes growing at the edge of a depression in the soil or unusual stone wall configurations brim with meaning and pose questions about who, why, and when. These places may be forgotten, but they are not entirely gone.

Although ghost towns are generally associated with the past, new ones can be created and can just as easily disappear. A few years ago, I walked down Stratford's Long Beach West, a peninsular spit of sand on Long Island Sound. Soon I reached a cracked, weed-wracked length of pavement running between over forty abandoned summer cottages that some were calling Connecticut's largest and newest ghost town. When I grew up nearby in the 1960s, it was a vibrant blue-collar getaway busy with bicycling children and fragrantly barbecuing bluefish freshly caught in the surf that could be heard just over the dunes. After a 1996 blaze irretrievably damaged a rickety bridge, making police and fire response problematic, the town decided not to renew land leases to these homes built on municipal property and rented for decades at a bargain.

Not a sheet of glass remained intact, and the street sparkled with prismatic fragments. Names and obscenities were spray-painted in bold graffiti across shingles and clapboards, and furniture, clothing, mattresses, and magazines looked hurricane-tossed. Several of the cottages had suffered arson, and metal pipe and wire, rusted bright orange with salt air, glowed among ashes and charred remains. After just over a decade of abandonment, a federal grant helped pay to bulldoze the derelict site, remove the wreckage, and restore the beach to a natural state.

Given the prodigious rate of development and redevelopment experienced in Connecticut, it is amazing that so many ghost villages have survived into the twenty-first century. They are irreplaceable treasures that add mystery and texture to our countryside.

But their value is not merely as mute testament to a rich past. They are reminders that, though we sometimes look at life in this fortunate part of the world as one of inevitable growth and progress, there have been false starts, dead ends, and short-lived places that once had an air of permanence. We are best served by their intimation that landscapes are ever changing and that even our most earnest endeavors may, in the long run, turn out to be more ephemeral than we imagine.

Ghost Streets and Routes Less Taken
Abandoned Roads

Though it's been a major thoroughfare between Hartford and Boston, the Connecticut Path can't be driven on. Built through a wilderness in the 1600s, it was the interstate highway of its day. The road was bypassed about fifty years before the Declaration of Independence was signed; it became a secondary route, and it eventually faded into obscurity.

From a sharp elbow on Meehan Road in Woodstock I struck out on a faded lane across a rough pasture, walking past a decrepit farmhouse and a large gambrel-roof barn verging on collapse. Sitting on a knoll, the dwelling faced not the paved road, but the ancient track running perpendicular. Making my way on a slightly elevated causeway traversing the wet field and crossing a stream on a bridge of huge fieldstone slabs, I entered the woods where the path, lined by stone walls, became a little uneven, paved with grass, mud, and leaves. In the oak forest beyond the walls, an ancient plow was caught among the trees, as if suddenly rusted in place like the Tin Man of Oz. Momentarily I was transported back to the days when rough roads made even short trips arduous. This may be the last place along the path where such time travel is possible, as the remainder of the route has been subsumed by pavement or developed out of existence.

Roads are so reliably a part of our daily lives that we think of them as indelibly tattooed on the landscape. Though Connecticut is tightly laced with an ever-growing network of increasingly congested routes, there are myriad that have fallen out of use. To the surprise of many, abandoned roads exist throughout the state, but they often remain unnoticed, hidden in plain sight.

Like the Connecticut Path, a lot of these corridors are ancient and obscure. They may have been Indian trails, date back to the dawn of

European settlement, been post roads or the main streets of small nine-teenth-century farming or mill villages that have long since become ghost towns. A cat's cradle of them is often found on the watersheds of large reservoirs, where they lead to villages drowned for city water supplies decades ago. Often bumpy, steep, and winding, these roads were not only the means by which people traveled, they were how our predecessors saw the world. We no longer travel or view our surroundings the same way, but our desire for mobility and connection among communities has remained constant and has led to straighter, faster, more permanently embedded avenues of passage.

But all the permanence of steel, concrete, and lofty engineering enjoyed by modern highways is not always sufficient to save a road from disuse, as the monumental "stack" above I-84 in Farmington demonstrates. Anticipating a confluence of roads that were never built, this four-level interchange stood vacant for more than twenty years following its completion in 1969. Today, a portion is used for access to State Route 9, but most of it is otherwise empty, the haunt of mischievous teenagers and a haven for skateboarders. Built for the ages and dwarfing everything around it, it seems like the twentieth century's nod to a Roman aqueduct. Walking feels eerie on the faded yet virgin concrete, where no aggregate has been exposed by wear, the guiderails are tangled in underbrush, and weeds grow in cracks. I kept expecting a car to whiz by at fifty or sixty miles per hour.

While much of the stack goes unused, stone wall-lined Old Rock House Road in Easton has long been impassable to vehicular traffic, but has found a most modern and valuable purpose with a fiber optic cable running beneath its irregular dirt surface. Following it along a tributary of the Aspetuck River through woodlands of oak and beech, I found mill remains and a small walled cemetery not far from the pavement of State Route 58.

Afterward I crossed the highway to Den Road, which was lined with the houses of about thirteen families in the mid-nineteenth century. It runs through an uneven country, lumpy and ledge-filled with pockets of lowland where skunk cabbage was in full glossy leaf on a March afternoon. Thickly forested, but with a parklike understory trimmed by deer, there were numerous old foundations hidden by vegetation and collapsing into the earth. Remains of animal pens, barns, root cellars, and wells were also visible. I walked into a stone-lined, cavelike root cellar imagining in miniature an object belonging at Stonehenge.

Abandoned roads tell stories and can be read as an ersatz collective biography. They say something about where people went and wanted to go, the pace and rhythm at which they experienced life. Their location and design speak to topography, cost, modes of travel, business development, techno-logical innovations, shifting population patterns, and social conditions.

It took years of political wrangling between a legislature promoting business and towns that feared the cost of upkeep before the eight-mile Wolcott Road was built in the 1700s along the east bank of the Farmington River between New Hartford and Colebrook. Part of the route is now East River Road in Barkhamsted, hugging the Farmington and passing through People's State Forest.

From the fishing access at the Pleasant Valley Bridge a few years ago I took the abandoned portion of the road south in the company of the late Walt Landgraf, a rangy, bespectacled educator and historian of unbounded enthusiasms. A crude path in dense woods, the road ended upon reaching the industrial area of New Hartford at a brick factory where everything from sailcloth to Ovation guitars have been made. Along the way, the old road kept the Farmington River at a distance on one side and steep slopes close on the other. It rose and fell through stands of oak, pine, and birch, where Walt pointed out more than two centuries of infrastructure. There were concrete footings that had supported towers carrying electrical lines; a series of stone walls and swales that once were canals and sluiceways for a sawmill, fulling mill, and tanbark factory; and the foundations of icehouses that had lined the shore of mile-and-a-quarter-long Greenwoods Pond, a river impoundment that blew out in 1936. With Landgraf's help, a series of low piers among the brush and leaves was transformed into a community of homes for workers who once squatted near the pond.

A carefully designed culvert and other stone work, as well as the deep cut made into the forest floor, distinguish this path from an ordinary woods road. At one time, this was a heavy freight artery on which refined iron, ship anchors, and chains were transported from furnaces in the Litchfield Hills to Hartford by oxen- and horse-drawn wagons. Rods destined for Newgate Prison, where the inmates would fabricate nails, also came this way. Cannon and other iron products moved along the route during the Revolutionary War. I'd walked this stretch of ground before, but through Landgraf's eyes I saw not just a place but a process of complex relationships, of forces moving at different paces from geologic aeons to a person's lifespan and the passing moment of a flood or fire.

Baldwin Drive in Hamden's West Rock Ridge State Park runs like a macadam spine for several miles along the mountain's crest. Unlike most roads, it was designed neither to facilitate commerce nor connect commu-nities or homes. Closed in the 1970s for security and maintenance reasons, it was built during the Depression as the state's answer to Skyline Drive in

Shenandoah National Park, and it is emblematic of an age of optimism about automobiles, when people drove for pleasure. I've made my way there via the blue-blazed Regicides Trail and found a straight ribbon of cracked pavement with leaf litter and weeds encroaching at the edges. Wire-and-post guiderails that once protected vehicles from the precipice are rotted and rusted, and mortared stone walls have cracked and fallen away. Especially to the west, I glimpsed spectacular views of rolling farmland and reservoirs through the trees. A road to nowhere across the ridge and deep in the woods, it felt like the remains of some long-gone alpine civilization.

Not far away, in the shadow of downtown New Haven, I found a series of urban ghost roads where only a twin line of trees marked the place where a street packed with houses once existed. At Greenwood Street and several others along Legion Avenue, homes and businesses were demolished during the 1970s in the name of urban renewal and an expressway that was never constructed. Today, a long mall of grass with its odd alignment of trees outlines a grid of streets that defined a neighborhood little more than a generation ago.

A similar ghostly feeling for a very different kind of road can be felt at the southern terminus of four-lane, interstate-like State Route 11, which suddenly ends and exits onto a two-lane blacktop in Salem. It was planned to connect with I-95, but construction ceased when money ran out over three decades ago. The residue of that intention, which may yet be fulfilled, is evident in a short stretch of unused pavement that extends beyond the traveled way, a rock cut exposing ancient geology, and the broad span of an unused bridge that crosses above State Route 82.

Roads are a synergy of natural conditions and cultural forces. They are not merely triumphs of engineering and surveying with long straightaways and Cartesian regularity. Instead, they respond to the landscape by rolling with our hillsides, winding along rivers, narrowing between rocks, and curving around wetlands. Such topographical imperatives are most pronounced along roads that have been abandoned.

Certainly I felt the landscape's anatomy on Bolton's narrow Bailey Road, once the main route connecting Hartford with Norwich, Lebanon, and other eastern Connecticut communities. Beginning in Andover, the pavement ended just beyond the Bolton town line in a neighborhood of modest homes from the 1950s and 1960s. It crossed an old rail grade and petered out into a muddy driveway. Here the road faded into brushy woods and then rose steeply as it twisted along a rocky slope of oak and hickory.

Crumbling stone walls about fifty feet apart frequently lined both sides, and where ledges crossed the road, pieces had been chopped away to accommodate travel. A stone culvert still channeled water, though it was clogged somewhat with leaves and debris. Some people maintain that this is the most authentic stretch of the route Rochambeau's French troops marched along in June 1781 on their way to join General Washington in his decisive victory at Yorktown, Virginia. Difficult as a footpath, it was hard to imagine wagons loaded with military materials making the trip. In fact, so rough was this length of road that supplies were delayed and the soldiers had to make do without tents that night. It's no wonder that the Frenchmen simultaneously marveled at our country's beauty while cursing its bad roads.

Corridors to nowhere in practical respects, abandoned roads not only take us into the past, they help us better appreciate how well current streets respond to our needs and the countryside. As new and improved roads are etched ever more enduringly upon the landscape, we would do well to contemplate the urgency and importance attached to long-gone routes that once seemed so critical.

Beneath the Lakes
Lost Worlds

Sparkling in sunlight or bathed in gauzy mist, lakes are among the most alluring elements of Connecticut's landscape. But the waters of some of our largest lakes, created by damming river valleys for drinking, flood control, or power production during the first part of the twentieth century, hide some unattractive secrets.

Because I live near 850-acre Nepaug Reservoir, which straddles the Burlington, Canton, and New Hartford town lines, I find myself frequently drawn to its forested shore and spacious expanse of sunlit, reflective water. It's a peaceful respite from the world of houses, cars, and utility poles. In winter I've spotted great horned owls lurking in tall pines and eagles cruising overhead. On summer strolls I've watched scarlet tanagers flit through the woods and heard the eerie call of loons echo across the water at night.

Protecting the drinking supply requires that thousands of acres surrounding the lake are closed, but the cracked remains of a macadam road, which was once the principal route to Torrington, still offers the public about a level mile for walking and biking. It crosses over the Nepaug Dam, where water often cascades from five arched portals 130 feet down a series of giant concrete steps to a rockbound gorge. It's an engineering work of art, and I frequently pause to admire its strength and clean geometric lines contrasting with the irregular ledges nearby. Unlike most Connecticut lakes, no cottages crowd its shore or old mills guard its outlet. Though it's inviting, no vessels ply the water, and only intrepid poachers enjoy the large trout, pickerel, and perch said to flourish beneath the surface.

Appearing like a gift of providence, Nepaug is actually pure human artifice created by plugging three watercourses. Less than a century old, it was built to provide water for Hartford and, when it was completed in 1917, it was the

state's largest lake. Before the flood, this was a lightly peopled place without a village center or businesses, a land patched in forest and fields where potatoes and other crops grew and dairymen milked cows. The reservoir's construction forced twenty-two families from their homes, some going back generations, and it required removal of a one-room schoolhouse and two cemeteries.

As I walk the Nepaug woods, once in a while beyond the proscribed bounds, I sometimes wonder about the lost landscape, the people who made their homes here, or the dead whose eternity was interrupted. There was a human toll not entered on any construction ledgers. But there were also serendipitous benefits to posterity unrelated to a city's craving for a drink. Gazing at treed hillsides and windswept water that conjures dreams of Vermont, I know that without Hartford's thirst I'd be looking at a network of paved streets, subdivisions, corner gas stations, and strip shopping plazas. Instead we've been bequeathed an accidental wilderness where bear, fisher, and turkeys roam, a place where, paradoxically, a person can sense what the landscape was like before Columbus.

Like Nepaug, Colebrook River Lake and Barkhamsted and Compensating Reservoirs in the Farmington Valley, and the Saugatuck Reservoir, Lake Lillinonah, and Candlewood Lake in the southwestern part of the state are among those water bodies made possible by drowning farms, small mills, homesteads, and entire rural hamlets. Land for these impoundments, created by both public and private entities, were acquired sometimes by condemnation, but mostly by purchases made in the shadow of eminent-domain powers. Taking private property for public purposes was big news then and remains controversial today, as demonstrated by New London's recent struggle all the way to the U.S. Supreme Court for Suzette Kelo's little pink house in an area slated for redevelopment.

Despite acrimonious and protracted legal battles over contemporary cases, their human impacts pale beside the development of the older reservoirs that displaced hundreds of people from their homes; closed schools, churches, and stores; rerouted miles of road; dismantled highway bridges; and even caused relocation of the dead to new cemeteries on higher ground. Tiny villages like Valley Forge in Weston, Colebrook River in Colebrook, and Hartland Hollow in Hartland were wiped off the map. Although some local bitterness remains, drinking water, flood protection, electricity, recreational opportunities, and vast tracts of open space have benefited millions of people for generations.

Typically cupped among hills, these manmade impoundments are so beautiful and look so natural that it's easy to assume they've always been there. Dams are the most obvious signs of human intervention, but even they can be well married to their location. When driving State Route 318 across the almost two-thousand-foot-long Saville Dam, I've often forgotten I'm atop a huge manmade structure because the concrete wall is hidden by a steeply sloping grassy berm. So well does the dam fit its surroundings that Kevin Murphy's book *Water for Hartford* called it "pure genius in its invisibility." One of Connecticut's most dramatic views, I never tire of looking north at the long, narrow Barkhamsted Reservoir covering a vast 2,323 acres, or south to uneven hills with Compensating Reservoir far below.

As with Nepaug, most watersheds are posted against trespassing to protect water quality, but all the reservoir lands reveal clues to the past that are visible from roads, trails, and other publicly accessible places. When looking carefully, I find evidence of long-lost communities abounding in truncated streets ending at the water's edge and crumbling foundations lying in the woods or beneath the waves.

Deep in the woods, along the blue-blazed Tunxis Trail on the east side of Barkhamsted Reservoir in Hartland, I've crossed a wide, linear swath of broken asphalt near the impoundment's north end. Here State Route 20 once descended into a hollow between hills now filled with water. A little further west in Colebrook, especially in late summer when the water is drawn down against potential tropical storms, I've driven a road usually submerged beneath Colebrook River Lake. A couple of side roads end abruptly where bridges once crossed the river, and at times a rusted steel truss span appears like a ghost near where Sawyer's Cotton Mill once stood. I've seen photographs of this quirky community of clapboard houses with a two-story school, a grange hall, an inn, and Ives & Baxter's Store. Trees that once grew here remain as stumps in the shallows and along the muddy shore.

During drought years I like to drive State Route 53 or Valley Forge Road along the Saugatuck Reservoir in Weston and Redding. Low water reveals a network of old roads, stone walls, and cellar holes that appears, Brigadoon-like, from the receding water. Valley Forge was a quintessential New England hamlet with stately Greek revival homes, fenced farmyards, rough shingled cottages, a one-room schoolhouse, a machine shop, and a sawmill. Sometimes when looking over the sandbars and mudflats I've imagined children laughing in the schoolyard, the smell of dinner wafting from a window, or the buzz of the mill.

As the dams were built, workers felled trees; demolished houses, shops, barns, and other structures; and burned the remains in huge crackling bonfires said to have licked the clouds. A few buildings were taken down and reconstructed elsewhere, like an old center-chimney colonial from Valley Forge, which was moved to Good Hill Road in Weston. Frank Barnes and his wife, whose home in Bristol had been recently destroyed by fire, took apart a Greek revival house slated for the bottom of the Nepaug Reservoir and transported it in pieces by horse and wagon to their lot on Jerome Avenue, where it stands today. Facing a busy street in a suburban area, the property bounds a small brook in a neighborhood of newer houses and reveals no sign of its unusual provenance. Some buildings were recovered many years later, like the tiny, white clapboard Barkhamsted Center Schoolhouse that now sits on State Route 181. About thirty years ago it was rescued from near the water's edge and restored as a historic site.

No place was sacred to the impoundment builders, and not even the dead were left undisturbed. New cemeteries were built and sometimes old ones were expanded to accept bodies exhumed from reservoir property. The cemetery in Barkhamsted Center feels formal with carefully laid stone boundary walls and handsome granite bollards joined by chains. It contains graves as old as two hundred years, but because the earliest remains were relocated here in the 1930s, the site is orderly and spacious with few stones cocked at the odd angles one expects to see in ancient burial grounds. Nearby, a bell taken from a church demolished to build Compensating Reservoir is perched on some large granite blocks.

After walking on a muggy day in mid-May through the graveyard built by the water company, I headed down a wide gravel road opposite the metropolitan district's headquarters in Barkhamsted, accompanied by district staff. The road to the massive water body passed several large field-stone cellar holes and a huge oak at what had been a village crossroads. Not far from the big tree we stopped to walk a patch of uneven ground beneath tall pines choked with a thick understory of hardwoods. Seen in old pictures with orderly rows of headstones and not a tree in sight, the old burial ground has been all but obliterated by forest, only the lumpy, furrowed earth and a single broken headstone evidencing what had once been hallowed soil.

Built for a hydroelectric pumped-storage plant that forces water to a hilltop from which it's released two hundred feet down a penstock to a turbine, Candlewood Lake, at over five thousand acres, is the state's largest water body. Although the area was sparsely settled, homes, farms, schools, churches, and two cemeteries were removed for construction, along with thousands of acres of timber. Today, much of the irregular shoreline is crowded with houses and other structures that have greatly altered the land-scape, making it difficult to find remains of the past. Nevertheless, SCUBA divers report discovering partial houses and barns, bridges, farm imple-ments, and even a Model-T Ford at the bottom.

It's not just the works of man that are forever altered by the flooding. Hills disappear, rivers lose their current, islands are created, and the typi-cally bony, glacially carved countryside is smoothed to a watery plain. Candlewood's companion hydroelectric impoundment, Lake Lillinonah, has swelled the boisterous Housatonic River to a slack-water as well as drowned the hamlet of Southville that once stood just downstream of the State Route 133 bridge with as many as thirty-four houses, a church, and a hat factory. Upstream of Southville is Lover's Leap Gorge, where by legend a white man jumped to his death as his forbidden lover, the heartbroken Indian princess Lillinonah, was canoeing toward certain destruction in the rapids. Not only have the roaring falls that Lillinonah sought been erased, but a traditional yarn has lost much of its impact.

The farms and small villages flooded during Connecticut's era of large reservoir building are places arrested in time. Like people dying young, they're remembered with a kind of youthful nostalgia through stories and photographs. But if we know what to look for, we can still detect their presence today, which provides not only insight into the past but valuable perspective on contemporary controversies about private property and public benefit.

Watery Ghosts of Manufacturing
Mill Ponds

Whenever I've glanced at a map or driven along highways and back roads, it quickly becomes apparent that Connecticut is bejeweled with lakes and ponds. Glistening in the sun or mirroring a cloudy sky, they infuse urban and wooded areas alike with space and light. They beckon to us for a swim, paddle, or simple relaxation and contemplation from the shore. One of the state's most valued natural resources, they are the most open of open spaces. No buildings can be built beyond their edges and no forest will ever encroach on their watery plains. "A lake," as Thoreau remarked, "is the landscape's most beautiful and expressive feature. It is earth's eye."

In my early twenties I got to live a Thoreauvian lakeside dream in a tiny cottage little more than a canoe's length from Middle Bolton Lake in Vernon. Though the shore was crowded with houses, I had a 121-acre sheet of water as my backyard. Summer meant diving off a homemade float and fishing for bass, bluegills, and perch. Autumn was colorful leaf reflections, gauzy mists, and migrating geese. And in winter I fished through the frozen surface, skated, and listened on frigid nights to the booming ice. Spring was a time for peepers and a lazy paddle on sunny afternoons. It took a few years before I realized that my lake paradise was no natural Walden Pond, but an artificial impoundment with a big dam.

Often, what at first blush seems a gift of nature has much to do with human tinkering. Many of our lakes and ponds are manmade reservoirs largely developed out of economic necessity for industrial and commercial purposes. Chemical contamination probably comes to mind first when we consider the effect of manufacturing on the environment, but the nineteenth-century makers of cloth, metal goods, and other items who relied on water power left myriad mill ponds as their longest-lasting legacy and perhaps finest products.

Lake building continued into the twentieth century, and our largest lake, Candlewood, was built in the 1920s to produce hydroelectricity. At over five thousand acres, its dendritic arms and bays lap at hillsides in five towns. Even Bantam Lake in Litchfield and Morris, our biggest natural body of water, at 947 acres, has been augmented by a dam. Connecticut has thousands of lakes and ponds, large and small, in the heart of cities and in the middle of nowhere. Most have a dam.

From the eighteenth century to the late nineteenth century, lakes and ponds of all sizes and shapes were commonly created by damming rivers and streams and harnessing the power of falling water to spin waterwheels and, later, turbines. From the earliest European settlement, many communities developed grist and saw mills. Later, the water powered machinery producing everything from furniture and axes to clocks, twine and textiles. Water bodies that today are cherished for their beauty and ecological attributes were the economic lifeblood of the state. "It would be difficult to conceive," the Connecticut Supreme Court noted in 1866, "a greater public benefit than garnering up the waste waters of innumerable streams and rivers and ponds and lakes, and compelling them with a gigantic energy to turn machinery and drive mills, and thereby build up cities and villages, and extend the business, the wealth, the population and prosperity of the state." As a result, today it's hard to walk along a stream in the woods and not find an old mill pond, or at least the remnants of a dam.

Although our state parks are usually considered pristine, even they had other uses prior to the twentieth century, and where there's a lake, it was likely created for industrial power. Few people swimming at Still Pond in Hebron's Gay City State Park realize it's an old mill impoundment, despite the existence of nearby ghost-town ruins that include a cemetery, house foundations, canals, and factory remains.

I've ice skated the "S"-shaped pond at Southford Falls State Park in Southbury, but I best like wandering the rocky ground below the spillway of the stone dam looking for old mill foundations. As early as 1805 there was a fulling mill, for thickening cloth, here along Eight Mile Brook. Later there was a flour mill, a couple of paper mills, a sawmill, an axe-handle manufacturer, and a cutlery shop. From 1901 to 1922 the Diamond Match Company employed as many as one hundred people in a large factory that made the stock for boxes and matchbooks. Today, a big lawn fringed in forest where people picnic, fly kites, and fish surrounds the quiet water.

On summer visits to Sand Dam Pond in Thomaston's Black Rock State Park I usually see fishermen along the wooded shore and boisterous children frolicking on the beach. In the days before widespread refrigeration its greatest use was in winter, when the Waterbury Ice and Coal Company harvested large chunks from its frozen surface. Wooded Mooween State Park in Lebanon, once a Jewish boys' camp, has a long shoreline on 127-acre Red Cedar Lake, where a broad earthen dam was built in the 1840s by the Hayward Rubber Company. Long and narrow, thirty-acre Higganum Reservoir in Haddam was created in 1870 by erecting a dam of giant granite blocks across Ponset Brook to supply water to a harrow-and-plow factory. The lakes in Huntington and Pierrepont State Parks in Fairfield County were built as part of neatly landscaped estates, though today their scraggly wooded appearance hides their lineage.

Many of the largest impoundments were created in the first half of the twentieth century. Rather than industrial power, the Hemlock Reservoir in Fairfield County, for example, was built to hold drinking water, Lake Lillinonah on the Housatonic River was built for hydroelectricity, and Colebrook River Lake was built for flood control. Their scale exceeded anything built for manufacturing, and it required tearing down and drowning entire villages, rerouting miles of road, and digging up cemeteries, all through the use or threat of eminent domain. During the same period, small ponds were also built with a new goal of restoring wildlife to a landscape that had suffered two centuries of abuse. Often they were developed by visionary individuals promoting forestry, like Norfolk's Wapato and Wampee Ponds in the privately held Great Mountain Forest, and Pine Aces Lake in Hampton, now part of Goodwin State Forest.

Our lakes and ponds still provide valuable products like water and electricity, but most people today connect to them through lakeside homes, picnics, fishing, swimming, boating, skiing, skating, wildlife watching, and shoreline walking. Few realize the man-influenced origins of these impoundments, though their genesis is sometimes betrayed by names such as Paper Mill Pond in Sprague or Factory Pond in Redding, or by long, narrow shapes mimicking drowned river valleys, like Aspinook Pond on the Quinebaug River and Lake Zoar on the Housatonic.

Although most impoundments were created by damming small streams and spring-fed swamps, some larger rivers have been repeatedly dammed into a series of bulging reservoirs that seem like tokens on the strand of a charm bracelet. The Pachaug River in eastern Connecticut, for one, includes Beachdale, Glasgo, Pachaug, Hopeville, and Ashland Ponds. Once a workhorse grinding grain, sawing lumber, and manufacturing cloth, the impoundments are now aesthetic and recreational amenities.

On a hot summer day I visited each, and though their waters are linked they exhibited distinctive characteristics as a result of topography, differing dam sizes and design, and nearby development. Glasgo and Pachaug

Ponds, for instance, have clusters of houses along their edges and tiny name-sake villages near their outlets, but their thickly forested shorelines offer a bucolic appearance. I was especially taken with the stone dam at Glasgo, whose thin, twenty-foot-tall curtain of water produced cooling breezes and softly hissed as it fell to the rocky pool below, where purple umbels of joe-pye weed grew in the shallows.

As I approached the old mill town of Jewett City, I could see that the long and twisting Ashland Pond was, by contrast, lined with houses. At the long, low dam, where fire had destroyed a large textile-mill complex dating back two centuries, was a bowl-shaped grassy area that had become a park. Several boys were jumping and swimming from a float just beyond one of the nearby houses.

While many former industrial water sources are accessible to the public through parks, there are even more that remain private, their development following a familiar pattern. Lake Williams in Lebanon was created for a saw and then a grist mill in 1816 by its namesake family, according to town historian Alicia Wayland. By the 1860s, the water was controlled by a textile firm several miles downstream, and the dam was rebuilt and enlarged. In the twentieth century, a seasonal hotel was established to take advantage of the lake's beauty, and after the Second World War house lots along the lake were sold, most often as summer places that in time were converted to year-round use. Along the wooded shore today is a campground, an elegant spa, and many private homes.

I pulled into a small rutted parking area and walked the dam, a long grassy berm armored with riprap beside State Route 207, which apparently provides the only public access. Several thickly treed islands were visible, and a few houses were well hidden by vegetation. There was a picnic table, a dry hydrant, a small boat landing, and a sign warning of the dangers of Eurasian milfoil, a nonnative invasive aquatic plant that has clogged the lake's shallows in recent years. The dam had been rebuilt not long ago, and the old stone spillway augmented with concrete left a dry creek bed below. A bypass structure composed of a couple of cement rectangles with an aluminum superstructure had brought modern engineering to the old mill pond.

As impoundments, many of our lakes and ponds are particularly fragile. Because they are often shallow and supported by large watersheds to ensure ready water, they are especially subject to filling with sediment, pollution from runoff and sewage, and choking by invasive weeds. If dams are not maintained, the water bodies may disappear altogether.

A few years ago I stood for the first time on a high berm behind a redbrick nineteenth-century factory near the Farmington River in New Hartford. I was with Walt Landgraf, who could see through time and understood better than anyone I've ever met the small-scale synergies between cultural and natural forces. The quirky building then housed Ovation Guitar, but it was once the home of the Greenwoods Company, manufacturer of cotton duck sailcloth and tenting. In 1844 the firm impounded the river, creating a one-and-a-quarter-mile-long, half-mile-wide water body. A 1936 storm washed away the dam stretching across the Farmington, leaving the lake a rapidly fading memory hidden in plain sight.

Atop the dam we were at the second-story level of the mill, overlooking the empty lake basin, now an elongated bowl of meadow growing up rapidly in trees. As we listened to the frequent calls of redwing blackbirds, Landgraf described a lively place where water was used not just for industrial power, but also for swimming, skating, fishing, and harvesting ice. There were docks and sailboat races. Along its shore was a small community of workers' homes and icehouses. For years I'd paddled the river as it wound through the old lake bottom totally unaware that the area had been underwater even though the landscape and vegetation are different than that in the reaches above and below.

While dam failures are not common, they still happen, and they leave the possibility of losing a lake. Floods in 1982, for example, broke seventeen dams and damaged thirty-one others.

The impoundments that dot our landscape are as of much value today as they were to businessmen of yore. The fact that our lakes and ponds are frequently a partnership between man and nature not only gives rise to fascinating stories of entrepreneurial energy and lost communities, it should heighten our awareness of the need to care for them.

Steeped in Mystery
Gungywamp

If you think there's little mystery in a place as long settled and well peopled as Connecticut, then you haven't been to Gungywamp. Situated in the northern reaches of Groton just a few miles from traffic-clogged I-95, over one hundred acres of densely forested and bony land beckons with a startling collection of unusual stone structures. Among the ledges and trees that line a swamp are low rows of standing stones, subterranean stone chambers, rock mounds, and a double circle of quarried stones about a dozen feet in diameter. Archaeologists see the remains of a colonial farm, but other hypotheses abound. Some people envision Native American stone temples or the ruins of a Celtic or Viking settlement. Gungywamp has been associated with Druid and Wiccan rituals and there are theories involving Egyptian, Norse, Phoenician, and even UFO influences.

Hitting the trail in the full light of a sunny summer morning, I felt a mixture of trepidation and excitement, and I remained on my guard for the serendipity of something unexpected, despite this being my third trip to the site. With stonework that even casual hikers find arresting, it was difficult to keep my imagination tethered as some of the wilder stories played in my mind like catchy song riffs. Fortunately for intrepid adventurers, this privately owned YMCA property is accessible with the aid of knowledgeable guides from Mystic's Denison Pequotsepos Nature Center, who ably navigate both a complex network of trails and a tangled web of suppositions surrounding the site's origins and uses.

A well-worn but unmarked path on the property's south end passed beneath a thick canopy of oak, maple, and yellow birch. Thickets of laurel and fields of fern flickered under shifting sunshine. A rock wall appeared, but, unlike all the others I've seen threading through New England's woods,

this one had periodic standing stones embedded in its length, perhaps for stability, a technique used in some old walls found in Ireland and Britain. Soon the wall devolved into a series of low, upright stones lined up like uneven granite dominos. Had the rocks between them been harvested for another purpose, or was this the site of prehistoric lunar ceremonies, as some have claimed?

Taking a trail that wound among low ridges and around lichen-crusted bedrock outcrops, I struck out for the stone circle, which sits on a small plateau near the center of some of the site's most intriguing structures and controversies. In this double wheel of roughhewn granite some people see the heart of a 1,500-year-old Native American ceremonial area celebrating the moon and sun. Old charcoal at the site leads others to envision a ritual altar. Archeologists look at the ring as a mill for crushing apples or bark used in leather tanning, although evidence of a center post for pivoting the grindstone has never been uncovered. Charred sticks, a few pieces of foil, broken glass, cigarette butts, and some crushed beer cans were mute testament to its continued use as a focal point for teen parties. At Gungywamp, stories are layered one upon the other like soil horizons.

Given the sometimes bitter polemics over the site's function and history, it's perhaps fitting that the very name "Gungywamp" is shrouded in mystery and susceptible to multiple interpretations. Some claim the word is ancient Gaelic for "church of the people." Others maintain it's a Pequot term for "swampy place," Mohegan for "place of ledges," or that it means "place of snakes" in some other Native language. There's even been an assertion that "Gungywamp" is merely a corruption of the words "spongy swamp."

Just south and downhill of the double stone circle I walked into a narrow, stone-lined underground chamber a few yards long. The opening was doorway sized with a boulder defining one side. A roof of large stone slabs was mounded with moss-covered earth. It was like entering a shallow stone basement, a slightly claustrophobic space that smelled dankly of soil and amplified the voice. Just to the right of the entry was a low, beehive-like room large enough to accommodate two or three people, though its small opening belied that possibility. At the far end of the structure opposite the entry was a small rectangular opening, a window of sorts furnishing light and air. It also acts as a solar calendar, for at the spring and fall equinoxes a beam of sun shines on the side chamber entrance.

This Stonehenge magic with sunlight, along with similarity to ancient subterranean structures in Britain, fortifies those who envision a settlement of Irish monks crossing the Atlantic in the style of Saint Brendan. Acknowledging that settlers from the British Isles would build in the manner of their homeland using materials at hand, archaeologists maintain that the chamber is a colonial root cellar equipped with a solar calendar to remind the farmer of planting and harvesting time, as well as the possibility of stored crops freezing in winter or rotting in summer's heat.

West of the root cellar was a low chamber, shaped like a turtle shell with an opening like a cave mouth. Undiscovered for years, its entrance was exposed at the base of a tree uprooted in a windstorm. Another root cellar? An icehouse? A place of ancient worship? A refuge against enemies? All possibilities have been suggested.

Regardless of viewpoint, Gungywamp's density of unusual structures and artifacts makes it a place of endless enchantment. There are eighteenth-century house foundations where coins, glass, buttons, pipe stems, and shards of pottery have been found. Stepped stone walls climb steep hillsides, open rock-walled chambers might have been colonial lambing shelters, and a boat-shaped cairn of cobbles lies beached in the woods. A variety of standing stones are sprinkled throughout the site, and long flat stones straddling narrow swales could be scupperlike road drains or bridges to another world. In a place of scabrous natural beauty, the manmade structures have become naturalized, an integral part of the landscape. In any event, Gungywamp's folklore, regardless of its veracity, has become as enduring and engaging as the stones themselves.

Wandering northerly over the rock-jumbled ground, I crossed Slag Iron Brook, a narrow stream stained ferrous orange by bog ore deposits. A short walk found me beneath the towering Cliff of Tears, a long, three-story-tall horseshoe-shaped precipice with an uneven face of dark, foreboding gray rock. Visitors here are rumored to become suddenly sad or unaccountably depressed. Weeping, nosebleeds, and bleeding gums have been reported at the site.

It's speculated that Gungywamp may be at the vortex of an energy-generating electromagnetic field. In fact, instruments have detected such fields in the area. The nonprofit, educational Gungywamp Society maintains that these phenomena have nothing to do with paranormal activity, but exist in many places owing to the presence of iron deposits and other natural occurrences. Though the cliff's shadow loomed over me, I felt nothing but exhilaration in the fresh air and magic of this enigmatic countryside where stone walls wander like drunks. Maybe, I thought, we don't want everything to be explicable.

"People have a hierarchy about what is interesting," observes Central Connecticut State University archaeology professor Kenneth Feder. "We crave mystery and value spiritual interpretations over day-to-day experience. How much more exciting to envision ancient transatlantic mariners or Native Americans with their mystical connection to the land, than ordinary people scratching out a living on an unyielding piece of property." Indeed, we're infatuated with the aberrant and anomalous, even when mundane explanations might reveal more intricate and interesting scenarios that require piecing together the puzzle of lives not unlike our own.

Nothing at Gungywamp better illustrates the gap between the mysterious and mundane than the inscriptions found on certain of the property's ledges. Some people perceive in these crudely scratched letters Chi Rho christograms, Greek characters used by early and medieval Christians to symbolize Jesus. But others see English letters indicating a property survey or boundary marker. The figures are roughly incised and often difficult to make out on the uneven stone. I lean strongly toward the prosaic explanation, but I revel in the existence of both, which gives the landscape added intrigue.

Perhaps much of Gungywamp's mystery arises from objects being both out of time and place. Thick forest on once cleared land, the loss of all but stone portions of structures, and persistent cultural amnesia about obsolete technologies leave us panting for explanatory stories and patterns. Maybe visiting a landscape susceptible to multiple explanations and layered meanings can help us better understand and piece together the divergent, often chaotic aspects of our everyday encounters by enabling us to look at common objects and places on multiple levels. How, we may well wonder, will our lives look to the future based on what we leave behind.

Containing both unusual natural and manmade stone objects that are sometimes hard to distinguish, Gungywamp offers a transcendent consanguinity of man and nature. Though no Bronze Age artifacts or shards of medieval European culture have been unearthed, there's no doubt that the place has endured millennia of human occupation. At the very least, it's been an Indian hunting ground, colonial farm, and twentieth-century recreation facility. Today it's become a refuge of austere outdoor beauty that feeds our imaginations. In the twenty-first century, you'd be hard pressed to find a better use for the land.

Space-Age Ghosts
Nike Missile Sites

For those old enough to remember ducking under a school desk or other air-raid drills of the early 1960s, the word "Nike" evokes not just a stylish shoe with a trademark swoosh but a system of conventional and nuclear missiles aimed at the threat of Soviet bombers. Connecticut had six Nike sites ringing Hartford and another half dozen around Bridgeport, which, combined with those in New York, Massachusetts, and Rhode Island, made us the nation's only fully covered state.

Emblematic of this dramatic Cold War epoch in American history, the sites also have much to say about Connecticut's landscape and how it changes. Some Nike locations have been wholly obliterated by development or have been reborn as parks; others are merely rubble piles, concrete pads, or little ghost towns in the woods. At several sites, the old buildings continue to be used for education, science, recreation, offices, and even agriculture.

Named for the Greek goddess of victory, about 250 Nike batteries were constructed around the nation from the mid-1950s to the early 1960s. Each consisted of two parcels: an integrated fire control area, housing radar and computer systems used to track enemy aircraft and guide missiles to their targets, and a launcher area at least one thousand yards away, where missiles were stored horizontally in underground magazines. Usually located on high ground, the control area typically contained administrative facilities like offices, barracks, a motor pool, and mess and recreation halls.

Habitable buildings at both control and launch areas were typically long and low, constructed of concrete block with a slightly angled roof. Radar towers came in various designs and were fabricated of concrete and metal. Like the backyard bomb shelters of the era, the buildings reveal a low, hunkered-down architecture of fear. In an atmosphere of doom and gloom officials reassured us that "whatever tomorrow brings … Nike will be watching, always ready."

At launch areas, missiles were brought to the surface via elevator and manually pushed on rails to a launcher, where they were raised to a nearly vertical position for firing. Ajax missiles were the first deployed. About thirty-four feet long, solid and liquid fueled, with a range of about twenty-five miles, they were fitted with three individual high-explosive fragmentation-type conventional warheads. By the early 1960s, the Ajax was obsolete, and the larger, solid-fueled Hercules missiles were deployed at some sites. They had a range three times that of Ajax and could carry nuclear warheads with up to twice the destructive power of the bomb that obliterated Hiroshima.

Nike bases began closing in the mid-1960s due to changes in Soviet tactics and technical capability that favored intercontinental ballistic missiles over bombers, and because of shifting American priorities like the Vietnam War. Arms-limitation treaties forced the deactivation of all sites by 1974. Fortunately, no Connecticut site ever fired a missile, not even as a drill.

Along rough dirt roads, on the blue-blazed Shenipsit Trail, or by taking a host of informal paths, I've spent many hours wandering Portland's Meshomasic State Forest, finding stone walls, the remains of old mines, and caved-in farmstead foundations evidencing the land's past uses. The woods are home to endangered rattlesnakes, a pine plantation of giant trees over a century old, and clear streams feeding a public water supply. Accidentally discovering the ruins of a rocket-age military installation deep among the trees jolted my imagination.

My curiosity piqued by a driveway of broken pavement blocked by a rusting yellow gate on my first visit two decades ago, I climbed from dirt Del Reeves Road to the remnants of a hillside control area. A rusting flagpole presided over a cluster of ruined buildings tangled in brush and looking as if they had suffered a bomb blast years ago. Broken pieces of masonry, half-ruined walls, chunks of wood, metal pipe, tangles of wiring, and other detritus littered the ground while chickadees sounded in the trees and a couple of turkey vultures kettled far overhead. Concrete steps led me to foundation slabs of long-since-demolished buildings. I felt as though I'd stumbled upon an apocalyptic science fiction movie set depicting the last outpost of a ruined civilization. I've returned several times over the years, but the spot is slowly fading away as trees retake the site and foresters gradually clean up the mess.

Not far away on North Mulford Road, the launch area has almost disappeared. I remember crawling into some of its concrete bunkers years ago, and the state police bomb squad is said to have detonated devices there. On my last trip, the area was hard to find in the brush. A few concrete slabs and the rectangular sand-filled magazine mouths were all that remained of a once mighty defense site.

While hiking the blue-blazed Metacomet Trail high on a traprock ridge in Plainville, I passed a rusting chain-link fence topped with barbed wire. Uneven macadam paths led nowhere, and the forest had healed around pieces of concrete and the few rusting metal remains of a control area. The once busy site was quiet and contemplative, with a view of green ridges through the trees. A companion launch site in the valley below had long ago been bulldozed for the large, boxy buildings of the Stanley Works Access Technologies Division on U.S. Route 6 in Farmington.

Many of the launch sites, with their dangerous underground magazines, have long disappeared, leaving behind few clues. But the array of uses to which some of the control facilities have been put illustrates the adaptability of their simple buildings and the allure of their hilltop locations. They effectively demonstrate the way in which we constantly reinvent our built environment.

Westport's control site, adjacent to the Merritt Parkway, houses the offices of the local health district in telltale concrete block buildings along Bayberry Lane. Behind them I discovered the town's compost facility, with mounds of material surrounding another typical Nike building. On top of the hill were two forty-foot-tall corrugated metal cubes that once supported radar. Though one rusted away in the woods, the other stood in a neat field, where it had been outfitted with an observatory dome and telescope by the local astronomical society.

Parks are a common fate for old Nike sites, including those in West Haven, Shelton, and elsewhere. I reached Manchester's Nike Site Recreation Area at the end of Garden Grove Road, which climbs gently to a parking lot with several classic Nike block buildings. Some had overhead doors signifying garage use; others seemed used for storage or maybe offices. But one building's severe facade was painted with a bright mural depicting a rainbow, trees, puffy clouds, and smiling children. In a striking departure from the structure's original use, it was now the home of Nike Tykes, a well-respected preschool. On the hilltop above the buildings were ball fields with a view of downtown Hartford. A concrete pad near the tree line probably supported a radar tower.

Nike sites were located in all sorts of terrain. Perched among sharp traprock ledges and dense hemlocks on a ridge overlooking the Farmington Valley, I found the Talcott Mountain Science Center in Avon still utilizing

Nike buildings, though they've been outfitted with new roofs and siding. The well-maintained guard shack had become a tool shed. On One Rod Highway, not far from the beach in Fairfield, beside a *Phragmites*-choked wetland, a control site housed the Elias Fire Training School, a dog pound, and a sewage plant. On the other side of Pine Creek was the old launch area, where a block building sat behind a metal fence. Beside it was a big tentlike bubble hosting an indoor tennis facility, while across the street was a golf course.

Many Nike buildings are used in agriculture. Autumn View Equestrian Center in Woodbridge has several launch-site buildings painted white, blue, and red. Jones Family Farms in Shelton once hosted a control center and uses the old mess hall for wine production, the control building for equipment storage, and a barracks for a hay barn.

Surrounded by new ranches and raised ranches where farm fields and a grass airfield once created a secrecy buffer, Ansonia's control area on Ford Street retains a semblance of Cold War–style high security. When I made arrangements to visit a few years ago, its chain-link fence, topped with barbed wire, was intact, and I entered through an electronically controlled sliding gate after speaking into a squawk box. Although the guard shack near the entrance was decrepit and strangled by vegetation and the radar platforms had long since been demolished, most of the original buildings remained as a quarantined laboratory where the U. S. Forest Service engages in biological research on gypsy moths and other invasive insects. It was a bucolic hilltop field where oaks and scraggly cedars grew among structures erected mostly between 1956 and 1958. Old Glory flew from the more than fifty-year-old flagpole, and new stucco-covered exteriors and gable roofs did little to disguise the buildings' provenance.

Experiments with nonnative insect pests, such as the Asian longhorned beetle and the emerald ash borer, are conducted in one of the long, low buildings. I was escorted through a double airlock equipped with an entry keypad and insect light traps. Once inside, I had to sign my name and don a Tyvek jumpsuit and slippers. It was probably the closest a person could still come to military secretiveness at an old Nike base.

Out back I was shown an unrenovated but still watertight bunker with block walls two feet thick. It was a dank building with few windows and a warren of rooms used for storage. I was at once struck by how sturdily this relic was built and reminded how the passage of time is not just a matter of years, but cultural and technological change.

Behind a big-box discount store and just beyond the Stop-and-Shop supermarket on a hilltop along heavily traveled State Route 372 in Cromwell,

I found a campus of derelict block buildings and radar platforms that felt like a ghost town. Squatting in a fenced field surrounded by condominiums, the windows and doors of the battered structures were long gone, and the graffiti-decorated walls had been left to drown in trees and scrub. It was eerily quiet as I walked into the debris-ridden mess hall, with its frayed wiring and broken pipes. A metal counter stood with a gap where a sink or steam table had been. An exhaust hood remained where stoves once were. The boiler house contained old pipes and broken electrical boxes, and on the highest ground were platforms of concrete and steel where radar once scanned the sky for Soviet bombers.

So much of the vandalized site remained intact that I felt a chill creep up the ladder of my spine, remembering a seven-year-old-boy cowering beneath his desk in October 1962, having overheard adult fears that Russian missiles in Cuba would soon destroy the world in a fireball. No doubt the soldiers here, wired on coffee, were scanning the heavens with radar. Missiles a few thousand yards away on Mile Lane in Middletown, where a military recruiting station was later built, were at the ready.

Those Nike defenders, whose regular routines must have been shattered by moments of extreme apprehension that autumn, are long gone. The mission of protecting our nation has evolved with advances in technology and new political realities. It has changed in as many ways as have these antiquated remnants that were once at the forefront of homeland defense.

Perpetual Care Isn't Forever
Neglected Graveyards

Traveling on State Route 179 along the Farmington River in Burlington a few years back, I was detoured by a traffic accident onto Ford Road, just a couple miles from my home in Collinsville. Driving slowly on the unfamiliar pavement, I noticed among the trees a blackened marble obelisk memorializing the street's namesake family. Standing at the macadam's edge, where a few houses were tucked into the woods, it blended into the unkempt, forested area like an oak trunk. Several people were buried there, the last in 1901. Though right at roadside, it seemed abandoned in plain sight, a memorial for the ages that had been lost to time and become invisible.

My accidental drive that day forever altered the way I looked at cemeteries. Beforehand, they seemed an unchanging fixture of the landscape. The dead rested for eternity, and the barest facts of their lives were carved in enduring stone for edification of the living. With their orderly rows of headstones typically set on manicured lawns, I saw them as tranquil islands of stability in a world of transformation and movement.

But the more I looked, the more I found that the postcard image of perpetual care beside a white steeple or within neat stone walls was too often at odds with reality. Of Connecticut's 2,000 to 2,500 graveyards, several hundred are neglected, abandoned, or forgotten. Their markers are often cracked and broken by decades of weathering or senseless vandalism. They are frequently overgrown, hidden in deep woods, or obscured by roadside undergrowth.

Perhaps the state's most obscure graveyard is on a small oblong rise squeezed between two Farmington streets. A remnant of the reservation to which the tribe was confined more than two centuries ago, the Tunxis Indian Cemetery lacks a gate, is enclosed by no walls, and doesn't even have

a path leading to its sacred precincts. Getting there required a short bush-whack upslope through pines and mixed hardwoods to a plateau. Beneath a few stately white oaks that got their start before second growth encroached, several brownstone nubs signifying burials poked through leaf litter. No one knows how many bodies lie here or exactly where they are. There's only one inscribed slab, which stands beside a suburban driveway at the proper-ty's edge. Without this memorial to Eunice Wimpey, who died in 1667, few standing here would realize there's a cemetery. The very condition of the graveyard seemed a cultural artifact, a poignant reminder of a people often idealized but in reality more comfortably forgotten.

Orphaned by time and circumstance, many neglected graveyards, like the Ford site, are small family plots established on the clan's property when the state's countryside was quilted with farms. Some are community ceme-teries established in places long since abandoned by the living. Still others are plainly visible in areas with modern homes and businesses, evidencing the inhabitants' limited retrospection and local budget priorities.

Cemeteries are collective, public biographies planted on the landscape. Their location, monuments, and design illustrate technology, social trends, wealth, ethnicity, and settlement patterns in different places and eras. Though evocative of the past, their condition says more about the present. While willfully damaging a cemetery is a felony, letting one slowly go to ruin remains unpunishable.

Accessible only via a network of bumpy, potholed dirt roads in the deep woods of Winchester, Danbury Quarter Cemetery is the last visible piece of a nineteenth-century community that was once home to as many as two hundred families. Inasmuch as cemeteries are established where people live, finding a graveyard in the middle of the woods was eerie, a remnant of a world that had itself become a ghost. Although the grass seemed occasionally cut, many of the finely carved tombstones surrounded by a stone wall had been damaged by hooligans and the ravages of time. Someone's token care for this remote place was sadly visible in a couple of broken headstones propped up with rocks likely taken from the wall. Though it was silent when I visited, beer bottles, candy wrappers, and cigarette butts nearby illustrated the popularity of the site for drinking parties and bonfires. Isolation doesn't necessarily mean quiet, and distance doesn't always protect. I found Revolutionary and Civil War soldiers among those whose sleep might be disturbed by such carousing, including twenty-nine-year-old Charles Gilbert, who died in 1862 of wounds received at the battle of James Island, South Carolina.

In People's State Forest another obscure cemetery exists on a laurel-tangled hillside high above the Farmington River in Barkhamsted. Not long ago I took the short but steep hike from East River Road on the Jessie Gerard Trail to the flattened area where the legendary Barkhamsted Lighthouse community's graveyard was marked only by chunks of rough fieldstone that indicate about fifty burials. Not a single marker was inscribed, and the logic of their placement was a mystery. Nearby were stone clusters and cellar holes marking the dwellings of this poor community of mixed-race outcasts, whose lit homes served as a "lighthouse" guiding stagecoach drivers when this was a remote region around the turn of the nineteenth century. The cemetery seemed not so much forgotten as naturalized into its surroundings, a place so indistinct that most people on the trail pass right by it unawares.

I've seen no better illustration of the notion that where you stand in life determines how you lie in death than in Moosup. Well-groomed Union Cemetery rises in terraces up a hillside with handsome, substantial, and intricately carved monuments sharing a view of the old textile village. But on the other side of Grove Street is a linear patch of headstones lying in thick trees and hidden behind a guardrail above the Moosup River. Many of the markers have been damaged, and most are just chunks of native rock. State archeologist Nicholas Bellantoni estimates that about forty African Americans, buried over a century ago, lie here beneath brush and dried leaves. Disenfranchised in life, these anonymous individuals remain so in death.

The ignominy of burial in an overgrown and vandalized cemetery extends even to members of well-known families. From Woodtick Road in Wolcott, a middle-class neighborhood of ranches and capes, I walked down rocky and rutted Beecher Road, which has never seen pavement and is now impassible by vehicles. Louisa May Alcott, author of the classic *Little Women*, has family buried in two neglected cemeteries along this onetime thoroughfare, which first saw service around 1753. Her father, Bronson, was a friend of Ralph Waldo Emerson and Henry D. Thoreau and the subject of a Pulitzer Prize–winning biography by Odell Shepard. Both graveyards contain shattered, eroded, tilted, and bramble-choked markers attacked by trees and frost. Shepard well knew such places and in the mid-1920s wrote that "nothing could symbolize the insolent trampling of life upon death, of the present upon the past, more vividly than the way in which these robust oaks and maples made free with God's acre, elbowing the tombstones aside, splitting coffins, riving skulls, and drawing their sustenance from what had once been human."

Pike Hill Cemetery was a small burial ground overrun by brush and surrounded by a cheap, mangled wire fence. I could have easily missed it if I hadn't been looking. There were a few broken stones with epitaphs as early as 1776. One dark slate bore the name Allcox, a variant of Alcott.

It took about five minutes of steep descent on the eroded path to reach the much larger Northeast Cemetery, fenced with rusting chain-link deep in the woods. Bluets grew profusely there, as did poison ivy, and more stones were broken and lying horizontally than standing upright. The headstone of Joseph Alcott had a quarter-sized bullet hole through it. Among Revolutionary War soldiers and at least one who fought in the War of 1812 is an eleven-year-old "killed by the fall of a tree." He remains anonymous because the top of his stone is broken and lost. One family was so frustrated with the condition of this graveyard that a few years ago they had several of their ancestors exhumed and moved elsewhere.

Despite being unkempt, many of these plots retain an emotional resonance that highlights the poignancy of their poor condition. Shrouded in scrubby woods above the Quinnebaug River in Plainfield is a tiny cemetery with about a dozen burials, most of which are indicated with fieldstones. I spent the better part of an hour searching for it on a confusing tangle of old trails and woods roads just north of where State Route 14 crosses the river. Greenish with age, a marble stone marks the grave of David Kinne, who died in 1808 at age seventy-two. Beside him is Nathaniel Kinne, whose flaking slate slab tells of his death crossing the icy river in April 1807 during his thirty-first year. Broken and lying horizontal on the ground next to it is the stone of Nathaniel, son of Nathaniel, who died in 1804. Standing before these silent stones while listening to wind in the trees and a sparrow chipping, I imagined the anguished elder Kinne witnessing the deaths of younger loved ones he thought would sustain his legacy. The grief seemed to cascade down the centuries and pool in my heart, which suddenly filled with concern for my own children.

Derelict cemeteries vary considerably in size, location, and condition. The Weeks family plot, with a few stones overwhelmed by trees deep in Eastford's Natchaug State Forest, was fairly remote. On the other hand, Griswold's Hopeville Cemetery lies on a well-traveled road not far from an interstate highway. But its monuments, ranging from eighteenth-century sandstone slices with death angels to simple concrete markers from the 1950s, were obscured by three-foot-high desiccated grasses that I had to brush aside before reading the epitaphs. We say nice words over the dead, but the future doesn't always remember. We give lip service to perpetual care, but eternity is a long time.

Cemeteries are also neglected in cities. Hartford's seventeen-acre Old North Cemetery on North Main Street was established in 1807 and contains a striking, diverse cross-section of nineteenth-century personalities. There are national luminaries like Frederick Law Olmsted, the father of landscape architecture in America and the designer of New York's Central Park, and Daniel Wadsworth, founder of America's first public art museum. There are over twenty black Civil War veterans, as well as soldiers who fought in every conflict from the Revolution to World War II. Immigrants include people from the Russian, Italian, Irish, and Jewish communities.

Despite Old North's rich heritage as a time capsule of Hartford life, when I first visited in the late 1990s the graveyard was overgrown with weeds, and broken tree limbs were left where they fell. A grassy island in a dense urban neighborhood, it had become seedy and ill kempt, a haunt of drunks and druggies. Grave markers were broken and defaced with spray paint; some had disappeared in a riot of vegetation. Although still far from ideal, by virtue of both municipal and volunteer efforts, the grounds today are much better groomed, and a modicum of dignity has been restored to the stately monuments.

Some communities have programs that encourage scout groups, garden clubs, civic organizations, and families armed with clippers, rakes, lawnmowers, and other tools to adopt or help clean up neglected graveyards. A few, like East Hartford's three-hundred-year-old Center Cemetery, have active friends groups that work on planning, maintenance, and restoration. While more of this enthusiasm and energy needs to be recruited, lack of funding can frustrate even the most passionate advocates, as was the case with Berlin's Cemetery Committee, which stopped meeting less than two years after it was established in 2008.

Maintaining cemeteries is an act of devotion that doesn't just honor the dead; it teaches the living about their origins. More artifacts of our humanity than pious slices of real estate, cemeteries are not just burial grounds, but peaceful green spaces, outdoor art museums, and walkthrough books of history and culture. Unfortunately, without proper care, cemeteries, like people, can die prematurely.

Haunting Stones of Metal
Zinc Grave Markers

It's no surprise that we use stone to mark burials. Hoping to keep the memories of loved ones alive, we demand this most enduring material. But sandstone flakes, inscriptions on marble are washed away by acid rain, and even granite darkens and can become pitted or splotched with lichen and moss. Fortunately, our cemeteries often contain distinctive bluish-gray monuments that have proved in many respects more durable than stone. Their lettering and images remain remarkably sharp after almost a century and a half. Tapping a finger on their surface causes a peculiar pinging sound because, while looking like stone, they are actually hollow and made of metal.

Marketed as "white bronze" to make them seem more impressive and attractive to buyers, these monuments are neither white nor bronze. Made of almost pure, corrosion-resistant zinc, and sandblasted to a matte finish resembling stone, they have telltale seams at the corners and a distinctive soft silvery-blue color resulting from natural oxidation.

Found across North America in cemeteries that were active between the end of the Civil War and the onset of World War I, they are frequently encountered in Connecticut, their principal place of manufacture. White-bronze grave markers were a product of the Monumental Bronze Company of Bridgeport, established in 1874, and its subsidiaries elsewhere across the country, including in Detroit and Chicago, and in Canada. By some accounts all the casting was done in Bridgeport, while assembly and some finish work was left to other sites. The metal memorials were made until 1912, although the company continued to produce zinc and other nonferrous castings for automobiles, radios, and other products until it went bankrupt in 1939.

Though most of us have seen many white-bronze grave markers, few people realize it. Once a person learns to recognize them, however, they become a common sight. Their light cyanic color seems to glow among the duller browns, grays, and pinks of conventional monuments, even on cloudy days. I can spot "zinkies" from behind a windshield at fifty miles an hour, and ever since first discovering them I can't resist looking, much to the chagrin of passengers in my vehicle. If I see more than a couple, I'm compelled to stop. It's an opportunity to become lost in a world of names, dates, and geometric shapes that tell stories to which I'd otherwise be deaf.

I've found zinc monuments in places as diverse as Torrington's urban Center Cemetery behind city hall and a small, stonewall-surrounded country graveyard in North Colebrook. There are at least five in Norwich's tree-shaded Maplewood Cemetery on the city's outskirts and no fewer than eight in the rolling pastures of Watertown's Evergreen Cemetery. A couple of zinc markers memorializing some of Unionville's most prominent citizens are terraced into a steep hillside overlooking the village's old brick firehouse and the green truss bridge across the Farmington River.

Although company catalogs depicted a wide variety of basic styles, each monument was custom made to order, a marriage of mass-produced industrial efficiency and personal artisanship. To keep costs low, there was no showroom for customers to view the stock. Potential purchasers could leaf through a catalog or hoof it out to a graveyard to see the real thing. Shunned by traditional stone-monument outlets, which may have resented a product that was not handcrafted, they were sold by independent local agents. Prices in 1890 ranged from six dollars for a simple unadorned tablet to five thousand dollars for large elaborate versions. Since many cemeteries include only a single zinkie, some believe that a site's first one may have been sold at an introductory discount to attract business. But even some small country cemeteries, like the one in Colebrook center, have several of the metal stones, a sign of a good aggressive salesman.

Perhaps the most popular designs were obelisks of differing heights and rectangular columns topped with various urns. The metal could be formed with architectural features such as dentils, quoins, and triangular pediments. Some markers also included decorative aspects that looked like roping or draped cloth. Crosses were ubiquitous, and medallions of clasped hands, anchors, roses, wreaths, sheaths of wheat, lilies of the valley, or angels were not uncommon. The bases, where sometimes the company name was cast, were often formed to look like rusticated stone.

A monument could be as simple as the two-foot-high curved-top tablet in memory of Andrew and Henry Jordan, one of two zinkies in Voluntown's tiny Douglas Cemetery near the Rhode Island state line. I found it accidentally one autumn afternoon along a rough dirt road while hiking in Pachaug

State Forest. Surrounded by a fieldstone wall with two upright granite posts at the entrance, it's another of Connecticut's neglected graveyards overgrown with pole-sized oaks, mountain laurel, and blueberry.

Zinkies could be as big and elaborate as anything created by stonecutters. The Dawson-Dakin monument in Woodbury's meticulously maintained North Cemetery is a detailed six-foot-high square pillar topped by a life-sized statue of a woman in classical robes, grasping an open book in one hand while the other arm is raised with an index finger pointing heavenward. The largest and most intricate were works created for public spaces like Stratford's huge Academy Hill Civil War memorial, which starts with a tiered base beneath a Greek temple above which is a tall shaft crowned by a standing soldier grasping a flag. Zinc monuments are found on even the most sacred public ground, including the battlefield at Gettysburg, Pennsylvania.

Horizontally oriented rectangular models were also popular and often highly articulated. The Beckley memorial in Thomaston's aptly named Hillside Cemetery includes classical columns and other features reminiscent of Greek temples. Like many fancier models, it serves as a family marker surrounded by low zinc wedges cast with the names or initials of individuals. The nearby Mullin monument has the same basic shape but with a pagoda-like aspect.

The back of the Beckley marker was missing a panel the day I visited, providing me with a rare inside view. The interior had an uneven, pebbled finish and a faint three-digit number inscribed. My breathing seemed amplified when I stuck my head in the opening. Legend has it that cemetery maintainers would store rakes, shovels, and other hand tools in the larger monuments, and that they have been used as hiding places for thieves or bootleggers during prohibition. Their odd-shaped, cramped interiors suggest that such uses were rare if they occurred at all. Nevertheless, clues once led me to a letterbox ensconced inside a small zinkie in Naugatuck.

In the late nineteenth century, the zinc-monument-making process was a cutting-edge technology, and an 1885 issue of *Scientific American* devoted space to the topic, including a pictorial illustrating design, casting, and finishing. The work began with a company artist's wax model, which was used to produce a plaster cast. The plaster figure was then cut into pieces and utilized to shape the sand molds into which the heated metal was poured to form the zinc pieces. Instead of soldering, the assembled parts were fused together by the novel technique of poring molten zinc into the joints. Sandblasting then left a porous finish, which lightened the color and caused the product to resemble stone more than metal. Finally, a trade-secret sealant was brushed on the surface.

Epitaphs were often cast on individual plates and fitted into the monument with ornamental screws. Larger works typically had four of these spaces. Decorative or blank plaques were left in place until a new name was added.

Wandering through a cemetery looking for zinkies is part treasure hunt, part history mystery, and part art exhibit. Since they're uncataloged, I never know what I'll find. It's akin to rifling through the shelves of a used bookstore.

Slamming on the brakes when I saw a few zinkies as I drove back from visiting a friend, I once lost myself for an entire afternoon on the gentle slopes of Watertown's Evergreen Cemetery, a bucolic stretch of ground set in a residential neighborhood. Stumbling on the unusual Atwood monument not far from a winding, channelized brook, I was intrigued with its gabled top, which formed a triangle much like the shape of a Victorian coffin. Decorated with cast tasseled roping, it read, "Friends, Come Up Higher." Next I came upon the Dains memorial, a pillar with a fireplug-like lantern top. The stout, urn-topped Vera marker had a New Testament quote on one side and "In God We Trust" emblazoned on the other, seeming to mix the spiritual with the patriotic. The Slade monument bears a Grand Army of the Republic medallion that late in the day was starkly outlined in full sunlight.

Searching for zinkies may seem a dull pastime, but I felt energized rushing from one find to another as if I were fitting together pieces of a puzzle or filling out the last items in a collection. The Dubois marker included ivy strands and oak clusters and was crowned with an urn graced in a garland. Despite the day's warmth, I felt a shiver when among the names and dates I was reading there was listed an unnamed infant whose age was forty-five hours.

The company's boast that its products were more durable than stone has largely proven true. After more than a century, the decoration and lettering remains in high relief, and the pearly-blue finish is still uniform and satiny. However, the metal is brittle and easily damaged by falling tree limbs and other mechanical impacts. Vandals sometimes steal the screwed-in plates, and larger monuments often suffer from sagging, bulging bases, and separating seams caused by supporting the weight above them.

In a world of neglected, overgrown graveyards in which stone inscriptions are rapidly fading, we are lucky to have these long-lived marvels of the industrial age. The past is not just a matter of legend or book knowledge in a cemetery, but of stories made palpable by the stones around us, as zinkies in the quiet North Colebrook Cemetery attest.

One quiet, overcast winter day I stood before a modest obelisk set at the edge of thick woods, memorializing the Terrell family. Drowned on their way to school in mid-December 1881, Wallace was one day shy of his twelfth birthday and George was less than a fortnight away from turning ten on Christmas. Despite the passage of well over a century, the anguish of their parents, who had lost a nine-week-old baby just a couple of years earlier, was palpable. I imagined the boys giddily taking a shortcut to class on the thin ice of Sandy Brook, and subsequently a house whose Yule and New Year were riven with pain. I was grateful for the clear lettering that left no doubt as to what had happened.

Sprinkled throughout Connecticut, these singular monuments add a little grace and beauty to our communities. Practical works of art, their durability is both suitable to eternity and emblematic of industrial-age Yankee ingenuity. They symbolized faith in a higher power and in technology, both of which offered the promise of a better world.

Trash Talk
Landfills and Landscape

On a low dirt plateau in the northwest part of Windsor, bulldozers were busy covering piles of freshly dumped garbage with soil. Pizza boxes, blue poly tarps, bright plastic toys, kitchen scraps, a battered lampshade, and a pile of old clothes were quickly disappearing. Nearby, birdwatchers looking for a rarity focused their scopes on the flocks of gulls that rhythmically landed and took flight. With muck clinging to my boots, I walked wide-eyed around the rutted, muddy Windsor-Bloomfield Landfill with its gently sloping shoulders rising about 212 feet above old tobacco land. Adjacent to a large park along the Farmington River and not far from new housing subdivisions, a couple of deteriorating barns at the edge of the mound revealed the site's history as they awaited slow demolition by the weather.

Consisting of fifty acres of garbage and five more of construction and similar wastes, the vast mesa of exposed dirt was punctuated by plastic gas pipes recovering methane. Long windrows of composting leaves filled one corner, and a big brush pile ready for chipping lay near the middle. The rumble of machinery and the harsh squawk of birds darting overhead filled the air as site manager Mark Goossens pointed to a couple of eight-foot-tall fiberglass cows his staff had saved from burial. A big man with a crew cut, generous smile, and soft voice, he sheepishly acknowledged that the most unusual waste they'd ever received was a load of elephant dung from the circus. Nevertheless, the area around the bunkerlike masonry office displayed other treasures, like wagon wheels, garden gnomes, and broken toys.

At one time every town in Connecticut had at least one landfill for the interment of household trash, but Windsor's is the last. Although there are places still taking demolition debris and other special materials, environ-

mental concerns have wisely made landfills for ordinary garbage increasingly difficult to locate and operate. What we throw away after composting and recycling now goes mostly to waste-to-energy plants.

Landfilling garbage may be a thing of the past, but the state is riddled with hundreds of old dumps, many of which have settled into their surroundings and long been forgotten. Some have dramatically changed our topography, as any passing motorist can see from the precipitous mountain of garbage that rises 120 feet above I-91 north of Hartford where there once was a low spot along the Connecticut River. Over the past few years as the site took its last loads and finally closed, I've ventured to the top with an intrepid group of birders for the annual Christmas count. From below it appeared to be a single eminence, but as I gained elevation, I realized it was a massif with small hills. In places steep slopes bled mattresses, plastic pails, chunks of lumber, foil, and the remains of garden tools. With the dark and waxy river on one side and traffic whooshing along pavement on the other, the landfill offered the best view of the Connecticut Valley between Springfield, Massachusetts, and the traprock heights of Meriden.

Cradled between low ridges to the distant east and west, the towers of Hartford looked like a fairyland in the thin winter light. A bald eagle cruised over the water, and among an astounding variety of birds we found about seventy increasingly rare horned larks on a grassy patch of ground near giant rolls of plastic and pipes. From some angles the landfill's snow-splotched slopes looked as forbidding as anything in the White Mountains.

Whether large or small, these areas remain artifacts of our culture, and many people hunt for bottles, buttons, ceramics, and other treasures at long-closed sites. Landfills are the cemeteries of our material world. Houses may be demolished, whole villages may disappear, and roads may be rerouted and rebuilt, but trash, though often hidden, remains as the most enduring signature of human occupation since the age of Native American rock shelters.

Trash exists wherever people have dwelled, and sometimes what is thrown away lasts longer than what is valued, as is the case with aboriginal shell middens left thousands of years ago. Eighteenth-century trash was broadcast out a home's windows and doors, and that's where tobacco pipes, coins, and glass have been found at Suffield's gambrel-roofed Phelps-Hatheway House, which dates from the 1760s. In fact, the apertures of even long-gone colonial homes can be platted by where garbage lies. As the landscape became more crowded in the nineteenth century and an industrial society with an increased standard of living generated more goods and garbage, farmers collected trash in wagons and barrels and dumped it in depressions on the back forty. Today they are often called bottle dumps for the prized object most commonly found there.

Before the turn of the twentieth century, smaller house lots and increasing garbage from a burgeoning consumer society made municipal dumps a necessity. No longer did a trash pile tell the story of a particular family or home site, but instead it told of an entire community. Through the 1950s, such locations were useable almost indefinitely because trash was reduced to ashes by burning. Air pollution concerns ended the practice. This resulted in the development of sanitary landfills where garbage was covered with soil and ultimately mounded and shaped to shed rain and reduce pollution of aquifers and streams. Materials became practically entombed in the absence of air and water. Newspapers in excess of forty years old can still be read when unearthed, according to the Connecticut Department of Energy and Environmental Protection's David McKeegan. As these local dumps reached capacity, garbage was brought to regional facilities like Hartford's.

Old dumps are frequently found at the edge of slopes, terraces, and rivers and in wetlands, gullies, and ravines. Any spot where the topography looks a little unnatural or vegetation abruptly changes is worth investigating.

Evidence of farm and family dumps is commonly found wherever there is an old cellar hole or colonial homestead in a relatively undisturbed area. Walking along the state forest road at the end of Shetucket Turnpike in Voluntown not long ago, I found bits of pottery, rusted hardware, and glass fragments not far from old fieldstone foundations hidden among the trees. Beyond a low stone wall at the edge of playing fields on State Route 82 in Salem where the Dolbeare Tavern once stood, pieces of wire, rusted metal, and the remains of shoes and bottles can still be discovered in the humus.

On the low side of State Route 138, as it runs along a hillside just west of Jewett City, is a steep declivity that descends in a series of uneven humps. This natural-looking hubbly ground actually results from mounds of trash covered by decades of leaves and detritus. The road is partially built on an old dump, and treasure seekers have dug away at the slope, uncovering machine parts, rusting cans, animal bones, wood fragments, coal ash, oyster shells, and myriad other objects.

Deb Labrie, an energetic retired nurse who wears her gray-blonde hair in a ponytail, is a self-described scrounger "obsessed with digging for stuff" in obscure places. Her home is filled with thousands of artifacts, from bottles to bone-handled toothbrushes, arrowheads, figurines, and old nails. On a November day she led me over the guardrail and down the slope where leaf litter had been cleared and several holes had been dug alongside and beneath the road and among the roots of large trees. Medication and beverage bottles, half a teacup, a knife handle, rusting galvanized pails, and clinkers from coal burning indicated late nineteenth- and early twentieth-century activity. Particular types of objects like cinders and milk bottles often lie within layers, Deb said. As she digs, she feels as if she is plummeting through time. Dumping continues here today in the form of brush and leaves, or an old refrigerator or car battery tossed down the embankment. It's as if there were something in the ravine that draws junk.

Not far away, the old redbrick Slater Textile Mill, with its twin stair towers, sits in the angle formed by Route 138 and the Quinnebaug River. Riverbanks have a long tradition as dump sites and, until the mid-twentieth century, industries that lined them often made full use of the opportunity to dump in and along the river. Labrie said that a friend of hers canoes from dump to dump, seeking treasures along the Quinnebaug, which once powered myriad factories.

Walking through a dirt parking lot we crossed the railroad tracks and entered a lumpy landscape thick with briers, brush, and trees tangled in vines. What was probably once a floodplain was raised considerably above the river from years of trash disposal. The ground was a series of uneven and misshapen mounds, and in places bottle hunters had left elaborate excavations. There was a great deal of coal ash and some goodly clinkers, likely from the factory boilers. Bottles and glass and pottery fragments, clamshells, pieces of iron pipe, bowls and basins, shoe leather, and machine parts were among the detritus. Newer objects had also been chucked into the knotted vegetation, including golf clubs, a broken carpenter's level, a food processor, and the ubiquitous plastic bottles, wrappers, tires, and foam cups.

Late twentieth-century landfills often appear as large grassy hills and ersatz drumlins. In addition to the Hartford site, obvious examples include one in Shelton along the Housatonic River north of the Sikorsky plant at what was once a gravel pit, the mountain that looms behind Seaside Park in Bridgeport, and New Haven's old dump, which rises like a Gibraltar out of a *Phragmites* swamp beside the old incinerator stack along I-91 near exit 8. Some sites exist without detection, even though thousands of people pass them daily, like the low mound on the median of I-91 near the Charter Oak Bridge at the south end of Hartford.

These and other big dumps have transformed the landscape by creating grassy hills where once there was a depression, and yet they remain almost invisible in plain sight until you know what you're looking for. But they are not just about what our countryside looks like. As archeologists know, you can tell a lot about a people by their trash. The landfills dotting Connecticut's landscape are accidental libraries of cultural information likely to fascinate future generations.

But these preternatural landforms are not just waste spaces. Old landfill sites have been recycled as athletic fields, parking lots, and even public and commercial building sites. Windsor's will eventually be made a part of the park next door. The old Milford landfill—rising fifty feet above the beach at Silver Sands State Park—offers a spectacular view of Long Island Sound and Charles Island. Someday visitors will be able to hike, ride bikes, or drive cars via a narrow roadway that will spiral around the landform to a summit featuring a pavilion for picnics and weddings. A toxic dump between North Hillside and Hunting Lodge Roads at the University of Connecticut has been capped with a parking lot providing access to a new park with two miles of trails and a couple of overlook decks. Old Saybrook's Coulter Street landfill is also now a park with a view of North Cove and delicate coastal wetlands at the mouth of the Connecticut River.

It's not hard to stumble across old landfills, whether in rural or urban areas, once you know what you're looking for. Some people may think that garbage dumps, like the trash in them, are best kept out of sight and out of mind. But rather than a dirty secret, they are endlessly intriguing places that add complexity, interest, and texture to our natural and cultural landscape.

Through Artists' Eyes

If eyes were made for seeing,
Then beauty is its own excuse for being.

—Ralph Waldo Emerson, "The Rhodora"

Our world is shaped more than we commonly realize by artists—writers, painters, sculptors, poets, photographers, and others—because they mold the ways in which we see the built and natural landscape. They infiltrate our imaginations. We may never experience their work directly, but their images seep into the culture and affect even those who have never heard of them.

Wallace Nutting is a name all but unknown today, yet through his photographs, furniture making, books, and other enterprises early in the twentieth century he popularized the quaint, nostalgic image of colonial New England that continues to drive the region's tourism machinery. The white clapboard houses, hardscrabble farms, neat town greens, and winding country lanes we still envision are the result of his antiquarian evangelism. While today we value authenticity over his idealized approach, no doubt he energized the public about its past and fueled the historic preservation movement.

Nineteenth-century Hudson River School paintings, with their grand, human-dwarfing landscapes, were the first American works in a truly native style. They continue to shape our view of the country's topographical beauty and natural resources. Connecticut played a significant role in constructing this national self-image, and the state was not only the subject of paintings, but also the home of its most ardent patrons and the birthplace of its most renowned artist, Frederic Church.

Early in the twentieth century, the state was an epicenter of impressionist painting, which focused not on grandeur, but on the fine details, colors, and moods of our varied landscape. Today we can look through the eyes of these geniuses by means of signboard images of their work posted near where they painted, or by visiting the farm of J. Alden Weir, whose Branchville home was his muse. It's the only unit of the National Park Service devoted to an American painter, and the link between life and landscape is vivid.

Four influential Connecticut-based nature writers continue to shape the way in which our nation views forests, fields, and wildlife and their relationship to the built environment. In the mid-twentieth century Pulitzer Prize winner Edwin Way Teale, essayist Joseph Wood Krutch, women's magazine columnist Gladys Taber, and Hal Borland, who wrote *New York Times* nature editorials for well over a generation, conveyed to a national audience and beyond a view of nature for which Connecticut was the benchmark. They helped sensitize millions of people to the natural world and readied them to receive Rachel Carson's critical warning about pesticides in *Silent Spring*, the book that launched the environmental movement.

An educated, intellectually curious, and tolerant population has enabled Connecticut to foster artistic genius. Little along our roadsides signifies this incubation of imagination so much as used bookshops. The survival of even a few in an era of big-box stores and increasing Internet sales is a tribute to a public that demands more than surficial sensory experience. Never knowing what I'll find at them, used bookstores are among the last serendipitous retail encounters. Unlike most businesses that have locational formulas, they appear in country barns, on commercial strips, in old factories and downtown storefronts, anywhere rents are reasonable. They are a measure of culture imprinted on our landscape.

Reinventing the Colonial Landscape
Wallace Nutting

A few years ago I made my first visit to Southbury's Heritage Village to see a dear friend who had retired to its sprawling pastoral campus. Styling itself the "best active adult community," it was developed in the late 1960s and the 1970s, and it covers over one thousand well-landscaped acres with meticulously maintained condominiums. Its winding streets are bounded by manicured lawns dotted with shade and flowering trees, shrubbery, and flowerbeds. My friend liked to tinker in the woodworking shop, where he fashioned bookcases and chairs with more tools than he'd ever had in his old garage. He boasted that there were four swimming pools, an eighteen-hole and a nine-hole golf course, a library, and art studios. As I was leaving, he handed me a couple of tomatoes he'd grown in his own garden along the Pomperaug River. It was as close to paradise as he'd come, he said.

As I was driving away, I noticed what looked like an eighteenth-century center-chimney farmhouse overlooking a pond. I assumed it was a repro-duction, but its white clapboarded elegance stood in such contrast to nearby buildings that I decided to take a closer look. The foundation and moldings told me it was the real deal. An older woman inside said it was called the Meeting House, used as offices and for functions. Peeking in the rooms, I glimpsed big fireplaces and fine wood paneling. "It was built in 1740 and was once the home of Victor Borge," she said proudly. "You know, the famous pianist." Later I would find out that it was once also known as "Nuttinghame," the home of Wallace Nutting from 1906 to 1912. Though largely vanished from the popular consciousness, he remains principally responsible for our perception of old-time New England as depicted in tour-ist brochures, *Yankee Magazine*, and our own imaginations.

Connecticut's clusters of eighteenth-century homes are often protected within historic districts. Our country roads and old town centers are peppered with antique shops. But respect and even commercial zeal for these vestiges of bygone days was not always a staple of life. As the twentieth century dawned, with its whirlwind of inventions like electric lights, automobiles, movies, and radios, remnants of our deep past seemed to many people an expendable luxury, even a positive hindrance to modernization. That one hundred years later the value of antiques and historic architecture has penetrated beyond elite circles to much of society is largely Nutting's legacy.

Wallace Nutting was a Congregational minister who, having retired at the age of forty-three due to frail health, avidly pursued his hobby of photography as a therapy. He soon parlayed his nostalgic pictures into a business that would eventually include writing, antique collecting, museum operations, and reproduction-furniture making. From the 1910s until his death in 1941, Nutting was an impresario of the colonial who, like Martha Stewart today, was not only a doyen of good taste, but also a promoter of personal aesthetic judgments to the advantage of interrelated businesses that harnessed a growing consumer culture.

Nutting got his full commercial start over a century ago in a barn beside his home that he converted into a photography studio where he worked for six years and employed about twenty people. The Connecticut countryside was probably the perfect muse because, as he would later write, "were we to sum up the most distinctive and most attractive features of Connecticut, we should say that for quaintness the state is unsurpassed."

Nutting's softly focused platinum prints, often hand tinted by the young female colorists he began hiring while at Nutinghame, illustrate rural farmsteads with pasturing sheep or cows, and colonial streetscapes with ancient clapboard houses and overhanging elms. Many featured carefully staged interiors, usually with women working at spinning wheels or engaged in other hearth and home tasks. Among those inside views is an image of Nuttinghame's parlor, with its ladder-back and Windsor chairs, braided rugs, candlesticks on the mantel, and a roaring fire in the hearth beside which a woman in Williamsburg-style colonial garb holds a teacup.

The most evocative photographs are landscapes of lonely country lanes flanked by stone walls, streams reflecting sky and trees, orchards in bloom, waterfalls, stands of white birches, and isolated country houses set at the edge of fields and forests. "It is hard to find anywhere," Nutting effused in the mid-1920s, "more beautiful drives than those we see from Hartford through Waterbury and Danbury to Norwalk; from Hartford northwest through Winsted to the Berkshires; from Hartford easterly past Bolton Notch to Willimantic and thence to Norwich and New London." The places Nutting found still exist along those routes, but typically through a narrowly focused lens, for contemporary distractions are most always juxtaposed nearby.

Nutting's landscapes are the Connecticut we imagine existed a few generations ago, pockets of which we hope still endure. Yet they are sanitized places, lacking dust or mud on rural roads, absent rainy days, and without junked farm equipment around barns—just an eternal springtime of hope. Certainly there are no modern intrusions. In fact Nutting was known to retouch prints by eliminating utility poles and wires, making it look as if the countryside were posing for the camera.

For a rising middle class overwhelmed by rapid industrialization, such images were the perfect antidote to their anxieties. The photographs sold by the hundreds of thousands for about two dollars apiece. In addition to providing soothing images to comfort those weary of life's ever-quickening pace, Nutting's photographs were also a way for people of modest means to own a piece of art for significantly less than the cost of an oil painting.

Though once scorned as romantic kitsch, Nutting prints can be found today in antique shops, and they often hang at inns, restaurants, and other businesses seeking to evoke an old-time feel. A quick immersion into Nutting's world can be had in most libraries by opening a copy of *Connecticut Beautiful,* one of a series of rambling books he wrote about the states. Through these pages a person can gaze at a dirt lane in Middletown, a hillside homestead in Coventry, sheep on a Middlebury roadside, a lily pad pool in Torrington, and blossoming trees in Hartford. They are places forever preserved in the photographer's careful composition, places we still long to discover. "A field road," depicted as a grassy Windham County lane with a stone wall, split-rail fence, and apple tree in bloom, "will lead the way to all sorts of joys, if only we allow the imagination to build and inhabit its structures," he wrote with trademark dreamy yearning. With his books, images, and furniture, Nutting commodified and enabled us to possess that mythical past.

Wethersfield's Webb House provides an opportunity to literally step inside Nutting's world. Located in the heart of Connecticut's largest historic district and in proximity to many other eighteenth-century buildings, the grand old structure is like a time machine.

Built in 1752, the white gambrel-roof house with twelve-by-twelve divided-light windows was one of five properties that Nutting purchased and then converted into a series of museums he styled a "chain of colonial picture houses." With the Webb House facing possible demolition or conversion into a library, Nutting's 1916 purchase can be credited with saving the place where Washington and Rochambeau spent several days in 1781 plotting the final strategy of the Revolutionary War. Along with the other museums, the Webb House enabled Nutting to tap into rising middle-class automobile tourism and provide a venue for the sale of his products.

In typical fashion, Nutting made changes to the house, not just to remove modern alterations but also to suit his notion of what a colonial residence should look like. He removed original woodwork and substituted fancier material from a nearby house that had been torn down. He also commercialized the structure, painting the walls with murals that depicted idealized scenes of the war council held at the house and of the siege of Yorktown. The images convey how Nutting thought events *should* have appeared, but they are at best fanciful. Now restored in order to illustrate not just the house's origins, but its full history, the one in the southeast parlor depicts British General Cornwallis presenting his sword to Washington, an event that never happened. In the northeast parlor is a glorified colonial scene, also more daydream reverie than reality. I've looked out the small panes of wavy, bubbled glass and wondered if Nutting ever peered out the same window, imagining the scene painted on the wall.

Nutting exalted quaintness over authenticity. The result is a house that may reveal more about our romantic notions of the past than actual history. In a world where Disneyesque depictions of our heritage are multiplying, the house as he reconstructed it may offer more valuable lessons than it would if it had been precisely restored.

Unlike his photography, furniture making, and books, Nutting's house museums, already financially shaky, were dealt a fatal blow by diminished tourism during World War I. Fortunately for Connecticut, the National Society of the Colonial Dames subsequently preserved the Webb House as a museum.

In addition to reading his books and visiting the Webb House, I've steeped myself in Nutting's world with a visit to Hartford's Wadsworth Atheneum. The financial difficulties that led the nation's premier connoisseur of antiquities to close his colonial houses, combined with the generosity of J. P. Morgan Jr., brought Nutting's collection of seventeenth- and eighteenth-century furniture to the capital city. No longer needing the originals as models for his factory reproductions, the donation gave Nutting invaluable credibility and, according to the Atheneum website, made Hartford "home to the largest and most comprehensive assembly of Pilgrim-century furniture in the United States." It's intriguing to wander past the blanket chests, tables, spinning wheels, cupboards, cradles and other items displayed antiseptically in the museum, where they feel more like works of art than household items.

Nutting "mixed morals, aesthetics, and economics in his views of the New England landscape," according to scholar Thomas Andrew Denenberg. His photographs are often dismissed for sentimentalizing a bygone era, and his house-restoration techniques are an anathema in these times when we prize originality and accuracy. Evangelist of a mythic yesteryear, he enticed people to explore the landscape and imagine the past.

Without Nutting's entrepreneurial antiquarianism generating public interest in the first half of the twentieth century, it's likely we would have a lot less of our colonial heritage today. No doubt he would have decried the ironically named Heritage Village and the fate of his beloved Nuttinghame. Still, I wonder what photographic magic he might work in its art studio, or what creative furniture reproductions he might craft in its workshop.

A Fresh Way of Looking
The Hudson River School

I'm not one to look for reasons to spend a lot of time indoors, nor to encourage others to do so, especially where interiors have few windows. But I make an exception for art museums whose collections can change the way we see our surroundings, improving the acuity of our vision more readily than the most skilled optician. Connecticut is blessed with a remarkable number of fine art museums, but when I need a visual tune-up I usually head to the two closest to my Collinsville home—Hartford's Wadsworth Atheneum, the nation's oldest public art museum, and the New Britain Museum of American Art, the first in the country devoted to American works.

My attraction is not merely a matter of proximity, but because I'm drawn to their extraordinary collections of nineteenth-century Hudson River School paintings bursting with grandeur, optimism, color, and drama that open my eyes so wide that when I walk outside every object seems as if it's just been coated with a fresh layer of paint. You might think that after viewing the sheer cliffs and jagged snowy peaks in Albert Bierstadt's *In Yosemite Valley* or the untrammeled purity of the splashing cascade captured by Thomas Cole's *Katterskill Falls*, the world outside the museum might seem diminished. In fact, it is enhanced by a reinvigorated sense of color, detail, space, and light.

On a recent visit to the Atheneum I was struck by how Connecticut, a small state with modest topographical features, has exerted a great deal of influence on the way in which the nation views its landscape. The most cursory peek at the paintings hanging in the quiet, well-lit galleries leaves no doubt. The works of Connecticut natives Frederic Church of Hartford, John Trumbull of Lebanon, George Henry Durrie of New Haven, John F. Kensett of Cheshire, and John Denison Crocker, who was born in Salem but lived most of his life in Norwich, are well represented. But just as significant to Connecticut's artistic legacy as the paintings is the enlightened support of these and many other painters by Connecticut art patrons Daniel Wadsworth and Elizabeth Jarvis Colt. By commissioning and collecting the works of Cole, Bierstadt, and their colleagues, they encouraged and sustained the artists, enabling the painters' visions to fully flower.

The result is a legacy that not only helps us understand our past, but also infuses all who view the works with a visceral sense of the American landscape's splendor, fostering a deep-rooted attachment to the country. I cannot, for example, stand in the presence of Church's *Rapids of the Susquehanna*, with its roiling sediment-laden waters, threatening charcoal clouds, and tiny figure in the foreground, without awe and a lump in my throat sweeping me up in a kind of topographical patriotism.

Works in the collection range from Cole's *View of Monte Video*, a dramatic depiction of Wadsworth's home atop Talcott Mountain in Avon, where hilly forest and cultivated fields lie beneath a cumulous-dominated sky, to the tranquility of two people strolling on a seaside beach in Kensett's *Coast Scene with Figures*. Sometimes the image is allegorical, as in Church's divine-light-suffused depiction of Hartford's founding in *Hooker and Company Journeying through the Wilderness from Plymouth to Hartford, in 1636*. Other scenes are more domestic, such as Crocker's *Home in the Wilderness*, which depicts a family beside their streamside log cabin. Natural features are pristine and massive. Humans are small by comparison, their activities seemingly in harmony with and dwarfed by nature.

The museum is rife with magnificent paintings and intriguing information about the artists and their methods. But anyone who walks out the door and down the steps of the turreted gothic fortress on Main Street having only a better familiarity with the works and techniques of these great artists, and their role in reflecting and shaping the nation's sense of itself, will not fully grasp their teaching. These paintings do not just illustrate scenery, they offer us a portal of perception, a means of looking at the world. It is not merely a matter of unflattering comparisons between today's tamed and sometimes abused landscapes, and images of untrammeled nature on canvass. Rather, the paintings tutor us to simultaneously see sweeping horizons and a rich collection of carefully observed details. To an amateur art lover and inveterate landscape observer like me, this mode of seeing seemed like the greatest lesson these works have to offer, and it suggests that many of these artists were driven not just by a love of craft, but by genuine affection for the countryside itself.

Perhaps Frederic Church, America's most popular painter by the mid-nineteenth century, best illustrates an artist's dedicated love of landscape. I've had the opportunity twice to directly experience his passion by visiting Olana, his hilltop home overlooking the Hudson River in Hudson, New York. Here Church used his painter's eye to craft both a river and a mountain view by means of architecture and landscaping. It was his largest work, requiring the last thirty years of his life, and was, like Thomas Jefferson's Monticello, completed only at his death. Olana is Church's ultimate statement about the relationship of a person to the countryside, an interaction too large to be enclosed by any frame or hung on a museum wall.

So passionate was he about landscapes, Church found that it was not enough to paint them, he had to create one. Beginning in the 1860s, he transformed an agricultural hillside into a large ornamental garden. On 250 acres he planted thousands of trees, created meadows, and dug a lake whose contours reflected those of the river far below. Over five miles of carriage roads, artfully composed to provide openings for pastoral views over fields and quiet bodies of water, wind lazily through the property. Some of the spaces are intimate, like outdoor rooms, and others have panoramic vistas of the mountains across the Hudson. His roads pass through sunlit hardwood forests and plunge into near twilight beneath thick stands of hemlock.

Near the top of the hill, Church built a startling mansion of brownstone and brick that looks like a Middle Eastern castle replete with towers and turrets, recessed spaces and projections, shifting rooflines, ogee arches, decorative tiles, and painted bricks. He designed the interior rooms down to the color and furniture. It is a fancy and fussy but magical house that invited me in and transported me to the lost world of a genius' imagination.

As his popularity waned with changes in artistic fashion and arthritis made it increasingly difficult for him to paint, he threw himself even more into the creation of Olana. "I can," he said in the mid-1880s, "make more and better landscapes this way than by tampering with canvas and paint in the studio." But even as he was creating a landscape around him, he continued sketching and painting the house, trees, meadows, and views in all seasons. It was a remarkable synergy of art depicting life while life simultaneously imitated art.

Visiting Olana enabled me not only to see the Church landscapes that hang inside, but also to briefly inhabit a landscape he created. I arrived on a warm autumn day brimming with the clear and pure light emanating from many of the master's canvasses. The pond sparkled with wind-driven fish-scale riffles. Beyond was a forested prospect interrupted only occasionally by a smokestack or building. To the west rose the rugged sawtooth Catskills, and far below, the broad, winding Hudson threaded through steep hills like a silver ribbon. The view was mesmerizing, and I sat transfixed for over an hour, steeping in hillsides mottled with fall color and dark evergreens as a cluster of ladybugs crawled up the stone wall beside me. The sky seemed as large as any Church ever portrayed, and I felt Lilliputian. Momentarily, it seemed as if I had stepped inside one of the great man's paintings.

With Hudson River School works commanding princely sums today and exhibitions raking in big numbers at the box office, it is hard to believe that by his death in 1900 Church was relatively obscure. In the early 1960s Olana was faced with demolition. But by the middle of that decade, fresh scholarship renewed interest in Church, and dedicated citizens joined with New York State to save the mansion.

Of course, more than academic reassessment and architectural preservation were at work. The time had come when Americans again needed Church's vision. In a catalog created for a posthumous 1900 exhibition, Charles Dudley Warner, once editor of the *Hartford Courant*, observed that Church's greatest achievement was inspiring average citizens with "an enthusiasm for landscape art . . . as an expression of the majesty and beauty of the divine manifestation of nature." After a century of exploitation and despoliation, Church reminded people of a once boundless, expansive, and optimistic view of nature.

It seems no coincidence that his revival came only a few years after publication of Rachel Carson's *Silent Spring* detailed the horrors of unbridled pesticide use and kicked off the environmental movement. As ecological awareness gained ground, Church's reputation grew. It grew not just out of nostalgia, but through a wellspring of inspiration about what our landscape was and could be. Today we need Church and his Hudson River School colleagues as much as ever, both for what they invite us to see and how they motivate us to act.

In a State of Plein Air
Artists Outdoors

I'd traveled in the echoing twilight of the Merritt Parkway tunnel hundreds of times before really seeing West Rock. Certainly the massive wall of greenery and sharp, burnt-orange cliffs through which the road passes were visible, but the great traprock barrier seemed more obstacle than object, a mental blur obscured by the novelty of suddenly having plunged into the narrow passage. It wasn't until discovering Frederick Church's 1849 painting *West Rock, New Haven* in the New Britain Museum of American Art that the rugged beauty of the ridge truly struck me.

I was captivated by the notion that a master had painted an ordinary Connecticut scene. But even more captivating was the mountain's dramatic appearance in sunlight with puffy clouds and tiny figures haying in the foreground, which lent it a majesty I'd never imagined. Sure, the bucolic view Church captured was vastly different from the sea of houses and shopping plazas now arrayed below the escarpment, but nevertheless every trip afterward was an encounter with The Rock. The mountain had been transformed from backdrop to vivid reality.

If large features like West Rock can be passed in a trance, it is small wonder that we hardly notice the hills, streams, villages, and cities we view each day on our way to work or while running errands. But a landscape that seems dull and familiar to most has intrigued painters for two centuries.

Perhaps Connecticut reached its zenith as a place of interest to painters several decades after Church captured West Rock, when impressionist artists flocked to the state for what a tourist brochure called "its beauty and charm." Museums in Connecticut and around the nation boast images of Wallingford, Bridgeport, Simsbury, Salisbury, Farmington, Hartford, Willimantic, Old Lyme, Ridgefield, East Hartford, Greenwich, and Warren

painted by impressionist geniuses such as Childe Hassam, John F. Kensett, Willard Metcalf, John H. Twachtman, Charles Ebert, and Henry Ward Ranger. And the numerous places they illustrated remain less than an hour's drive from galleries where their works are hanging, like Hartford's Wadsworth Atheneum, Old Lyme's Florence Griswold Museum, the Bush-Holley House in Cos Cob, and the Bruce Museum in Greenwich. They were largely painted early in the twentieth century, when nationally renowned art colonies sprang to life here. These paintings don't merely record the details of a place; they convey its mood and sentiment. Studying them refreshes interest in the familiar, teaching us to see common objects anew. "An impressionist aesthetic," noted Bard art history professor Julia Rosenbaum, "functioned as a unique means to register the value of the land and the belief in the connection between soil and character."

Perhaps there are no better places to stretch our way of seeing than the five "viewpoint'" stations established during 2002 in Burlington, Westport, Hadlyme, Willimantic, and Kent under the aegis of the state's Commission on the Arts and the Department of Environmental Protection. At these spots, signboard reproductions of paintings from early in the twentieth century can be seen near the locations depicted. As points along Connecticut's Impressionist Art Trail, these sites enable us to look through our own eyes and the artist's simultaneously.

More than once while waiting to board the boat, I've gazed from the east end of the Chester-Hadlyme ferry landing across the broad Connecticut River dotted with vessels to a hilly horizon while glancing at the signboard reproduction of William Chadwick's *Connecticut River*. It renders a similar scene, captured in autumn, in a brilliant shadowless sunlight that highlights shapes and color in the actual view that I otherwise might not have noticed.

Sherwood Island State Park's viewpoint is more than just pretty scenery. In the formal beach attire of a century past, but otherwise enjoying the shore much as people do today, a mother and two daughters in Edward H. Potthast's *Ocean Breezes* stand on sundrenched sand with dark blue water and a dazzling sky behind them. The painting does not reveal every detail, instead focusing on light and the texture of objects. But for the antique clothing, his painting is not unlike what I've often seen while walking along the sand. The startling sight of long dresses and high-topped shoes, like farmers haying in the foreground of Church's *West Rock*, reminds me that these places exist in time as well as space, providing a sense of both continuity and change.

Mill towns are as essential to Connecticut's identity as hills and shore, and J. Alden Weir's *Factory Village*, located at the Windham Mills, illustrates the typical manufacturing town of Willimantic. Though remarkably like the view encountered today, with its stone mill buildings, smokestack, and church spires, the painting's colors and slight alteration in perspective always keeps me glancing from signboard to scene, both of which seem to reveal something new with each turn of the head. Of course, after having been to Weir's Branchville farm, I was startled by an image so different from the pastoral sights he painted there.

Although it's an image of another place, Willard Metcalf's *November Mosaic* is evocative of the meadow, stream, and hillside visible from the signboard at the edge of the parking lot at Kent Falls State Park. The bronzed palette offset by pockets of evergreens and a few worn buildings is just what I've encountered on late fall days in New England's top foliage town. I'm especially drawn to his dreamy depiction of trees growing at the edge of the woods. Metcalf's trees and the work of other impressionists also greatly influenced Wallace Nutting's old-timey photographs in the first half of the twentieth century. They in turn set the tone for our archetypal images of the rural Yankee world. "Nutting delivered a product that performed the same cultural work as Metcalf's painting, but at a price the expanding middle class could afford," wrote scholar Thomas Andrew Denenberg.

Connecticut's landscape continues to engage painters, and it likely always will. Even in the most frequently pictured places, there is no lack of subjects or enticement. As Frank Dumond, director in the early twentieth century of the prestigious Lyme Summer School of Art, observed: "If artists continue to go there for 2,000 years, they will find something new to paint, and each one who comes finds something that has been overlooked by everybody else." Indeed, "painters make us see, feel, and value the beauty of Connecticut," wrote professor and politician Odell Shepherd, "and the inexhaustible variety of her moods, colors, contours, and nuances."

The passage of time has proved both Dumond and Shepherd right, and the plein air tradition of painting outside in all weather that the impressionists popularized is thriving. On a warm, hazy morning last summer I ran into a group of artists at their easels a couple blocks from my house. Perched above a bulge in the Farmington River at the Collinsville mill pond, each painted a remarkably different scene, though they were set up within a raised voice of each other. Walter Kendra, Carolyn Newell, Estrid Ekland, and the others had met through a common teacher at the Lyme Academy College of Fine Arts and were getting together on Thursdays to paint at sites across the state. Outdoor work required them to move briskly, I was told, capturing the essence of what is at hand and leaving little time to idealize a subject. Color is integral to form, which doesn't require precise images.

Brisk work was especially required when painters Rob Meyers and Sara Gagan spent a couple of frigid days daubing at their canvasses in front of my house in January 2011, the snowiest and one of the coldest months on record. Bundled in coats and wearing fingerless gloves, they captured on canvas both clapboard and brick buildings and bare tree branches starkly outlined by the snow. Meyers praised the winter light for its subtle colors, long shadows, and bright horizons.

While bicycling along the Farmington River Trail several years ago, I stopped at the viewpoint signboard of Dawson Dawson-Watson's *Early Morning on the Farmington*. Its sleepy portrayal of trees along the river reminded me of many misty summer mornings hereabouts. Pausing momentarily, I pedaled home in gathering dusk and passed a brightly lit house hugging the road near the old Collinsville railroad bridge. Through the windows I saw paintings of river scenes covering the walls. I knocked and was greeted by Judith Reeve, who was working at her easel. She lived there, she said, to be closer to her favorite subject, the Farmington River, and she successfully captured its moods from a spring freshet's hurried urgency to the brooding winter flows beneath clouds suggesting snow. Though I'd spent nearly twenty years living a block from the water, I saw it differently in the scenes she'd painted.

The power of a painting to renew my perception of well-known objects most struck me when I was gifted a watercolor depicting my home of over two decades. Painted by the late Wick Knaus, who spent many years in San Francisco but was one of Collinsville's Factory Five artists in the 1960s, it's a winter scene whose soft colors suggest the bearhugging comfort of the place. Tree trunks frame the house's sides while branches emphasize clapboards and rooflines. The painting uncannily captured my sense of home, yet in a way I'd never noticed.

Images painted of my own neighborhood seemed like proof that art is not just a pretty picture, but a way of seeing what's hidden in plain sight. Through artists' brushstrokes, the most ordinary objects can resonate with wonder, and scenes we encounter daily can be transformed into images with uncommon power to stir our own imaginations. It's no surprise that painters at their easels in Collinsville slow traffic and cause pedestrians to stop and stare. What in the world, the passersby wonder, could be worthy of art? That we find it hard to believe the everyday streets of our daily existence can inspire artists only makes their presence more valuable.

Where the Landscape Is Art
Weir Farm

My reaction years ago when I first set eyes on Weir Farm was to wonder how a piece of ground so bony, uneven, and seemingly inhospitable to agriculture could be called a farm. When I later learned that the 238 acres were producing alfalfa, hay, and enough apples to produce several barrels of cider annually at the turn of the twentieth century, it seemed sufficient to establish the place's historic agrarian credentials, but not enough for anyone to earn a living producing food and fiber. Still, I was struck by the timeless, elemental landscape that conveyed the hardscrabble gentility of a century past. It wasn't just uneven grassy fields, a twisting road, and stone walls, but the house, barn, and other outbuildings that suggested defiance of age and harsh weather.

Perhaps I was sensitized by the contrast with a hodgepodge of garish commercial structures I'd seen while driving along U.S. Route 7 just down the hill, or the large and sometimes ostentatious new houses that had been bulldozed into the woods nearby. My official state road map indicated that I was in the Branchville part of Ridgefield, but since it lacked a post office and a definable village center, I wouldn't have known where I was if I hadn't accidentally pulled off Route 7 into the small railroad station that bears its name.

Of course, in 1882, when J. Alden Weir agreed to trade a stillife painting he had just bought at a New York gallery for $650 in exchange for the farm's original 153 acres, he hadn't heard of Branchville either. Even then, with its rich patchwork of fields and woods, stone walls and antique buildings perched on gently undulating ground, the property was a glorious and radiant landscape of quintessential, rustic Connecticut domesticity. On inspection, its subtle beauty caught Weir's painterly eye, and for another token ten dollars at closing, he found the site that would be his principal subject and muse until his death in 1919. Ever since, the farm's principal crop has been works of art.

Now a part of the National Park System, Weir Farm National Historic Site has brought a measure of worldwide renown to obscure Branchville, and it has enabled new generations of painters to draw inspiration from the woods, fields, and buildings that Weir so loved. It's Connecticut's sole National Park System unit where I could get a brochure, enter a visitors' center, and receive a tour by a uniformed ranger wearing the traditional Smokey Bear–style campaign hat.

Unlike the traditional park, however, Weir Farm is not some remote and majestic landscape, but a long-used plot of ground in the well-settled suburbia of Fairfield County. In contrast to Yellowstone, which is the nation's first national park and itself the size of Connecticut, Weir Farm encompasses only about sixty acres, part in Wilton and part in Ridgefield. Designated in 1990 after well over a century of nationwide park development, it made the state nearly the last to gain such recognition. But late recognition, diminutive size, and nearby location are not reasons for feeling discouraged or inferior. They are causes for celebration, because Weir Farm so perfectly captures the essence of Connecticut's rapidly disappearing rural landscape and remains the only park devoted to an American painter.

An old clapboard house once the home of Weir's daughter has been transformed into the visitors' center, where helpful park service staff answered my questions and flicked on a video explaining how the farm's allure transformed Weir from a well-trained and skilled portraitist to a nationally recognized figure and a landscape artist for the ages. According to litterature I received, "Weir painted scenes of his family and nature in soft blues, greens and silvery grays that evoked a feeling of security and permanence." That image of Connecticut's countryside remains a dominant perception of the state's bucolic precincts regardless of one's familiarity with Weir's work, or whether such a landscape still exists outside the four corners of the artist's canvases.

In subdued colors and flickering brushstrokes, Weir depicted sloping summer pastures with bare ledges, stone walls, and a few large trees. He painted hardwoods under a quilt of snow, white oaks still clinging to a few bronzed leaves at autumn's end, along with stark, bare birches. He captured a tawny open field through overhanging green foliage, recorded simple domestic scenes of drying laundry outside his house, and painted barnyards with chickens or horses. Unlike Hudson River School artists, Weir and his fellow impressionists sought not grandeur, but an intimate view of the landscape that would demonstrate the beauty in everyday life. Rather than a portrait of a place, they sought to evoke a moment and mood by means of light and color.

I've toured the studios and other buildings at the site, but what keeps me coming back is a desire to wander the grounds, where at times I feel as if I'm stepping into a painting. Along with The Nature Conservancy's adjacent preserve, there are about 170 acres where, as Weir observed, "one cannot help but feel that wonderful something that the landscape in nature suggests, somewhat like the soul of a human being."

On summer days I've walked down a gentle slope through the meadow's mown path to the pond where Weir went to paint and fish. The tall grasses are always vibrant with flowers—daisies, blackeyed Susan, Queen Anne's lace, goldenrod, and others, depending on the month. Surrounded by woods, the trail around the pond can be muddy, and I've enjoyed breathing deeply the scent of muck and sunbaked vegetation. From the grassy earthen dam at the far end, I've sat watching cloud reflections sweep over the water, listening as the banjo twang of frogs occasionally echoed.

In autumn, when the hills are pied with color like impressionist brushstrokes, I've usually headed in the opposite direction from the pond, past the overgrown pastures along Pelham Lane, which are rapidly succumbing to red cedar and black birch. West of the visitors' center, the trail winds through a craggy woodland of tall oak, beech, hickory, hemlock, and red maple where sassafras, autumn-blooming witch hazel, moosewood, and stunted chestnut sprouts grow in the understory. The paths follow and cross tumbled stone walls, reminders of long-gone agriculture. Uneven ledges lean out of the ground at every angle, sometimes affording views of wetlands thick with tall cinnamon fern that has been partially bronzed by frost. Huge glacial boulders lie beneath the trees like sleeping elephants, and impenetrable thickets of laurel cling tenaciously to rocky ground. Once I heard a loud hammering, and just as it stopped a pileated woodpecker darted away in a blur of black, white, and red. In October, it's not uncommon to spot kettling hawks as they follow a migration path along the edge of Long Island Sound.

Weir was not alone in drawing inspiration here. Other great artists came to spend time with him and paint. Childe Hassam depicted open meadows traversed by stone walls along the narrow street in *Road to the Land of Nod*, and Albert Pinkham Ryder created an almost mystical, dusky rendition of fruit trees called *Weir's Orchard*. I've seen both at the Wadsworth Atheneum. One summer morning after viewing them I hurried to the car and drove over an hour to the spots where they were painted to see if I could capture with my eyes the same light and color. While vegetation has closed the once open countryside, I nevertheless felt a connection between canvas and place that was exhilarating. John Twachtman was fascinated by this gently rolling landscape of rough pasture, and John Singer Sargent, William Glackens, and Theodore Robinson were among the others who found their muse at the farm. Over 250 artworks have been created here at more than sixty sites.

The capacity of this place to inspire did not end with Weir's death in 1919. His daughter Dorothy continued to paint the farm. She married sculptor Mahroni Young in 1931. Young, known for small bronzes of muscular athletes and laborers, built a spacious studio with a ceiling rising over two stories and banks of tall windows facing north, where the light is most even. Here he created the twelve-foot-tall statue of his grandfather, Brigham Young, that now stands at Emigration Canyon outside Salt Lake City. His marble likeness of the Mormon leader graces the U.S. capitol. In 1957, when Mahroni Young died, artists Sperry and Dorothy Andrews purchased the farm and continued to paint the landscape as it increasingly transformed from pasture to woods. Almost every time I visit the site I see contemporary artists at their easels, continuing the plein air tradition on what to them is sacred ground.

Weir Farm is beautiful, not just for its scenic qualities or its tradition of fostering artistry, but also for the grassroots way in which it was preserved. No great revelation of park service staff or infusion of cash from Washington secured this humble farm for posterity. It was the hard work of neighbors and nearby citizens concerned with protecting Weir's legacy and stemming encroaching development that resulted in the place being rescued.

As early as 1963, advocates of the farm alerted the press and enlisted experts in historic preservation, art history, and open-space conservation. They continued the arduous tasks of increasing public awareness, raising funds, and working political connections into the next decade. In the 1980s, they formed the Weir Farm Trust to organize and focus efforts to protect the property. The nonprofit Trust for Public Land aquired some of Weir's original land and then sold it to the state. The National Park Service conducted a study to assess the farm's eligibilty for park status. An act of Congress established it as a park in 1990, and, in a reversal of the usual circumstances, the state of Connecticut donated its land to the federal government when the park service took possession of the site in 1992. As a young legislative staffer, I had a tiny role in preserving the farm by helping shepherd the transfer bill through the state's general assembly.

This extraordinary effort by ordinary citizens has allowed the artistic traditions of Weir Farm to flourish. Daytripping painters are not uncommon, and opportunities at the farm range from art classes for children to an artist-in-residence program that offers lodging and studio space. A pamphlet with directions and prints of paintings allows even the rankest art amateur to literally stand in the footsteps of geniuses—in the orchard, by the pond, along Nod Hill Road, and at the edge of fields—and compare today's view with depictions by Weir, Ryder, and Hassam.

At Weir Farm, art and landscape have merged. The depictions of man and the works of nature support and amplify each other. Weir taught us to appreciate the beauty all around us, the prospect out the back door and down the street. He enabled us to value the familiar and the near at hand. In doing so he illustrated what is most intriguing and emblematic about Connecticut's landscape: its marriage of nature and culture.

Poetic Space
James Merrill's Apartment

It seems as if he must have stepped out for just a moment, maybe to run an errand down the street. Pulitzer Prize–winning poet James Merrill died in 1995, but his apartment in the thickly settled seaside Borough of Stonington is alive with his presence. Its informal domesticity makes a visitor feel like a neighbor stopping by unannounced for a quick hello and perhaps the offer of a drink.

Born in 1926 in New York City, the son of a founding partner of the Merrill Lynch investment firm, Merrill grew up in privilege, served in the U.S. Army during World War II, and graduated from Amherst College in 1945. With his great wealth he was widely traveled and could have lived anywhere in the world. At various times he had homes in New York, Greece, and Key West, but for over forty years he also lived very modestly in Stonington with his partner, the painter David Jackson. It was the place he came back to most often as he grew older.

Surrounded on three sides by water, Stonington Borough is about a third of a square mile of land projecting into Little Narragansett Bay in the state's far eastern reaches. The village is dominated by eighteenth- and nineteenth-century wooden buildings weathered with years of salt air and standing shoulder to shoulder on narrow streets. Despite its small size, the compact architecture yields a measure of urbanity. Becoming increasingly gentrified in recent decades, there is still a goodly mix of old Yankees, fashionable summer people, and Portuguese families who for many years have led Connecticut's last offshore fishing fleet, which is docked in the harbor. In his 1971 book, *In the Village*, resident and author Anthony Bailey found a unique place where "sympathies of mind and temperament are more important than years and careers." Perhaps that is what attracted Merrill.

The poet's apartment is on the third floor of a large nineteenth-century wooden structure at the corner of Union and Water Streets in the heart of the borough's cluster of old houses and small shops. It's toward the end of the commercial area now dominated by restaurants and boutiques. The first floor is fitted with plate-glass storefronts, including a barbershop and two upscale women's clothing stores. It's a bulky but handsome building sided with clapboards and scalloped shingles. At the corner above street level is a round tower.

Merrill's affection for Water Street is evinced in his 1962 book, which adopts the street name as its title. The welcoming, sweet hominess of the apartment is reflected in the final lines of "Tenancy," the last poem in the volume where he described inviting visitors to sit and the hope that they would feel at home in the place where he lived.

I entered the building amidships through a handsome doorway with a transom window and a divided pediment over the entry. A discreet and likely seldom-noticed plaque beside it recognizes the poet's occupancy. Merrill was a world-renowned master craftsman whose work transformed ordinary words into deep phrases of shimmering elegance. He won practically every major American literary honor, including multiple National Book Awards. Though the space where he lived and wrote some of his finest work is available to the public, it remains virtually unknown, a place hidden in plain sight.

Worn wooden steps creaked as I climbed, announcing my presence without the need of a knock, so I wasn't surprised when Lynn Callahan, chair of the James Merrill House Committee, which cares for the place, and poet Michael Snediker, a former writer in residence, were ready for me as I reached the apartment's open door. On his passing, Merrill unexpectedly donated the property to the nonprofit Stonington Village Improvement Association, which has preserved the apartment and sponsored scholars and poets in residence under the auspices of the house committee.

"Ninety-five percent of what is here was here when Jimmy died, but not everything that *was* here remains because of specific bequests on his death," Callahan told me as she gestured into the rooms. Works of art, books, and records were among the items that left the apartment when the poet gifted them to relatives, friends, and museums. Recently, inheritors of the library made plans for returning books and records to the apartment.

After a brief introduction in which Callahan described herself as the "chief administrative clerk, organizer, house cleaner, and laundress," she and Snediker left me to roam the place like an old friend. No velvet ropes, no descriptive signs. Their use of the familiar name "Jimmy" seemed to further erase any distance between Merrill's space and me.

The apartment is neither large nor grand though it sometimes seems so because it's filled with light and decorated with wit and color and objects that grab for attention. I was most drawn to the dining room with its bay window and coral walls that Merrill described as "now watermelon, now sunburn." But the real treat for the eyes is the white, pressed-tin ceiling dome detailed with gold wreaths and fleur-de-lis from which hangs a floral globe chandelier. Below is a round wooden table beneath which the hardwood floor has a circle of lighter wood mimicking the table's shape, like a reverse shadow. It's a kind of architectural rhyme, Snediker observed.

The living room wallpaper features bats, clouds, and oriental fans. It was designed by a friend of Merrill's to match motifs in the Chinese rug. The bats, Callahan told me, symbolized rebirth and eternity. A leather Charles Eames chair entices the weary, and an oversized and elaborate free-standing guilt-framed mirror injects humor, light, and space into the room. As Merrill describes in poetic rhythms, the "immense Victorian mirror" was hauled by Jackson from "the grandest home in town" when the owner made "up her mind to renovate." At a window are colored bottles, which toss prismatic colors onto the floor and walls. In his 1978 *Mirabell: Books of Number*, Merrill tied his living room to the larger community by describing the interest of village neighbors in his eccentric wallpaper and calling the notion of "small town" life largely a state of mind.

I entered Merrill's small study through a "secret" bookcase wall. Here he is said to have worked almost every day from early morning until noon. It's a tiny, Spartan room with a simple writing table, an antique standing desk, shelves of books, and an open dictionary on a stand at a window overlooking the street.

The bedroom features a brass bed and a floor painted a startling and humorous lime green, which is duplicated in some of the bureau drawers. In the kitchen, where framed reproductions of his many awards hang, there's a cork floor, Formica counters, and dated appliances, which not only locate the room in time, but give it a timeless humanity. Merrill's dishes, cooking utensils, and cutlery are still stored in this room. Unlike the usual literary residence with its formality and reserve, there is something disarmingly whimsical and welcoming here. I could move right in and feel at home.

The fourth-floor studio, added by Merrill and Jackson during their first year of residence, is part renovated attic and part rooftop deck. The quirky interior space has a beamed ceiling that slopes at multiple angles, while the deck, like a crow's nest, looks out over Greek-revival rooftops to the harbor and its fishing fleet. There's a bright aqua couch, artwork, and a baby Steinway that Merrill liked to play. I longed to have been at the parties that Merrill and Jackson hosted from this high perch while watching the last light glisten on the water. Like the rest of the apartment, there were multiple objects collected from many times, places, and cultures that seemed to be in esoteric conversation with one another.

Fortunately, James Merrill's space remains a hothouse of creative ferment where writers are given working space, living quarters, and a stipend enabling them to produce a literary or academic work via a writer-in-residence program. Since 1995 over twenty-five writers have been able to enjoy the quiet and inspirational atmosphere of the place. Perhaps such ongoing writing is what keeps the apartment so vibrant and not merely a stale monument to greatness.

Part voyeuristic curiosity, part pilgrimage, I always feel a kind of magnetic pulse when visiting places where great writers have lived and worked. But Merrill's apartment is even more charged. It's the scene of the action. Here he conducted séances via Ouija board and recorded supernatural communications that were the basis of some of his finest work, including his dramatic book-length epic, *Changing Light at Sandover.* As Merrill reports in the book, he and Jackson contacted the spirit world using a homemade board of "heavy cardboard sheet" and a planchette described as "a blue-and-white cup from the Five & Ten." Who knows whether the spiritual presences they reached—W. H. Auden, Wallace Stevens, Gertrude Stein, Edna St. Vincent Millay, Pythagoras, Nefertiti, and many others—may occasionally return and linger?

Poet and publisher Rennie McQuilkin recalls visiting the apartment when Annie and Theodore Deppe were in residence in the late 1990s. They placed a cracked teacup, much like Merrill's planchette, in the sink one evening, and by morning they found it in an entirely different place without either of them having moved it. Cate Marvin, who stayed there in fall 2009, told the *Hartford Courant* that it was "a magical place." Perhaps "the problem of living in the James Merrill House" was best captured by Ivy Pochoda, writer in residence in 2008, who "knew I would never live somewhere so splendidly strange and so simply splendid again."

Some spaces are so imbued with the presence of a person that they become indelibly identified with that individual, impossible to imagine otherwise, though they existed beforehand and will continue to do so in the future. Merrill's home was not just the place where he lived and wrote, but an outward expression of his being and part of the very instrument through which he channeled inspiration that translated into words on a page. The space remains neither desiccated nor austere, but faithful to a writer of great erudition and mischievous humor. It's a place that yet glows with the man's complex charisma and wit, a perfect complement to the fun formalism still alive in his poetry.

Landscape and the Written Word
Nature Writers

Just outside the archetypal New England village of Hampton and at the end of a rutted driveway is an 1806 white clapboard farmhouse with a large center chimney. Fronting a pond and set in fields surrounded by forest lined with stone walls, it's a classic Connecticut scene that betrays nothing particularly remarkable. Yet the views from its divided-light windows and the scenery along the trails that wind around its wetlands and over its ledges have resonated across the nation. Known as Trail Wood for its many paths, this was the home of Edwin Way Teale—naturalist, photographer, and Pulitzer Prize–winning author.

Connecticut's landscape has had a remarkable effect on the way in which Americans today look at the natural world. From the 1940s until the mid-1970s, a cohort of four widely read state-based authors wrote about their encounters with nature, mixing homespun philosophy with keen observation. Grounded in phenomena witnessed around their homes, their views were calibrated in Connecticut's rural and suburbanizing precincts.

In addition to Teale, the state was home to Joseph Wood Krutch, Gladys Taber, and Hal Borland. Author of biographies and literary and social criticism, Krutch gained his most enduring fame as a nature writer likely inspired by his biography of Henry David Thoreau, which he wrote while living on a ledge-filled hillside in Redding. Taber was a prolific and enormously popular writer for *Ladies Home Journal*, *Family Circle*, and other publications on the subjects of nature and the tribulations and joys of rural life. In both books and articles, her Southbury home, which she dubbed Stillmeadow, was a leading character. For more than thirty-five years Borland wrote nature editorials for the *New York Times* as well as articles and books of fiction, poetry, and essays from his home along the Housatonic River in Salisbury.

Literary figures' houses have long been pilgrimage sites for readers, scholars, and tourists. But while an author's home may offer a sense of a writer's life, it rarely provides insight into their work. Nature writers, typically inspired by the places where they live, are an exception. A trip to their homes can be a journey into their words.

Calling it "the perfect habitat for a pair of naturalists," Teale and his wife, Nellie, moved to Trail Wood from increasingly crowded Long Island in 1959, when both were sixty. From then until his death in 1980, Teale wrote ten of his thirty-one books there, including the Pulitzer Prize–winning *Wandering through Winter* and *A Naturalist Buys an Old Farm*, which describes the world of Trail Wood.

Pulling into the uneven driveway at Trail Wood was like arriving at an old friend's home. All was as I expected from my readings and Teale's many photographs. Sitting on a knoll overlooking a pond, the house looked less like a museum than a lived-in place, as indeed it is. Occupied by a caretaker, the surrounding 168 acres of wetlands, forest, and ponds is now a Connecticut Audubon Society sanctuary. Visitors are welcome—Teale wrote that "the trees own the land almost as much as we do." Regardless of changes such as the maturing forest, increasing invasive plants like Japanese barberry or winged euonymus, or the prevalence of deer, the notion that a "sense of guardianship, of responsibility, surpasses that of ownership" remains evident and imbues the place with a peaceful, timeless beauty and wonder.

Teale was born, was raised, and attended college in the Midwest. After a couple of years teaching in Kansas, he went to Columbia University to pursue his education and a writing career. He served as a staff writer for *Popular Science* and published his first natural-history work, a book about insects, in 1937. Most famous for his four-volume series about traveling across America with the seasons, he became the nation's most influential nature writer, respected by critics and beloved by readers for his accessible prose, interesting photographs, and insatiable curiosity.

Walking down the stone-wall-bounded drive, where grape vines and hay-scented fern grew lushly, I stood on the high ground in front of the house surveying Firefly Meadow, the pond, and the woods beyond. Nearby trees and brush were alive with birdsong and the flitting of blue jays, cardinals, chickadees, robins, white-throated sparrows, and catbirds. Between forty-five and fifty birds, Teale wrote, nested within singing distance of his home. Heading behind the house, I entered a mown path traversing a meadow the Teales called Starfield. Queen Anne's lace, black-eyed Susan, daisy, and spotted knapweed grew among the tall grasses. Turkey vultures kettled overhead, dropping low and gliding with their fingertip-like wings outspread. Here at night Teale found that the stars "seem to draw closer, to burn with greater intensity, to increase into swarming multitudes."

Cutting to the woods, I walked among hickory, oaks, black birch, red maple, and ash beneath which ferns flourished. Teale found twenty-six species of ferns on the property, half the complement native to Connecticut. Looping around, I came to the occasionally muddy pond shore. Alders grew thickly in spots and pickerelweed stalks were abloom with purple flowers. Near Teale's tiny Thoreauvian writing cabin, a log structure with four small divided-light windows, I saw beaver-chewed tree trunks. I peered inside the cabin at the simple wooden table where an oil lamp, a couple of books, a pen, and some papers lay. It seemed the great man had just left for a walk.

Limekiln Road in Redding is a winding, narrow street that rises and falls through thick woods. Between 1932 and 1950, Joseph Wood Krutch lived in an eighteenth-century center-chimney house perched on a rising slope on nine and a half acres, according to town historian Charley Couch. A lanky, middle-aged man in a checked shirt and a ball cap out of which hung a long gray-streaked ponytail, Couch was given a copy of *The Twelve Seasons* at age twelve or thirteen by his mom. Krutch's first nature book, published in 1949, it's a month-by-month examination of the year's progress in nearby woods, fields, and swamps.

Born in 1893, Krutch grew up and went to college in Tennessee. He got his Ph.D. from Columbia and was drama critic for the *Nation* from 1924 until 1950. Articulate, with a keen intellect and strong powers of observation, he was well known in literary circles when he ventured into nature writing. *The Twelve Seasons* was praised for beginning the year with spring's reawakening and for the cerebral, contemplative nature of observations that drew wider conclusions about man's place in the world. "Those who see Nature merely as a spectacle or a picture," he reasoned, are "not among those who share her own moods." Not long after his first foray into nature writing Krutch moved to Arizona for health reasons. There he gained renown as a chronicler of the Sonoran Desert until his death in 1970.

Couch and I wandered the woods behind the house where maples and oaks grew above an understory of laurel thickets and witch hazel. Fields had contracted since Krutch's day, he noted, as we crossed through waist-high sweet fern while skirting a power line. Walking down Limekiln Road, we came to a large *Phragmites*-dominated swamp where Krutch had been entranced by the otherworldly sound of spring peepers, the first subject in his book. "I wonder," he wrote, "if there is any other phenomenon in the heavens above or in the earth beneath which so simply and so definitely announces that life is resurgent again."

Gladys Taber's Stillmeadow was only a few minutes from exit 15 off I-84, but Sanford Road's narrow pavement became hard-packed dirt as I approached the big center-chimney house, parts of which are said to date to 1690. Situated in an area growing through an awkward adolescence from rural to suburban, the immediate surroundings still retained much of the hardscrabble but quaint old-time feel Taber evoked in her writing about nearby meadows, patches of forest, and old barns. Sitting on a low knoll behind a white picket fence, the story-and-a-half clapboard house with its twelve-over-eight divided-light windows seemed emblematic of an idealized rural Connecticut.

Born in 1899, Taber spent her early life west of the Mississippi. She came east to college and eventually settled in New York, where she taught English at Columbia. Seeking a respite from harried city life, Gladys and her friend Eleanor sought a country house, finding their dream on an icy February day in 1931. By her death in 1980, Taber had authored fifty volumes, including poetry, novels, and short-story collections, but she is best remembered for writing about Stillmeadow. The house was a platform not only for nature observation, but also for tales of family life, gardening, cooking, home repair, and her beloved dogs. "A home in the country is no place for the idle," she wrote.

Not long ago, I sat facing the big stone fireplace in Stillmeadow's parlor, chatting with Taber's granddaughter, Anne Colby. The beehive oven works, Anne knew, because her grandmother once used it to cook a TV dinner for her mother when the power went out. A lithe, energetic woman with a welcoming smile, Anne's passion is land conservation. About a decade ago she was instrumental in saving the neighboring farm, where friends of Gladys worked the fields and taught her about rural life. The biggest changes over the years have been new houses and trees. "Gladys could look out the window and see more than a mile to Route 67," Anne said as we peered through wavy glazing to a view terminating in tangled woods at the lawn's edge.

Outside, Anne pointed to cracked clapboards and peeling paint as she described planned repair projects and showed me an area undergoing meadow restoration, as well as a stagnant pond slated for revival. The house and its environs were still the center of attention, keeping the people who loved them busy. Not much that was important, it seemed, had changed at Stillmeadow.

"Gladys believed nature could provide continuity and solace through the ups and downs of life," Anne told me. Indeed, Taber could domesticate and draw comfort from the drabbest and most foreboding season. "All the browns, a thousand browns, come out," she wrote of November in *The Book of Stillmeadow*. "The sky over all is soft and hazy, and there is a feeling in the air that winter is coming ... . This is a peaceful, serene land, and never quite so peaceful as now, with the crops in, wood piled high, houses snugged down, brooks running slow with leaves."

Sometimes I discover a writer's work and their home almost simultaneously and by pure serendipity. Having climbed the state's high point on Mount Frissell on a cold autumn day, I took refuge among the well-lit, carefully organized shelves of Johnnycake Books in the center of Salisbury. I began leafing through a copy of Hal Borland's *This Hill, This Valley*, and almost instantly proprietor Dan Dwyer was beside me. "Borland was a local," he said. Suddenly we were launched into a conversation about area writers and changes in the landscape. I left with directions to Borland's place on Weatogue Road. "Used to be painted red," Dwyer told me. "Think it still is. A huge new house went up nearby."

Born in 1900 and raised in Colorado, Borland became a journalist, moving to New England in 1945. By his death in 1978 he had over twenty-five books to his credit, including several novels. But the essays that grew out of life on his hundred-acre Salisbury farm have proved most enduring. Neither naturalist nor farmer, Borland styled himself a "countryman," a lover of semirural places where wildness was still accessible. Calling the profit motive a "superstition" and preaching engagement with one's surroundings, Borland urged a practical philosophy of life where people and nature were in a relationship. "Man," he wrote, "is a live and sentient part of the whole earth community."

Borland's place is a modest red structure with white trim that sits close to a road bounded on the other side by the broad, sluggish Housatonic River. There's a screened porch and a few small outbuildings. Along the street are the fields and woods he described. Corn had been cut to a stubble and beef cattle and horses pastured nearby. Standing on the riverbank, I watched cloud reflections in the dark water like Borland once did and "had, for a few moments, a sense of foreverness that now seems so uncommon. Time stood still for a little while and the day ahead seemed endless."

Beyond were hills that once inspired the author, and I imagined him gazing at Canaan Mountain, where I'd climbed to the state's most remote place. The new house Dwyer mentioned stood strangely apart. Its palatial proportions and sprawling suburban design seemed a warning Borland would have understood all too clearly.

Drawn from far away to the beauty of Connecticut's natural and built environments, this state's nature writers taught several generations of Americans how to look at and appreciate the outdoors. Their reach was broad, from the pages of the *New York Times* and *Audubon* to women's magazines. Among them they appealed to city dwellers, suburbanites, and rural folks, to intellectuals and average readers. The respect and understanding of the natural world they championed enabled people to realize what was at stake when Rachel Carson and others sounded the alarm bells about impending environmental disaster in the 1960s and 1970s. With its seasons, hills, swamps, and seashore as well as its cities and exploding development, Connecticut became the national benchmark for Americans' relationship with the outdoors.

Buy the Book
Used Bookstores

Writing and reading are reflexive, so it's no surprise that I find bookstores an irresistible attraction. Last autumn, while on the prowl for old milestones along U.S. Route 1, the old Boston Post Road, I took a sudden left near the center of Clinton and pulled into the lot of a used bookstore I'd never noticed before. In an area of old houses gone commercial, plate-glass storefronts, and strip shopping outlets, the Bookloft is a long, narrow, barn-red building across from a Friendly's restaurant. Part of the structure was once a farm stand and another portion was a corncrib. Inside was a maze of nooks and small rooms walled with books. The uneven floors creaked, and the place smelled vaguely of furniture polish and old newspapers.

Enjoying a collection heavy on history, it seemed the typical, staid Yankee bookshop until I gazed at a shelf devoted to World War II. There among volumes on the battles of Midway and D-Day was a toy military flatbed hauling a full-size can of Spam. Startled, I involuntarily chuckled. Soon I was poking around books on the American West, where a small stuffed bear grasping an American flag sat on a twig chair. In the religion section was a shelf full of angel statues and a mechanical monkey that clapped cymbals when wound. There were tiny, brightly colored cars in the automotive area, and a wooden sailing ship model among the maritime offerings. Wherever I looked, there was some small object making a subtle, playful commentary on the reading material.

"Books induce conversations," said owner Bob Stein, a neat, gray-haired man in his mid-70s who makes people smile as they wander through his shop, giving them a memorable experience that will bring them back. Book selling started as a hobby, and he now carries about fifteen thousand volumes. Eschewing online sales and computers altogether, the whole point for Bob is to meet people "because there is no better way to learn about strangers" than through the books that interest them. He works part time at a retail clothier to make ends meet, but the bookshop gives him an excuse to read and, he emphasized, keeps him alive.

Connecticut is well known for a highly educated population, and we are thick with colleges and prep schools, some of which enjoy worldwide renown. From the eighteenth-century poets known as the Connecticut Wits, to Mark Twain and Wallace Stevens, to contemporary writers like Philip Roth, the state has a rich literary legacy, so it shouldn't be astonishing that bookstores, especially used ones with unusual stock, continue to persist despite distractions from other media and the movement of retail sales to the Internet. In a world of chain stores and increasing product homogeneity, independently run used bookstores are a last bastion of shopping seren-dipity and adventure, a kind of lottery in which the right book is as hoped for and as unexpected as a winning ticket. Books might not be a necessity on par with groceries, but as attorney Norm Pattis, owner of the venerable Whitlock's Book Barn in Bethany, has said, a book can suddenly change your life. "Set Yourself Free," he posted on a wooden sign above the shop entrance soon after buying the place in 2005.

The dirt drive to Whitlock's Book Barn was bumpy and potholed, and the two spare, rectangular wooden buildings set in a meadow where horses grazed seemed more barn than book, but stepping over Whitlock's threshold was magical. The long room, the floors and walls of which lean slightly in several directions simultaneously, was crowded with shelved and stacked books that induced calm, and the place felt more like an old country library than a business hungry to move product. Elaine Sargeant and Audrey White have each worked there for over a quarter century and seemed more like librarians than salespeople. Like matchmakers, they want to fix visitors up with the right book.

They spoke reverently of their longtime boss, the late Gilbert Whitlock, who passed away in 2004 at eighty-eight. A taciturn, old-fashioned Yankee gentleman with a wry wit, he started the business in 1948 in the same barns where he first tried to raise turkeys and sheep. Though they continue to keep general stock, Whitlock's increasingly specializes in scholarly books because of its proximity to Yale, which Sargeant hopes will keep the business from being swallowed by the Internet. Knowing that Pattis bought the shop less as a financial proposition than as a way to save a community institu-tion, she considers him an "angel." "I love it here," she said. "Every day is like Christmas because you never know what you're going to find when you open a box of books."

"There is no Frigate like a book/To take us Lands away," Emily Dickinson wrote. The same is true of used bookshops, which can take us to many different landscapes. Unlike most businesses today, which have a formulaic location type, these shops that depend on the passion of their owners and loyalty of their customers can pop up most anywhere. They can be in isolated rural settings like the Colebrook Book Barn or in cities as diverse as New Haven and blue-collar Waterbury. They can thrive on main commercial arteries close to shopping centers like Canton's On the Road Bookshop along U.S. Route 44, in rural village centers like Salisbury's Johnnycake Books, or in old mill town factory buildings like Books by the Falls in Derby.

Used bookshops have dwindled in the past few years, and some store owners fear that Internet sales and digitally downloaded books may spell the end of traditional storefronts. Others have harnessed the Internet to support their shops and feel that nothing will ever replace the pleasure of browsing or the tactile relationship people have with print and paper. Many have tried to recast the traditional "books only" approach and transform the experience into a species of entertainment.

Across from the post office in downtown Waterbury, the John Bale Book Company is in an elegant, old-fashioned storefront with hardwood floors where stationery and musical instruments were once sold. It's a spacious, well-lit shop where I was instantly greeted by the welcoming smell of brewing coffee and steaming soup. You can get breakfast, a sandwich, or a snack while reading or browsing in a cozy, unhurried atmosphere. Owner Dan Gaeta, who loves the book business for its nineteenth-century gentleman's-handshake values and knows the need for a strong back, also recognizes that the store probably wouldn't work in that location without the value-added experience of the café.

David Duda believes that the combination of books and food at his Book Trader Café, situated in the heart of the Yale campus, is the key to its strength as a community institution that generates loyalty and even affection. People not only buy books, but also feel comfortable lingering and talking. Book conversation often leads, he said, to deeper relationships, even among people meeting casually. Many of his regulars feel like family. On occasion he makes house calls to deliver or pick up books for people who are homebound. I enjoyed the soothing, low hum of conversation from the café side of the shop as I slowly worked my way down the orderly rows of shelves. The sound reminded me that while reading and writing are solitary preoccupations, books are all about people and about sharing the ideas and emotions given life on the page.

The Book Barn on State Route 156 just west of Niantic is a series of book-packed outbuildings, shacks, tent-like structures, and sheds built around a large shingled barn with stone pillars in the basement. Fabricated of wood, cinderblock, corrugated metal, plastic, and canvas, the outlying structures go by names like Hades, The Last Page, The Haunted, and Ellis Island, an immigration station for newly arrived volumes. Even the property's original outhouse has been fitted with shelves. Among the buildings are a series of gardens with pools and fountains, arbors and trellises, gargoyles, benches, and bridges. There is playhouse and swings for children. Summertime customers picnic on the grounds, though they sometimes have to share their meals with one of several goats or the twenty-odd cats that call the place home.

With its 350,000 books, an eccentric layout, and pervading tongue-in-cheek humor, the Book Barn is a browser's paradise. Whenever I visit I lose myself for the better part of a day, and for a few hours both time and ordinary worries disappear. I've wandered entire continents and walked through generations of learning in a moment. I've sat in a stuffed chair petting a marmalade cat while thumbing through an old geological treatise, or enjoyed the free coffee and cookies while delving into a few stanzas by contemporary Connecticut poet Rennie McQuilkin.

"It's a quirky business, always with the excitement of a treasure hunt because you never know what you'll find," said owner Randi White. He gets almost all his books, sometimes as many as ten thousand volumes a week, from people coming to the shop. It's a destination to which customers will drive a couple hours not just for the books, but also for the amusement and adventure of wandering the grounds, where they can unwind and enjoy. But the store also attracts a devoted cadre of regulars whom he affectionately calls "old faithfuls." They stop by often to pass the time with conversation about books or the daily headlines.

"Traveler FOOD and BOOKS," reads a towering sign at exit 74 along I-84 in Union, Connecticut's smallest town with a population of about seven hundred people. It hovers above a spacious restaurant with wooden tables and chairs that possesses a homey 1960s vibe. But the walls and a room divider are lined with books, and where there aren't shelves there are framed photographs of authors like Robert Parker, William Styron, and Dr. Seuss, some of them signed. In the basement is the "Best Cellar Bookstore," a typical used shop with several thousand titles. In the restaurant, however, up to three books are free with a meal. Having been there before, I know it's easy for dinner to get cold while one gets lost among the shelves, but last

February when the roof was still snow covered I stopped for a coffee, a slice of pie, and an opportunity to meet Art Murdock, who, with his wife, has owned the place since 1993.

He's a thin, soft-spoken man with warm eyes who grew up on a local farm. The previous owner got started by leaving free books on the counter "and things sort of took off from there," he told me. Now he gives away one hundred thousand books a year, and many people who travel between New York and Boston stop regularly. But it's also a local hangout. A heavyset, thirty-something couple from neighboring Holland, Massachusetts, told me they come often because "the food is great, and you never know what you'll find." When asked what lured him into the business, Murdock shrugged sheepishly. "I like food and I like books. What more is there to say?"

Our landscape is defined not just by architecture and topography, but by how we use and inhabit buildings and natural features. Selling neither necessities nor the latest fashion or marketed need, used bookstores speak volumes about culture, eccentricity, and interest in the past. There aren't very many of them, but they may be as critical to our identity as eighteenth-century colonial homes, redbrick mills, and stone walls.

Epilogue to Further Discovery
The New England Trail

On foot we experience the world in three dimensions;
we move at a speed that allows us to absorb and savor and reflect.
—Scott Russell Sanders, *A Conservationist Manifestor*

After a slow climb slabbing the hillside above State Route 66, I reached the south end of the Higby Mountain ridge and walked tantalizingly close to the jagged escarpment. Fortunately, the usual stiff wind blew out of the west, pushing me away from the precipice, which bowed and bulged with naturally sculpted outcrops. From one perspective the cliff looked like a face and from another a leaping animal. The angular fractures of traprock made the images appear as if nature was in a cubist mood. Just below the edge were jumbles of talus, chunks of fallen rock that had collected over centuries, most of it bare of vegetation, leaving a barren moonscape of rust-hued stone. Such slopes were natural sumps of water shadowed from the sun. At just such a place nearby my naturalist friend Les Mehrhoff had once delighted in showing me pockets of hidden ice in August and a rare plant that took advantage of the unusual summer cool.

From the shoreline town of Guilford to the Massachusetts border, the blue-blazed Mattabesett and Metacomet Trails wind along the steep traprock ridges that form central Connecticut's rugged backbone. These footpaths traverse sites as familiar as Meriden's Hanging Hills, which brood over I-91, and Talcott Mountain, whose Heublein Tower is an architectural icon attracting thousands of visitors each year for spectacular autumnal views of the Farmington Valley. President Obama's 2009 signature on a bill designating the 110-mile-long trails and a connected eighty miles through Massachusetts to New Hampshire as the New England National Scenic Trail provided widespread recognition and a modicum of protection to what is both a natural resource and cultural artifact.

For centuries the ridgelines were a barrier to travel, too barren for farming and unsuitable for industrial or other development. As a result, they remain remarkably wild even though they exist in some of Connecticut's most developed areas with1.35 million people living within ten miles of the trails. Since the 1800s, these mountains have been most prized for their ability to purify the rainwater that supports reservoirs and for their quarried and crushed stone that forms the base of thousands of roads. As recently as the early 1960s, these lands were so little valued for development that some could be bought for as little as ten dollars an acre. Though increasingly threatened with development for communication towers and homes with commanding views, their best use in today's increasingly hurried and indoor society is as places where people can refresh their spirits and challenge their bodies. The trail corridor has been likened to an elevated and feral Central Park.

With its mix of manmade and natural features, the New England Trail may be the footpath analog to the Merritt Parkway. But as a means of seeing what is hidden in plain sight, the trail has a big advantage—it demands that we move slowly. As deep travelers know, the velocity of travel is inversely proportional to what we observe. The slower we go, the more we see.

At the sixty-five or even thirty-five miles per hour I am used to traveling in my pickup, the textures and details of the landscape disappear. Call it speed blindness, but topographical distinctions are flattened, window chatter masks sounds, and smells are obliterated. But on foot the senses are on high alert, and I give myself time to savor and absorb sensations. To truly see, I need the body knowledge of my lungs and leg muscles working the hills and my feet feeling the difference between a rocky pasture and a muddy floodplain, lest I lose the small details that paint the larger perspective. "Walking, ideally, is a state in which the mind, the body, and the world are aligned, as though they were three characters finally in conversation together," writes award-winning author Rebecca Solnit. "The rhythm of walking generates a kind of rhythm of thinking, and the passage through a landscape echoes or stimulates the passage through a series of thoughts."

Though the cliff edges were rough and precipitous, immediately past the escarpments were broad, grassy meadows shadowed by chestnut oak, ash, and hickory. There was little underbrush, yielding an orderly parklike effect with sun filtered through the canopy and splashed on the virescent grass. Islands of wizened red cedar appeared in the boulder-studded glades among old bleached trees that had long ago fallen.

Being perched on the trail with natural pastures on one side and nothing but sky and air to the horizon on the other left me with a floating feeling, though I stood grounded on one of earth's hardest substances. I fancied a realm of dreams and expansive imagination.

Made of dense, erosion-resistant basalt, the ridges originated two hundred million years ago when the supercontinent of which Connecticut was part began to break up. As the landscape stretched and sunk to form the Central Valley, cracks deep in the earth's crust were created from which molten rock flowed to the surface, cooled, and hardened. Afterward, the basalt was covered with mud and sand from surrounding highlands, material that eventually became glued together as sedimentary rock. Two later lava flows were also covered with sediments. Over millennia, the softer sedimentary rock eroded, leaving the harder basalt as ridges. Because of a fault, or fracture in the earth's crust, the rocks tilted down toward the east, leaving sheer cliffs on the west and more gradual slopes on the opposite side. Iron in the rock gave exposed cliffs a distinctive rusty color.

The ridges are a world apart. Because they are different, their singular characteristics easily catch my eye and render them good places to practice acute observation of things not commonly seen. Though their thin soils, cold temperatures, and desiccating winds make them hostile for many creatures, they provide refuge for unusual species such as Jefferson salamanders, cliff-dwelling peregrine falcons, copperheads, and rattlesnakes. Bears, fisher, and bobcats, perhaps the most indomitable creatures living among us, have crossed my path along the trail. Such encounters have transported me, momentarily at least, to a wilder place than can be explained simply in distance, time, or density of nearby development. In spring I forever marvel at finely spurred red and yellow columbine, which thrives among the sharp edged rocks, while delicate rue anemone's small white petals hover over a whorl of slightly lobed leaves in the grassy meadows. By June, pink lady slippers grow so profusely I can count over a hundred blossoms on a half-day hike. Later in the year it's the waxy, ghostly white stems of Indian pipe that draw my attention.

Used as lookouts and revered as spiritual places by Native Americans, traprock ridges, both within the trail corridor and beyond, remained largely wild in colonial times, providing occasional hideaways for fugitives like Will Warren, who hid in a trailside cave after trying to burn down Farmington Village following a flogging for failing to attend church. Chief Metacomet, the ridge's namesake, led attacks on Connecticut Valley settlers in the 1670s and is said to have secreted himself in a lava tube just off the trail on Talcott Mountain.

Later the ridges enticed artists like Frederic Church and George Henry Durrie, who painted the cliffs near New Haven. As surrounding land became settled, a few residences were built on these high points, most notably the estates of nineteenth-century art patron Daniel Wadsworth and twentieth-century liquor magnate Gilbert Heublein. Public observation towers were also built on the ridges, including Meriden's Castle Craig and the fortress-like lookout on the Sleeping Giant's hip.

Hiking along the trail I've spotted old quarries, abandoned cemeteries, a Nike missile base, cellar holes, stone walls, and other evidence of long-faded human use. A ledge carved by patients marks the site of an old small pox hospital, and in a couple of places I walked abandoned roads once traversed by Rochambeau's troops or taken by George Washington. Near Farmington's Hill-Stead Museum, I've walked a ten-minute detour off the trail to see paintings by Monet, Degas, and other great artists.

Though they offer a complex tableau of man's relationship with nature, the ridges are so dominant that it's possible to acknowledge their presence and understand little else about them. We fixate on the grossest objects and phenomena, assume we have seen something, and stop actively looking. But deep travelers are collectors of details that accumulate to reveal the truth about a place and its people. There's a lot more than the devil in details.

The landscape we experience today, whether on the ridges or in the valleys, is the consequence of its ongoing relationship with humanity. Generations of people wresting a living on this humble patch of the planet and expressing their will through technology, fashion, imagination, money, and other devices have been constantly tested against, and have made accommodation with, geology, climate, hydrology, topography, and the plants and animals around them. From the pitch of our roofs to the depth of our basements, from the roads twisting along rivers to the stretches rolling and dipping as the macadam mounts hills and dives into valleys, we frequently experience, perhaps unwittingly, the evolving interaction between people and the landscape. The source of our drinking water, placement of factories and farms, and location of our communities and protected forests all illustrate an ongoing give and take with our natural surroundings.

From the top of Higby's ledges I saw the countryside arrayed like a living map, the buildings and trees seeming like the miniatures of an architectural model. I traced the routes of watersheds, the rugged topography of hills and mountains, the cloud reflections on lakes and ponds, and the messy meandering wetlands. Forested ridges ahead and behind me were a wall high above a world busy with power lines, houses, roads, office buildings, and shopping centers. To the north a large amphitheater-shaped quarry was chewing into the mountainside. Woods surrounded patches of pasture and orderly rows of orchard. Meriden's clustered downtown masonry was tucked in a green bowl and visible like a distant toy city. The interstate's drone rose toward me and over the ridge.

All the good, bad, and ugly of development and its relationship to the natural world was connected in a panorama that presented an opportunity to better understand where we have come from and where we are going. The best views, I supposed, have the power not only to awe us with drama and eye appeal, but also to inspire us to make the places we live better.

In the early 1930s, as development of the Merritt Parkway was in the works, a cadre of volunteers with the Connecticut Forest and Park Association developed the ridgeline trails that they continue to maintain with thousands of hours of annually donated labor. This visionary effort created not only a spectacular recreational resource "in the middle of everywhere," but a tangible and indelible link between people and their landscape.

Today the blue-blazed trail system extends over eight hundred miles throughout the state, roughly twice the distance from Boston, Massachusetts, to Washington, D.C. Combined with paths maintained by land trusts, municipalities, and others, Connecticut may offer more miles of hiking trail per acre than any state in the nation. These slow-paced highways for walkers with wandering eyes are the ideal training ground for deep travelers who practice searching for whatever is hidden in plain sight. Footpaths put us in intimate contact with some of our most inspiriting natural wonders, from windy high points to deep hemlock ravines forever in shaded twilight. They pass ghost towns, abandoned mill sites, drive-in theaters, old springs, hidden boundary markers, active and abandoned railroads, factories, and homes, giving ample opportunity to observe and savor the questions posed by the juxtaposition of land and people.

Perhaps the only flaw a deep traveler can find with the blue-blazed trails is that they don't penetrate the cortex and neighborhoods of Hartford, New Haven, and other urban areas, where there is so much to see. Such is the case even though the quality of our villages, cities, and towns might best be measured by the number of pedestrians on the street. Walkers can be seen as a kind of canary in the coal mine, and the presence of foot traffic often indicates that a place is safe, interesting, and lively. Looking holistically, we would do best to pierce traditional distinctions between interest in the built and natural environments, because one affects the other as surely as a reservoir built to slake city thirsts creates an accidental wilderness in an outlying area.

Unfortunately, walkers have traditionally divided into two camps: those who wander on the wild side and those who prefer settled precincts. John Muir and Henry David Thoreau, who likened walking—or sauntering, as he called it—to the medieval custom of going "'a la Sainte Terre,' to the Holy Land on a pilgrimage," are among the most famous peripatetic outdoorsmen. Lovers of urbanity look to inveterate city ramblers like twentieth-century social critic Lewis Mumford and writer Alfred Kazin, who once "stumbled on a connection between myself and the shape and color of time in the streets of New York." But true deep travelers are flâneurs, loafing amblers with omnivorous tastes for both the neighborhood and the woods, "passionate spectators," as French poet Charles Baudelaire put it. They know they will find things hidden in plain sight on woodland paths brightened with wildflowers or city streets energized with colorfully dressed pedestrians.

In a world in which few of us engage in the rituals of cutting wood to keep warm, walking to work, or even reading the sky for weather forecasts, we need more than ever to purposefully hone awareness and better cultivate our bond with the landscape. We need to realize that land is not merely territory or a resource, but is itself a kind of sustenance for our bodies and spirits. If we begin with simple but concentrated observations near at hand, it will not only enrich our lives with illuminating insights, it will provide the wherewithal to better meet the large-scale environmental and social challenges lying ahead. It will help us understand that like those of the past, the roads, buildings, industries, and monuments we build today don't just shape the world as we now see it now—they set a pattern for tomorrow.

Just the Right Place
An Explorer's Guide

Prologue to Deep Travel: The Merritt Parkway

- A drive along almost any portion of the Merritt Parkway is well rewarded. The portion in Greenwich was among the first areas to be restored and is one of the best places to observe some sense of the builders' original vision.
- All of the bridges are different and it's hard to choose favorites, but two of the best are at James Farm Road in Stratford, with its whimsical Nike Wings, and Lake Avenue in Greenwich, with its tangle of cast-metal grapevines. Of course, the iron railings with butterflies and spider webs at Fairfield's Merwin's Lane overpass is hard to exclude from a favorites list.
- The best book on the subject is Bruce Radde's *The Merritt Parkway* (Yale University Press, 1993). It's lavishly illustrated and well written.
- The Merritt Parkway Conservancy is a good source of information at www. merrittparkway.org.

Along the Roadside

Counting Miles in Four Centuries: Old Milestones

- Some milestones can be viewed at museums, such as the Canton Historical Museum in Collinsville and the Old State House in Hartford, where they can be seen without the hazards of traffic or the vagaries of weather. Sadly, however, they are out of context in such places.
- Milestones can be found along many of Connecticut's oldest major roads, such as U.S. Route 6, U.S. Route 44, State Route 10, and State Route 85. Quite a few original markers can be found along State Route 10 between Farmington's center and New Haven. State Route 85 between Colchester and Salem also has several markers, but they are 1970s replacements.
- Perhaps the mile marker most worthy of being a destination is the one celebrated by a small roadside park on U.S. Route 6 at Plymouth's border with Bristol. Further down U.S. Route 6 in Bristol at 1250 Farmington Avenue is the milestone in front of a Taco Bell that is wonderful for its juxtaposition with modern surroundings. At 100 Griswold Road in Wethersfield is the reproduction milestone created by Richard Lasher.

What's in a Name?: Reading Street Signs

Even a casual glance at a street atlas will show that every town in the state has intriguing names with historical and landscape resonances, or those that are playful or odd. My favorite road names are Skunk Misery Road in Haddam and Roast Meat Hill Road in Killingworth. Divining the meaning of names is often a lot more enjoyable than driving on the pavement. Two atlases that list street names are *Fairfield/Litchfield/New Haven Counties Atlas* (Hagstrom, 2007) and *Central/Eastern Connecticut Street Atlas* (Arrow Map, Inc., 2006). Local historical societies and municipal historians are often good sources for information on names. Connecticut Place Names, by Arthur H. Hughes and Morse S. Allen (Connecticut Historical Society, 1976), is another useful reference.

Seeing through Time: Roadcuts

- Roadcuts revealing bedrock are ubiquitous, and it's hard to drive even a few miles without seeing several that betray the area's deep earth history. My favorites are around the junction of State Routes 9 and 15, where layer cakes of colored sandstone are visible. State Route 9 between Haddam and Old Saybrook has many interesting cuts and is a great place to see the tilt and folds of the metamorphic rock underlying most of the state.

- For more about what you're seeing from the windshield, try *Roadside Geology of Connecticut and Rhode Island,* by James Skehan (Mountain Press Publishing Company, 2008). An informative and easily readable general treatment of the state's geology is *The Face of Connecticut,* by Michael Bell (State Geological and Natural History Survey of Connecticut, 1985).

- Traprock Ridges are among the most fascinating aspects of Connecticut's geology visible from behind the wheel. Two brief and excellent introductions are *Traprock Ridges of Connecticut: A Naturalist's Guide,* by Diana V. Wetherell (Connecticut Department of Environmental Protection, 1997), and *West Rock to the Barndoor Hills: The Traprock Ridges of Connecticut,* by Cara Lee (Connecticut Department of Environmental Protection, 1985).

Painted Ledges: Roadside Rock Art

Frog Rock on U.S. Route 44 in Eastford is the oldest rock art and also my favorite. The frog on U.S. Route 7 just south of Cornwall Bridge and Spotty, the dog on State Route 165 in Preston, are well worth visits. The eagle in Hebron and the turtle in Marlborough are just a few miles apart on State Route 66.

Last Picture Shows: Drive-In Theaters

The three existing drive-ins are: Mansfield Drive-In Theater and Marketplace, 228 Stafford Road, Mansfield (www.mansfielddrivein.com); Pleasant Valley Drive-In Theater, 47 River Road, Pleasant Valley (www.pleasantvalleydrivein.com); and the Southington Drive-In, 996 Meriden-Waterbury Turnpike, Southington (www.southingtondrivein.com). A number of closed drive-ins are still standing in various states of repair around the state. The easiest to see is the old Manchester Drive-In beside Bolton Notch Pond in Bolton. The blue-blazed Shenipsit Trail runs right by it. A Connecticut Historical Commission summer intern conducted a survey of Connecticut drive-ins and their history in 2002. *Drive-in Theaters of Connecticut,* by Anne Creevey Hall (Connecticut Historical Commission, 2002), is hard to find but available at the Thomas J. Dodd Research Center, University of Connecticut, Storrs.

A Cool Drink of Water: Roadside Springs

• For drinking purposes, roadside springs should be approached with caution. Regardless of whether you're there to slake your thirst, they are fascinating natural phenomena. Most worth a visit are Alex Cassie Spring, located in a park of the same name on State Route 195 in Windham; the Salmon River State Forest spring on the south side of State Route 16, just east of the Comstock Covered Bridge; and the spring at the junction of State Routes 184 and 49 in North Stonington. Some of the postings on www.findaspring.com are interesting, but any advice or recommendations should be skeptically received.

• Those interested in a filling up a jug at a commercial spring might try Triple Springs at 199 Ives Avenue in Meriden (www.triplesprings.com) or Schofield Spring on State Route 32 in Willington.

A Good Great Place: Diners

• True diners are prefabricated and movable, very rarely built in place structures (the Quaker Diner on Park Road in West Hartford is one exception to the prefabricated rule). Choosing a favorite diner is like choosing a favorite child. Among the ones I like best are the Main Street Diner at 40 West Main Street in Plainville, the Aero Diner on U.S. Route 6 in North Windham, O'Rourke's on Main Street in Middletown, and Collin's Diner on U.S. Route 44 in Canaan.

• To know more, see *Diners of New England,* by Randy Garbin (Stackpole Books, 2005). For additional information on diners and finding them, go to www.roadsideonline.com.

Places We Build

A Most Enduring Harvest: Quarries

• Operating quarries producing building stone are working places engaged in an activity with inherent dangers and so not generally open for public tours. Among those I visited were Portland Brownstone Quarries, 311 Brownstone Avenue, Portland (www.brownstonequarry.com); Stony Creek Quarry Corporation, 7 Business Park Drive, Branford (www.stonycreekquarry.com); Skyline Quarry, 110 Conklin Road, Stafford Springs (www.skylinequarry.net); and Tower Hill Granite Company, New London Turnpike, Glastonbury. The historic quarries in Portland are now a recreational water park. Information about Brownstone Exploration and Discovery Park can be found at www.brownstonepark.com.

• The best history of Connecticut quarries is *Flesh and Stone: Stony Creek and the Age of Granite, edited by Deborah Deford (Stony Creek Granite Workers Celebration,* 2000). Southeastern Connecticut quarries are treated in *The Granite Industry of Waterford,* by Willard A. Reed III (Waterford Historical Society, undated).

The People's Castles: Stone Lookouts

Connecticut's four stone lookout towers are easily found on public lands. Castle Craig is in Meriden's Hubbard Park and is accessible by vehicle April to October. Norfolk's Haystack Mountain, Litchfield's Mount Tom, and Hamden's Sleeping Giant Towers are all in their namesake state parks. A road comes close to the top of Haystack, but the other two require a vigorous hike. Learn more about these and other state parks from *A Shared Landscape,* by Joseph Leary (Friends of Connecticut State Parks, 2004), or at www.ct.gov/dep/stateparks.

King of Homes: Yankee Castles

• Castle-style houses are scattered throughout the state, but they are private homes and are not accessible to the general public. Most however, are visible from the street. Among those that can be glimpsed from a road are Crowley Castle at 125 Brookside Drive in Greenwich, Christopher Mark's castle at 580 Brickyard Road in Woodstock, and Aborn Castle on State Route 83 in Ellington.

• In addition to its breathtaking view over the Connecticut River, Gillette Castle is the most interesting and eccentric castle in the state. Located on River Road in East Haddam, the Gillette Castle State Park grounds are available all year for hiking and picnicking, while the structure itself is open for tours during the warmer months. Additional information is available in *A Shared Landscape,* by Joseph Leary (Friends of Connecticut State Parks, 2004), or at www.ct.gov/dep/stateparks. More can be learned about the ever-fascinating William Gillette in *Sherlock Holmes and More,* by Doris E. Cook (Connecticut Historical Society, 1970).

- For those who like the romantic mystery of a castle ruin, there's Hearthstone Castle in Danbury's Tarrywile Park. The crumbling structure is at the edge of the woods, far from the elegant mansion and gardens that are also on the grounds (www.tarrywile.com).

- Though published in 1889, Mark Twain's *A Connecticut Yankee in King Arthur's Court* remains an enjoyable, satirical romp poking fun at technology, castles, and castle builders and their lifestyles.

A Thousand Uses: Quonset Huts

- You can't see more Connecticut Quonsets in a single glance than on State Route 322 in the Milldale section of Southington, where seven Second World War–era models are used for business and storage. If you want to get inside one, Southworth's Wayside Furniture on Winsted Road in Torrington or Quonset Surplus on State Route 66 in Portland are good bets. If you want to linger, the café at 20 Church Street near the Guilford Green or the Half Keg Tavern in New London are the places to be.

- For more information about Quonset huts, see the definitive *Quonset Hut: Metal Living for a Modern Age,* edited by Jill Decker and Chris Chiei (Princeton Architectural Press, 2005). Well worth a visit is the Seabee Museum in North Kingston, Rhode Island, where you can see several different hut styles, along with lots of memorabilia (www.seabeesmuseum.com).

The Shape of Futures Past: Octagon Houses

- The greatest number of octagon houses in the shortest drive can be had in the state's midsection, where five can be viewed in less than an hour. Start with St. Peter's Hall at Holy Apostles College and Seminary at 33 Prospect Hill Road in Cromwell and then head to the two on State Route 66 in Portland. Finish the tour in East Hampton with one at 6 Middletown Avenue (State Route 16) and another in the center of town, on Bevin Boulevard.

- There is no accurate inventory of all of the state's octagon structures. Although it contains some errors, the most comprehensive survey is at www.octagon. bobanna.com.

- For those interested in the source of the philosophy and building design that started the octagon craze, there's a reprint of the 1853 book The Octagon House: A Home for All, by Orson S. Fowler (Dover Publications, Inc., 1973).

- Although Connecticut has none, there are several octagon house museums in other states that are open the public. Among them are those in Camillus, New York, and Hudson, Wisconsin.

Practical, Adaptable, and Disappearing: Barns

- Despite the precipitous decline in their number over the past few years, it's hard to go too far in Connecticut without seeing a variety of barns, even in urban areas. Among my favorites are the University of Connecticut's gambrel-roof dairy barn on State Route 195 in Storrs, the quirky Gallup barn at 91 Huntington Road in Scotland, and the massive and regal Hilltop Farm barn in Suffield.
- The Connecticut Trust for Historic Preservation has assembled what is probably the finest barn inventory in the nation, with about eight thousand entries as well as information on various barn styles and a general history (www.connecticutbarns.org). For more about tobacco sheds and the culture of which they are a part, there's *Connecticut Valley Vernacular: The Vanishing Landscape and Architecture of the New England Tobacco Fields,* by James F. O'Gorman (University of Pennsylvania Press, 2002). The classic treatment of connected barns is *Big House, Little House, Back House, Barn,* by Thomas C. Hubka (University Press of New England, 2004).

The Spirit of Community: Camp Meetings

Although visitors are often welcomed, camp meeting grounds are private property, and beyond the public street they should be approached as such. The Willimantic Camp Meeting Association in Windham has an informative website at www.willimanticcampmeeting.org, as does Camp Bethel in the Tylerville section of Haddam at www.campbethel-ct.com. The Pine Grove Spiritualist Camp in Niantic also has a helpful site at www.pinegrovespiritualistcamp.net. The best history of such a place is *The Heart Strangely Warmed: The Chautauqua and Methodist Campground at Plainville, Connecticut,* by Arthur K. Pope (Trafford Publishing, 2006), an affectionate story by a longtime resident.

Exploring Gasoline Alley: Racetracks

- Get race schedules, track history, statistics, and a lot more at www.staffordmotorspeedway.com for Stafford Motor Speedway, www.limerock.com for Lime Rock Park, www.speedbowl.com for Waterford Speedbowl, and www.thompsonspeedway.com for the Thompson International Speedway.
- There's no thorough Connecticut racetrack history, but "A Short History of Connecticut's Racetracks," by Allan E. Brown, makes a good start at the subject in the Spring 2008 issue of *Hog River Journal* (now *Connecticut Explored*). For the history of car manufacture in the state, the best source is *Connecticut Created Cars,* by Paul Pellerin and Daniel Nichols (Minuteman Press, 2010).

Seeing Green: Trees, Culture, and Agriculture

A Place for Common Ground: Town Greens

- The most surprising thing about Connecticut's town greens is their diversity. If I could visit only a few, I wouldn't miss the ones in Lebanon, New Haven, Guilford, Litchfield, Waterbury, Eastford, and Norfolk.

- The only complete inventory and the definitive source for the history and culture of town greens has been assembled by the Connecticut Trust for Historic Preservation at www.towngreens.com. For the northeastern part of the state and adjacent Massachusetts, the Quinebaug-Shetucket National Heritage Corridor published *For the Common Good,* a pamphlet that includes photographs and maps as well as descriptions of the greens in that area.

- The Institute Library is an old-fashioned membership library founded in 1826. It has been in its current home at 847 Chapel Street, just off the New Haven Green, since 1878.

Heart of Nowhere: Connecticut's Most Remote Place

- Canaan Mountain has no blazed trails, and a hike should not be attempted by the inexperienced. Most of the mountain is within the Canaan Mountain Natural Area Preserve, a part of the Housatonic State Forest. For more information on the preserve, contact the Department of Energy and Environmental Protection's Wildlife Division at www.ct.gov/dep/wildlife, and for information about the forest, contact the agency's Forestry Division at www.ct.gov/dep/forestry. For hiking information, try the Connecticut Forest and Park Association (www.ctwoodlands.org) or Great Mountain Forest in Norfolk (www.greatmountainforest.org).

- Cultural GIS expert William Keegan can be reached at wkeegan@heritage-consultants.com.

- For more information on Candlewood Lake and Connecticut's other water bodies, see *A Fisheries Guide to Lakes and Ponds of Connecticut,* by Robert P. Jacobs and Eileen B. O'Donnell (Connecticut Department of Environmental Protection, 2002).

- For more information on Falkner Island and Stratford Shoal lighthouses and others, see *The Lighthouses of Connecticut,* by Jeremy D'Entremont (Commonwealth Editions, 2005).

The Measure of a State: Connecticut's Highest Point(s)

- It's a strenuous climb, but Bear Mountain is easily reached via the Appalachian Trail, which crosses State Route 41 just north of Salisbury's center, or via the blue-blazed Undermountain Trail, which crosses the same road 3.5 miles north of town. Trail information can be found in the Connecticut Walk Book,

West (Connecticut Forest and Park Association, 2006) or in the Appalachian Trail Guide to Massachusetts-Connecticut, twelfth edition (Appalachian Trail Conference, 2010). Mount Frissell can be reached via a trail that starts on seasonally accessible Mount Washington Road in Salisbury at the Massachusetts line; it is described in the Massachusetts Trail Guide, ninth edition (Appalachian Mountain Club, 2009). For further information, contact Connecticut Forest and Park Association at www.ctwoodlands.org or the Appalachian Mountain Club at www.outdoors.org.

- For those interested in state high points generally, go to www.peakbagger. com.

Big Trees: Old-Growth Forests

- The best place to view large trees in Connecticut is Gold's Pines in Cornwall. There's a short interpretive trail that begins next to the firehouse on State Route 128.

- *The Sierra Club Guide to the Ancient Forests of the Northeast,* by Bruce Kershner and Robert T. Leverett (Sierra Club Books, 2004), has a description of and directions to Gold's Pines and several other sites around the state. A short, lyrical description of Gold's Pines can be found in *The Sylvan Path,* by Gary Ferguson (St. Martin's Press, 1997). The book is walkthrough of East Coast forests.

- The Connecticut Forest and Park Association was founded in 1895 and is the state's oldest conservation organization. It can be reached at www.ctwood-lands.org. The history of the organization is *Connecticut Woodlands: A Century's Story of the Connecticut Forest and Park Association,* by George McLean Milne (Connecticut Forest and Park Association, 1995).

- For further information on old-growth forests, contact the Connecticut Department of Energy and Environmental Protection's Forestry Division at www.ct.gov/dep/forestry.

A Sacred Grove: Hope for the Chestnut Forest

- The Chestnut Grove is part of Sleeping Giant State Park in Hamden. It's located along Chestnut Road, and there is a trail to it 0.8 miles from the junction with Mount Carmel Avenue. More information on the grove and chestnut-preservation efforts can be obtained from the Connecticut Agricultural Experiment Station at www.ct.gov/caes.

- The natural and cultural history of the tree is well covered in *American Chestnut: The Life, Death, and Rebirth of a Perfect Tree,* by Susan Freinkel (University of California Press, 2007).

The Perfect Street Tree: A Few Good Elms

- The best place to imagine what colonnades of elms were once like in our urban areas, however imperfectly under today's conditions, is the New Haven Green. Remnant large trees, such as Hartford's High Street Elm (visible from I-84), exist throughout the state, though they still do not reach the size of yesteryear's giants.

- *Republic of Shade: New England and the American Elm,* by Thomas J. Campanella (Yale University Press, 2003), is the best overall history of the tree and its impact. Those interested in the current status of the trees should consult Elm Watch at www.elmwatch.org or the Connecticut Agricultural Experiment Station at www.ct.gov/caes.

- Founded in 1903, the Connecticut Botanical Society is a group of amateur and professional botanists who share an interest in the plants and habitats of Connecticut and the surrounding region. They publish a list of big trees. For more information, see www.ct-botanical-society.org.

Inventing New England Autumn: Leaf Peeping

- The Numeral Rock Trail in Kent leaves State Route 341 a little west of Kent's center. It's a steep climb of about half an hour.

- Up-to-date progress on the state's fall foliage and related information can be found at the Department of Energy and Environmental Protection website at http://www.ct.gov/dep/cwp/view.asp?a=2697&q=322764.

- A concise history of the foliage craze is "Leaf Peeping," a short essay by Donna Jean Zane found in *The Encyclopedia of New England,* edited by Burt Feintuch and David H. Watters (Yale University Press, 2005). Henry David Thoreau's seminal essay "Autumnal Tints" is available in many collections, including Excursions, edited by Joseph Moldenhauer (Princeton University Press, 2007). An excellent analysis is found in *Landscape with Figures: Nature and Culture in New England,* by Kent C. Ryden (University of Iowa Press, 2001).

A Most Useful Tree: Season of the Witch Hazel

- To learn more about witch hazel products and American Distilling, go to their website at www.americandistilling.com.

- Witch hazel grows in many places throughout the state and is best distinguished during leaf fall, when its golden starlike flowers are in bloom. In western Connecticut, a good spot to see it is on the Tunxis Trail heading north from State Route 219 toward Indian Council Caves. On the other side of the state, try the Nature Conservancy's Burnham Brook Preserve on Dolbia Hill Road in East Haddam.

Tasting the Landscape: Cider Mills

- There is no comprehensive list of cider makers. The Connecticut Apple Marketing Board publishes a print and online brochure listing apple orchards. Many of these are also cider makers, though some who indicate they have cider do not press it themselves. The Apple Board is at www.ctapples.com.
- Because it's a National Historic Landmark and the oldest steam-powered mill in the country, B. F. Clyde's Cider Mill in Old Mystic is a worthwhile destination (www.bfclydescidermill.com).
- For cider history, lore, and making, see *Cider: Hard and Sweet,* by Ben Watson (Countryman Press, 1999), and *Cider: Making, Using and Enjoying Sweet and Hard Cider,* by Annie Proulx and Lew Nichols (Storey Books, 1997).

A Community Harvest: Agricultural Fairs

Connecticut is blessed with over forty agricultural fairs that vary widely in size, location, and emphasis. Each has its own special vibe and allure, so it's hard to pick favorites among them. For an old-timey feel I like the Hamburg or Riverton Fairs. Goshen and Durham Fairs have plenty of animals you can get close to, and for a big place with lots of excitement it's hard to beat the Woodstock Fair. These and other fairs are listed in a print and online pamphlet produced by the Association of Connecticut Fairs (www.ctfairs.org).

Ghost Towns and Graveyards

Forgotten but Not Gone: Ghost Towns

- Although many Connecticut ghost towns are on private property, Gay City State Park on State Route 85 in Hebron is accessible to the public, and it's one of the best. It includes old factory ruins, cellar holes, canal remains, and a cemetery. For more information on the park, consult *A Shared Landscape,* by Joseph Leary (Friends of Connecticut State Parks, 2004), and www.ct.gov/dep/stateparks.
- Ghost towns are subject to exaggerated legends and all manner of apocryphal, sensational stories, so caution is urged when looking at any print or online information sources. Gay City, Barkhamsted Lighthouse in Barkhamsted, and Dudleytown in Cornwall are treated in *Legendary Connecticut,* by David E. Phillips (Spoonwood Press, 1984). Gay City, Dudleytown, Bara-Hack in Pomfret, Hell Hollow in Voluntown, and some others are highlighted in *Abandoned Villages and Ghost Towns of New England,* by Thomas D'Agostino (Schiffer, 2008). The Connecticut Archaeology Center, a reliable source, may have limited information on some sites (www.mnh.uconn.edu).

Ghost Streets and Routes Less Taken: Abandoned Roads

- Of course, ghost towns have ghost roads, but they have not enjoyed the same widespread notoriety. There is no survey of ghost roads, and the best way to find them is by careful observation or by looking through old maps in libraries and town halls.
- Ghost roads are frequently found along the blue-blazed hiking trails, which sometimes utilize abandoned thoroughfares. The Regicides Trail north of New Haven crosses the broken pavement of Baldwin Drive six times in West Rock Ridge State Park. The Tunxis Trail is accessed via old State Route 20 at the junction with Walnut Hill Road in Hartland. Abandoned Wadsworth Farm Road, once used by George Washington, is crossed by the Mattabesett Trail about two miles north of State Route 68 in Durham.

Beneath the Lakes: Lost Worlds

Construction of all of Connecticut's large reservoirs involved moving houses and other structures, sometimes cemeteries and even whole villages. The best sources for information on some of the grandest projects are *Water for Hartford: The Story of the Hartford Water Works and the Metropolitan District Commission,* by Kevin Murphy (Shining Tramp Press, 2004); *Barkhamsted Heritage: Culture and Industry in a Rural Connecticut Town,* edited by Richard G. Wheeler and George Hilton (Barkhamsted Historical Society, 1975); and *Village of the Dammed: The Fight for Open Space and the Flooding of a Connecticut Town,* by James Lomuscio (University Press of New England, 2005).

Watery Ghosts of Manufacturing: Mill Ponds

Whenever you see a dam near a pond or river impoundment, you will often find remnants of an old mill site ranging from primitive saw and grist mills to nineteenth-century factories. Explanations of mill and mill pond development as well as clues to interesting sites worth exploring can be found in *Empire over the Dam: The Story of Waterpowered Industry, Long Passed from the Scene,* by Kenneth T. Howell and Einar W. Carlson (Pequot Press, 1974); *Industrial Heritage in Northwest Connecticut: A Guide to History and Archaeology,* by Robert Gordon and Michael Raber (Connecticut Academy of Arts and Sciences, 2000); and *Mills and Meadows: A Pictorial History of Northeast Connecticut,* by Bruce M. Stave and Michele Palmer (Donning Company, 1991).

Steeped in Mystery: Gungywamp

Gungywamp has probably been subject to more misinterpretation and wild suppositions that any other place in Connecticut. The property is privately owned, but tours are available through the Denison Pequotsepos Nature Center in Mystic (www.dpnc.org). The best source for information about Gungywamp is the Gungywamp Society at www.gungywamp.com.

Space-Age Ghosts: Nike Missile Sites

• Nike site remains exist in various conditions around the state. To see a ruin, visit the area in the Meshomasic State Forest, marked by a yellow gate and broken pavement, inclining up a hill along Reeves Road. Another site with not much more than concrete pads marking old building locations and rusting fences is found along the blue-blazed Metacomet Trail in Plainville, less than a mile and a half north of the trail's crossing of State Route 372. Sites with recycled uses include Manchester's Nike Park on Garden Grove Road and Rolnick Observatory atop an old radar tower off Bayberry Lane in Westport.

• For information on the Nike system generally, visit the Nike Historical Society (www.nikemissile.org). A short history is available at http://alpha.fdu. edu/~bender/N-view.html.

Perpetual Care Isn't Forever: Neglected Graveyards

• Sometimes you can spot a neglected graveyard from the road, but most often they're in the woods or hidden in tall grass. Two can be seen fairly quickly near the blue-blazed Woodtick Trail off Woodtick Road in Wolcott. Pike Hill and northeast cemeteries include ancestors of Louisa May Alcott. Hopeville Cemetery on Edmond Road in Griswold is visible from the pavement, although tall grasses obscure it.

• Information on old cemeteries is available from the Connecticut Gravestone Network (www.ctgravestones.com). The Hale Collection of Connecticut cemetery inscriptions documented in the 1930s is another useful resource (www. hale-collection.com). A portion of the state is covered in *The Colonial Burying Grounds of Eastern Connecticut and the Men Who Made Them*, by James A. Slater (Connecticut Academy of Arts and Sciences, 1996).

Haunting Stones of Metal: Zinc Grave Markers

Many cemeteries that were active from the Civil War and into the early twentieth century include zinc markers, also known as white bronze. Good places to see a variety of them include Woodbury's North Cemetery on Washington Avenue and Norwich's Maplewood Cemetery on State Route 82.

Trash Talk: Landfills and Landscapes

• Once you start looking for the large, treeless mounds that signify big landfills, they're easy to spot. Hartford's old landfill in the North Meadows and New Haven's landfill north of the city, beside the old incinerator stack, can be clearly seen from I-91. Perhaps the best one for viewing is the old Milford Landfill in Silver Sands State Park. On a much smaller scale, it's not uncommon to find "bottle dumps" from old farms in the woods, especially near foundation ruins. Reclaimed landfill sites can be in surprising places, like a part of Cove Island Park in Stamford and under the softball fields at Bulkely High School in Hartford.

- More information about current and historical landfills is available from the Connecticut Department of Energy and Environmental Protection at http://ct.gov/dep/search/search.asp?go.x=1&qu=landfill. The Connecticut Resources Recovery Authority operates the CRRA Garbage Museum in Stratford and the CRRA Trash Museum in Hartford, which have exhibits on contemporary and historical waste-management issues (www.crra.org).

Through Artists' Eyes

Reinventing the Colonial Landscape: Wallace Nutting

- Wallace Nutting's Connecticut Home is now the Meeting House in Southbury's Heritage Village (www.heritagevillage.org). One of his premier museums, the Webb House, remains open to the public as part of the Webb-Deane-Stevens complex at 211 Main Street in Wethersfield (www.webb-deane-stevens.org). The Wadsworth Atheneum at 600 Main Street in Hartford (www.thewadsworth.org) is home to Nutting's collection of seventeenth- and eighteenth-century furniture.
- *Wallace Nutting and the Invention of Old America,* by Thomas Andrew Denenberg (Yale University Press, 2003), is a comprehensive examination of Nutting and his cultural impact.

A Fresh Way of Looking: The Hudson River School

- Connecticut is fortunate to have a large and diverse collection of Hudson River School paintings, most notably at the Wadsworth Atheneum at 600 Main Street in Hartford (www.thewadsworth.org) and the New Britain Museum of American Art at 56 Lexington Street in New Britain (www.nbma.org).
- Hartford-born Frederick Church was an exemplar of the Hudson River style, and his home and its surroundings in Hudson, New York, well represent the type of landscape he and his colleagues often painted. Tours of his mansion, named Olana, are available April through October (www.olana.org).

In a State of Plein Air: Artists Outdoors

- The five impressionist art signboard viewpoints are at Kent Falls State Park in Kent, at the Chester-Hadlyme ferry landing in East Haddam, on the Farmington River Trail in Burlington, at Sherwood Island State Park in Westport, and at Windham Mills State Heritage Park in Willimantic.

- Impressionist art can be seen at several museums around the state, including the Wadsworth Atheneum in Hartford (www.thewadsworth.org), the Bruce Museum in Greenwich (www.brucemuseum.org), the Bush-Holley Historic Site in Cos Cob (www.hstg.org), the Florence Griswold Museum in Old Lyme (www.florencegriswoldmuseum.org), the Lyman Allyn Art Museum in New London (www.lymanallyn.org), the New Britain Museum of American Art in New Britain (www.nbmaa.org), and the Hill-Stead Museum in Farmington (www.hillstead.org). Additional information on the Connecticut Art Trail is available at www.arttrail.org.
- Among useful books are *Connecticut and American Impressionism,* by Paul F. Rovetti et al. (William Benton Museum of Art, 1980), and *Visions of Belonging: New England Art and the Making of American Identity,* by Julia B. Rosenbaum (Cornell University Press, 2006).

Where the Landscape Is Art: Weir Farm

Weir Farm National Historic Site, the first park to honor an American painter, is at 735 Nod Hill Road in Wilton (www.nps.gov/wefa).

Poetic Space: James Merrill's Apartment

- Information about James Merrill's apartment and visiting opportunities can be found at www.jamesmerrillhouse.org.
- Merrill's poetic rendering of his experiences in the apartment with his Ouija board are found in his book *The Changing Light at Sandover* (Knopf, 2006).

Landscape and the Written Word: Nature Writers

- Operated by the Connecticut Audubon Society, Edwin Way Teale's Trailwood has miles of footpaths open to the public. It's located at 93 Kenyon Road in Hampton (www.ctaudubon.org). The other writers' former homes are private residences not open to the public, but they are visible from the street. Joseph Wood Krutch lived at 70 Limekiln Road in Redding, Gladys Taber at 487 Stanford Road in Southbury, and Hal Borland on Weatogue Road in Salisbury.
- All these writers were prolific. Recommended books include:

Teale: *A Naturalist Buys an Old Farm* (Dodd, Mead & Company, 1974) is about his life at Trailwood; *Wandering through Winter* (Dodd, Mead & Company, 1965) was the final volume in his cross-country seasonal wandering series, and it won the Pulitzer Prize.

Krutch: *The Twelve Seasons* (William Sloane Associates, 1949), about his Redding environs, was his first nature book; *The Best Nature Writing of Joseph Wood Krutch* (William Morrow, 1970) is a compilation of his career's finest.

Taber: *The Book of Still Meadow* (Macrae Smith Company, 1948) and *The Stillmeadow Road* (J. B. Lippincott Company, 1962) are two of my favorites.

Borland: Sundial of the Seasons (J. B. Lippincott Company, 1964) is a compilation of *New York Times* nature editorials; *Countryman: A Summary of Belief* (J. B. Lippincott Company, 1965) expresses his philosophy.

Buy the Book: Used Bookstores

The best guide to used bookstores, besides word of mouth, is the Connecticut Antiquarian Booksellers Directory, which can be found at most used bookstores or on the web at www.bookdirectory.org.

Epilogue to Further Discovery: The New England Trail

For a hike along the New England Scenic Trail, known in Connecticut as the Mattabessett and Metacomet Trails, consult the *Connecticut Walk Book, West* (Connecticut Forest & Park Association, 2006) or the *Connecticut Walk Book, East* (Connecticut Forest and Park Association, 2005). The latest information, as well as maps and trail history, is available at www.newenglandnst.org.

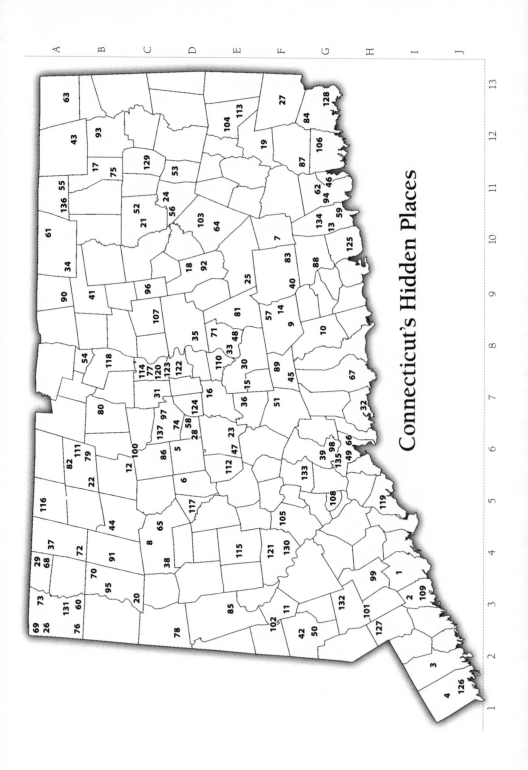

Connecticut's Hidden Places

Connecticut's Hidden Places
Map Key

Merritt Parkway
1. Merwins Lane Bridge, Fairfield (I4)
2. Rolnick Observatory, old Nike missile base, Westport (I3)
3. Guinea Road Bridge, Stamford (J2)
4. Lake Avenue Bridge, Greenwich (J1)

Milestones
5. U.S. Route 6, Bristol, at Taco Bell (D6)
6. U.S. Route 6, Plymouth, at Bristol town line (D5)
7. State Route 85, Colchester and Salem, replacement markers (F10)
8. U.S. Route 202, Litchfield (C4)

Road Names
9. Skunk Misery Road, Haddam (F8)
10. Roast Meat Hill Road, Killingworth (G8)
11. Obtuse Rocks Road, Brookfield (F3)
12. Satan's Kingdom Road, New Hartford (C6)

Roadcuts
13. Rocky Neck Connector, East Lyme (G10)
14. Sulfur-laden rock, State Route 9 (south of exit 8), Haddam (F9)
15. Traprock cliff, Mount Higby, I-91 (between exits 18 and 19), Middlefield, Middletown (E7)
16. Sandstone layers, junction of State Route 9 and Berlin Turnpike, Berlin (D7)

Roadside Rock Art
17. Frog, U.S. 44, Eastford (B11)
18. Eagle, State Route 66, Hebron (D9)
19. Dog, State Route 165, Preston (F12)
20. Frog, U.S. Route 7, Cornwall (C3)

Drive-In Theaters
21. Mansfield Drive-In and Marketplace, Mansfield (C10)
22. Pleasant Valley Drive-In Theater, Barkhamsted (B5)
23 Southington Drive-In, Southington (E6)

Roadside Springs
24. Alex Cassie Spring, Windham (C11)
25. Salmon River State Forest Spring, Colchester (E9)
26. Mount Riga Road Spring, Salisbury (A2)
27. Spring at State Routes 184 and 49, North Stonington (F13)

Diners
28. Main Street Diner, Plainville (D6)
29. Collin's Diner, North Canaan (A4)
30. O'Rourke's Diner, Middletown (E8)
31. Quaker Diner, West Hartford (C7)

Quarries
32. Stony Creek Quarry, Branford (H7)
33. Portland Brownstone Quarries, Portland (E8)
34. Skyline Quarry, Stafford (A9)
35. Tower Hill Granite Company, Glastonbury (D8)

Stone Lookouts
36. Castle Craig, Hubbard Park, Meriden (E7)
37. Haystack Mountain State Park, Norfolk (A4)
38. Mount Tom State Park, Litchfield (C4)
39. Sleeping Giant State Park, Hamden (G6)

Castle Houses
40. Gillette Castle State Park, East Haddam (F9)
41. Aborn Castle, Ellington (B9)
42. Hearthstone Castle, Tarrywile Park, Danbury (F2)
43. Christopher Mark's Castle, Woodstock (A12)

Quonset Huts
44. Wayside Furniture, Torrington (B4)
45. Farm, State Route 177, Durham (F7)
46. Half Keg Tavern, New London (G11)
47. Quonset cluster, State Route 322 at Clark Street, Southington (E6)

An interactive version of this map is available at
http://www.wesleyan.edu/wespress/maps/hiddeninplainsight/

Octagon Houses
48. State Route 66, Portland (E8)
49. Hallock Street, New Haven (H6)
50. Spring Street, Danbury (G2)
51. New Place Street, Wallingford (F7)

Barns
52. UConn Dairy Barn, State Route 195, Mansfield (C11)
53. Gallup Barn, Huntington Road, Scotland (C11)
54. Tobacco sheds, I-91 connector from Bradley International Airport (B8)
55. Connected barn, Rindge Road, Union (A11)

Camp Meetings
56. Willimantic Camp Meeting Association, Windham (private, seek permission) (C11)
57. Camp Bethel, Haddam (private, seek permission) (F9)
58. Plainville Campground, Plainville (private, seek permission) (D6)
59. Pine Grove Spiritualist Camp, East Lyme (G10)

Racetracks
60. Lime Rock Park, Salisbury (B3)
61. Stafford Motor Speedway, Stafford (A10)
62. Waterford Speedbowl, Waterford (G11)
63. Thompson International Speedway, Thompson (A13)

Town Greens
64. Lebanon Green, Lebanon (E10)
65. Litchfield Green, Litchfield (C4)
66. New Haven Green, New Haven (H6)
67. Guilford Green, Guilford (H7)

Remote Place
68. Canaan Mountain, Canaan and North Canaan (A4)

High Point
69. Bear Mountain and Mount Frissell, Salisbury (A2)

Old Growth
70. Gold's Pines, Cornwall (B3)
71. Big pines, Meshomasic State Forest, Portland (E8)

72. Great Mountain Forest, Norfolk (private, seek permission) (B4)
73. Sages Ravine, Salisbury (A3)

Chestnuts
(39) Chestnut grove, Sleeping Giant State Park, Hamden (G6)
74. Chestnut sprouts, Farmington Town Forest, Farmington (D6)
75. Chestnut hulk, Natchaug Trail, Eastford (B11)

Elms
(66) New Haven Green, New Haven (H6)
76. Hotchkiss School, Salisbury (B2)
77. High Street Elm, Hartford (C7)

Autumn Foliage
78. Kent (top foliage town per *Yankee magazine*) (D2)
79. Saville Dam, Barkhamsted (B6)
80. Heublein Tower, Talcott Mountain State Park, Simsbury (B7)

Witch Hazel
81. American Distilling, East Hampton (E9)
82. Tunxis Trail near Indian Council Caves, Barkhamsted (A6)
83. Burnham Brook Preserve, East Haddam (F10)

Cider
84. B. F. Clyde's Cider Mill, Stonington (G12)
85. Park Lane Cider Mill, New Milford (E3)
86. Hogan's Cider Mill, Burlington (C6)
87. Holmberg Orchards, Ledyard (F12)

Agricultural Fairs
88. Hamburg Fair, Lyme (G10)
89. Durham Fair, Durham (F7)
90. Four Town Fair, Somers (A9)
91. Goshen Fair, Goshen (B4)

Ghost Towns
92. Gay City State Park, Hebron (D9)
93. Lost Village, Pomfret (private, seek permission) (B12)
94. Pember Road, Waterford (G11)
95. Dudleytown, Cornwall (private, seek permission) (B3)

Ghost Roads
96. Bailey Road, Bolton (C9)
97. I-84 stack, Farmington (C7)
98. Baldwin Drive, West Rock Ridge State Park, Hamden (G6)
99. Old Rock House Road and Den Road, Easton (H4)

Beneath the Lakes
100. Nepaug Reservoir, Canton, Burlington, New Hartford (B5)
101. Saugatuck Reservoir, Weston and Redding (H3)
102. Candlewood Lake, Danbury, New Fairfield, Brookfield, New Milford, Sherman (F2)

Mill Ponds
103. Lake Williams, Lebanon (D10)
104. Hopeville Pond, Hopeville Pond State Park, Griswold (E12)
105. Papermill Pond, Southford Falls State Park, Oxford (F5)

Gungywamp
106. Gungywamp, Groton (private, seek permission) (G12)

Nike Missile Sites
107. Nike Park, Manchester (C8)
108. Ford Street, Ansonia (G5)
109. Bayberry Lane, Westport (I3)
110. Country Squire Drive, Cromwell (E8)

Neglected Graveyards
111. Lighthouse Cemetery, People's State Forest, Barkhamsted (B6)
112. Pike Hill and Northeast Cemeteries, Wolcott (E6)
113. Hopeville Cemetery, Griswold (E12)
114. Old North Cemetery, Hartford (C7)

Zinkies
115. North Cemetery, Woodbury (E4)
116. North Colebrook Cemetery, Colebrook (A5)
117. Hillside Cemetery, Thomaston (D5)

Landfills
118. Windsor-Bloomfield Landfill, Windsor (B8)
119. Milford Landfill, Silver Sands State Park, Milford (H5)
120. Hartford Landfill, Hartford (C7)

Wallace Nutting
121. The Meeting House, Heritage Village, Southbury (F4)
122. Webb-Deane-Stevens Museum, Wethersfield (D7)
123. Wadsworth Atheneum, Hartford (C7)

Hudson River School
124. New Britain Museum of American Art, New Britain (D7)
(123) Wadsworth Atheneum (C7)

Artists Outdoors, Plein Air, and Impressionism
125. Florence Griswold Museum, Old Lyme (H10)
126. Bush-Holley House, Greenwich (J1)
(124) New Britain Museum of American Art (D7)

Weir Farm
127. Weir Farm, Wilton (H2)

James Merrill's Apartment
128. James Merrill House, Stonnington (G13)

Nature Writers
129. Trailwood, Hampton (C11)
130. Stillmeadow, Southbury (F4)
131. Hal Borland house, Salisbury (A3)
132. Joseph Wood Krutch house, Redding (G3)

Used Bookstores
133. Whitlock's Book Barn, Bethany (G6)
134. The Book Barn, East Lyme (G10)
135. Book Trader Café, New Haven (G6)
136. Traveler Food and Books, Union (A11)

New England Scenic Trail
(15) Mount Higby, Middlefield, Middletown (E7)
137. Will Warren's Den, Farmington (C6)

Garnet Books

Fly Fishing in Connecticut:
A Guide for Beginners
by Kevin Murphy

Water for Hartford:
The Story of the Hartford Water
Works and the Metropolitan
District Commission
by Kevin Murphy

African American Connecticut Explored
Edited by Elizabeth J. Normen

Henry Austin:
In Every Variety of Architectural Style
by James F. O'Gorman

Ella Grasso:
Connecticut's Pioneering Governor
by Jon E. Purmont

The British Raid on Essex:
The Forgotten Battle of the War of 1812
by Jerry Roberts

Making Freedom:
The Extraordinary Life of
Venture Smith
by Chandler B. Saint and George
Krimsky

Welcome to Wesleyan:
Campus Buildings
by Leslie Starr

Barns of Connecticut
by Markham Starr

Gervase Wheeler:
A British Architect in America,
1847–1860
by Renée Tribert and
James F. O'Gorman

Connecticut in the American
Civil War:
Slavery, Sacrifice, and Survival
by Matthew Warshauer

Inside Connecticut and the Civil War:
One State's Struggles
Edited by Matthew Warshauer

Prudence Crandall's Legacy:
The Fight for Equality in the 1830s,
Dred Scott, *and* Brown v. Board of
Education
by Donald E. Williams Jr

Stories in Stone:
How Geology Influenced Connecticut
History and Culture
by Jelle Zeilinga de Boer

New Haven's Sentinels:
The Art and Science of East Rock and
West Rock
by Jelle Zeilinga de Boer and John
Wareham

About the Author

David K. Leff is the author of *The Last Undiscovered Place* (a Connecticut Book Award finalist), *Deep Travel*, and three volumes of poetry. His essays have appeared in the *Hartford Courant, Appalachia, Yankee, Canoe & Kayak,* and the *Encyclopedia of New England*. He lives in Collinsville, Connecticut. For more, go to www.davidkleff.com.